DELIVERANCE THROUGH RESTORATION OF HONOR:
SHAME AND HONOR
IN PSALM 22

JOSE MANUEL S. ESPERO

WESTBOW
PRESS®
A DIVISION OF THOMAS NELSON
& ZONDERVAN

WestBow Press books may be ordered through booksellers or by contacting:

WestBow Press
A Division of Thomas Nelson & Zondervan
1663 Liberty Drive
Bloomington, IN 47403
www.westbowpress.com
844-714-3454

Unless marked otherwise, all scripture quotations are taken from The Holy
Bible, English Standard Version® (ESV®), Copyright © 2001 by Crossway,
a publishing ministry of Good News Publishers. All rights reserved.

Scripture quotations marked KJV are taken from the King James Version.

ISBN: 978-1-6642-7327-6 (sc)
ISBN: 978-1-6642-7328-3 (e)

Print information available on the last page.

WestBow Press rev. date: 11/28/2023

ABSTRACT

TITLE: DELIVERANCE: SHAME AND HONOR IN PSALM 22

Author: Jose Manuel Sensano Espero

In Ps 22, the psalmist complains to God about his shame experiences. He prayed to God for his deliverance from shame and the restoration of his honor. The purpose of this study is to show the values and means in this psalm and the role of deliverance in the restoration of the psalmist's honor.

The psalmist experiences the shame of abandonment, mockery, and nakedness. The shame experience of the psalmist is caused by Yahweh's abandonment and the cruel enemies' desire for his ultimate shame. The psalmist uses several deliverance terms to indicate his desire for deliverance. The honor he desires is the restoration of his patronage relationship and kinship with Yahweh. The trust relationship of the fathers with Yahweh is the apex of deliverance, for Yahweh spared them from being shamed. The psalmist desires to have the same deliverance and to be spared from shame. The feast/meal became the transition point of the status of the psalmist, from shame to honor.

Chapter 2 shows an overview of some Mediterranean and Mesopotamian values of patronage, kinship/family, and trust and the means such as forsakenness/ abandonment, taunt speeches, nakedness, and feast/meal. The study revealed that these Mediterranean and Mesopotamian values and means have similarities and differences with the same values and means found in Israel. It also revealed that deliverance is in some ways attached to these values and means in their respective contexts.

Chapter 3 holds that David, the king of Israel's united monarchy, is the author of Ps 22. The analysis of Ps 22 revealed that the means of abandonment, taunt speech, and nakedness caused the psalmist shame. The value of patronage between Yahweh and the psalmist has to be reestablished to end the shame of abandonment and to restore relationship. The value of trust indicates the fathers' loyalty to Yahweh. The trustworthiness of Yahweh to deliver the afflicted led to the fathers' deliverance, causing them to avoid being shamed. The value of kinship indicates that Yahweh, as the psalmist's progenitor, cared for and protected the psalmist like a father. That relationship kept the psalmist honorable. The means of feast/meal is the transition of the psalmist's, together with those who were delivered, status from shame to honor. Also, the NT uses Ps 22 to portray the honor and shame of Jesus through the means of abandonment, taunt speech, nakedness, and the values of kinship/family and trust.

Chapter 4 surveys the different deliverance terms the psalmist used to convey his need for deliverance from shame. The deliverance terms indicate deliverance, rescue, salvation, protection, and victory over the enemies. Yahweh favorably answers the psalmist's prayer for deliverance, which is crucial to his restoration of honor.

Chapter 5 presents the theological analysis of the study. The analysis pointed that Yahweh acts as a faithful patron actively involved in the provision, protection, help, deliverance, salvation, and rescue of his people. Yahweh is holy, rejecting those who sin and putting them to shame but delivering the faithful from their shame. Yahweh keeps the honor of his people and does not leave them in utter shame. He is the host of the feast, allowing the transition of the afflicted from shame to honor.

to

my beloved wife

my patient mommy, and

my compassionate nanay

CONTENTS

AB	Anchor Bible
AJSR	*Association for Jewish Studies Review*
ANET	*Ancient Near Eastern Texts Relating to the Old Testament.* Edited by James B. Pritchard. 3rd ed. Princeton: Princeton University Press, 1969
AYBD	*Anchor Yale Bible Dictionary.* Edited by David Noel Freedman. 6 vols. New York: Doubleday, 1992
BA	*Biblical Archaeologist*
BCOTWP	Baker Commentary on the Old Testament Wisdom and Psalms
BDAG	Danker, Frederick W., Walter Bauer, William F. Arndt, and F. Wilbur Gingrich. *Greek-English Lexicon of the New Testament and Other Early Christian Literature.* 3rd ed. Chicago: University of Chicago Press, 2000 (Danker-Bauer-Arndt-Gingrich)
BDB	Brown, Francis, S. R. Driver, and Charles A. Briggs. *A Hebrew and English Lexicon of the Old Testament*
BEB	*Baker Encyclopedia of the Bible.* Edited by Walter A. Elwell, and Barry J. Beitzel. Grand Rapids: Baker Books, 1988
BibSem	The Biblical Seminar
BSac	*Bibliotheca Sacra*
BTB	*Biblical Theology Bulletin*
CANE	*Civilizations of the Ancient Near East.* Edited by Jack M. Sasson. 4 vols. New York, 1995. Repr. in 2 vols. Peabody, MA: Hendrickson, 2006
CBQ	*Catholic Biblical Quarterly*
CDWGTHB	*A Concise Dictionary of the Words in the Greek Testament and The Hebrew Bible.* James Strong. Bellingham, WA: Logos Bible Software, 2009.

INTRODUCTION

As early as the twentieth century, interest on the study of Scriptures in honor and shame perspective has significantly increased and considered honor and shame as the pivotal cultural social values in ancient Israel.[1] Although secular scholars originated the study on the honor and shame sociocultural concept, some biblical scholars have taken the honor and shame concept as the new lenses to study the Scriptures.[2] Studies on biblical narratives and Psalms that took these lenses show that Scriptures may be studied and interpreted from the perspective of honor and shame.[3]

The interest develops from the recognition that honor-and-shame-based societies influenced the writing of the Scriptures. The Scriptures were written in the Middle Eastern countries such as Egypt, Syro-Palestine, and Mesopotamia, as well as in the Mediterranean, where shame and honor concept is strong.[4] The influence is evidenced by the occurrences of the honor and shame terms in the Scriptures, more than 190 references to honor and a hundred references to shame.[5] The authors of the NT may have also been influenced by the first century culture because the "first-century Jews, Romans, and Greeks showed honor and shame in their thoughts, words, and actions."[6]

Studies relating the honor and shame social values to some specific psalms have indeed laid the foundation for further contributions on this matter. Some scholars have extensively looked into the various psalms that seemingly displays the honor and shame background.[7] Their studies mention Ps 22 in relation to the value of honor and shame in support of the concept.

Yet, the challenge in biblical studies towards more contributions on the theme of honor and shame remains. In particular, a careful consideration solely on the study of the sociocultural background of Ps 22 emphasizing the perspective of honor and shame has yet to be undertaken. In addition, since some psalms studies show that part of Ps 22 conveys honor and shame but have not seriously focused on the honor and shame lenses, this study intends to contribute to the honor and shame studies by revisiting this particular psalm and attempting to expound the values and means of honor and shame found in it.

Much of the research studies on Ps 22 focus primarily on messianic and christocentric themes. The studies range from serious biblical studies to application of the passage to mission. They focus on the suffering of the psalmist, linking it with the suffering of Christ and human beings.[8] Some highlights justice and salvation with emphasis on mission,[9] the identity of the "I" in its relation to the surrounding community,[10] and the similarities between Ps 22 and Deutero-Isaiah.[11]

Some scholars who argue for the messianic aspect of this psalm hold that the experience expressed in this psalm is Jesus's agony on the cross.[12] They connect the experiences of Jesus with the psalmist by comparing quotations and allusions from Ps 22 with selected passages in NT. They assert that Jesus experienced shame during his passion scene but later received honor in his glory. Yet, they barely focus on the theme of deliverance as Jesus's or the psalmist's restoration of honor.

Scholars, who cannot mistake that deliverance is central to Ps 22, hold that the relationship of the psalmist with God is significant. The relationship between God and the psalmist becomes the basis of the psalmist's deliverance from his abandonment and shame.[13] Shramek emphasizes that, indeed, the relationship is a matter related to honor.[14] Also, the social values of honor and shame govern "just about all relationships."[15] Yet, studies on Ps 22 that dig deep into the aspect of the relationship in honor and shame values are scarce. Significantly, this study looks into this aspect of honor and shame to help elaborate on the understanding of Ps 22.

Other studies on Ps 22 centers on identifying who experience the suffering in the psalm. There are various interpretation as to the identity of the sufferer: a) the exiles in Babylon;[16] b) the king who represents the community;[17] c) a person passing through deep distress in life who expressed in a liturgy;[18] and d) an anonymous individual or other individuals who experience the suffering in a new liturgical context such as those of Esther and Jesus.[19] Some deny that the suffering can be attributed to a person.[20] Others still hold to the authenticity of the superscript, thus attributing the psalm to David and his experiences in life, partly or wholly.[21] Still, others maintain that David may have experienced the suffering and the misery described in the psalm but not in its entirety. Rather, Jesus may have wholly experienced it.[22]

The differing opinions as to whom the experiences of the psalmist in Ps 22 should be attributed leads to the differing sociocultural contexts of the psalm. With these differences, connecting this psalm with the social values of honor and shame in the sociocultural context of the united monarchy of Israel poses a challenge. Thus, this present work assumes David as the possible sufferer in the psalm, that he went through the suffering portrayed therein and that the honor and shame sociocultural context in his time affected his writing of this psalm.

Aside from the honor and shame social values present in the psalm, the theme of deliverance and its parallel terms appear to be central to Ps 22. Deliverance in the midst of trouble and adversity is important as experienced by the psalmist in relation to his relationship with God, his enemies, and the people.[23] It is important against the threats of the psalmist's enemies and to the preservation of his relationship with God and his social relationship with the people.[24]

In relation to the work of the scholars on the theme of deliverance in Ps 22, this present work retraces the theme of deliverance in Ps 22. It also proposes to strengthen the understanding of deliverance through the lenses of honor and shame. In addition, it focuses on the connection of deliverance with the preservation of honor and avoidance of shame, which seems to be scarcely dealt with other studies on the psalm.

Further, the motif on humiliation in Ps 22 connects with the shame concept. Scholars diverge on who had suffered the humiliation as exposed in the psalm. The points of view are the following: a) all of the descriptions of humiliation in the psalm refer to Jesus and not to any other. David underwent through such humiliation in a modified sense. Jesus, having identified himself with human beings, pass through the same humiliation.[25] b) David himself experienced the sufferings and vindication. The language used to describe David's experience is also appropriate to describe Jesus's suffering.[26] With the differing views, it may be safely deduced that David's and Jesus's experience of humiliation are linked with the context of honor and shame.

In retrospect, the studies in honor and shame in the Psalms may have taken Ps 22 into consideration, but an in-depth study on Ps 22

CHAPTER 1

HONOR AND SHAME IN SOME MEDITERRANEAN AND MESOPOTAMIAN LANDS

Every human society has its own culture which varies from other groups. Culture enables a person or group of persons to live. It is shaped by historical experiences and framed by geographical settings. It shapes how a person thinks, reasons, evaluates, and behaves. It gives the person a sense of belonging, comfort, security, and identity within the social body. It is also a means of social control. From culture comes out religion and the sense of right and wrong.

Culture is the "total integrated sum of learned behavioral traits that characterize the members of a society."[1] Simply put, it is "the total way of life of a people."[2] Interhuman relationship, etiquette, conversation, and spiritual development are all part of life. One's way of life includes beliefs and customs.[3] Also, the way of life of people is influenced by the economy, technology, ideology, "arts, manners, and morals."[4] Kroeber states that the "specific human societies are more determined by culture than the reverse, even though some form of social life is precondition of culture."[5]

David, the writer of Ps 22, did not live in a vacuum. His demeanor, expressions, and words reflected in the psalm betrays the influence of the culture in which he lived. The following sections show examples of specific social values of honor and shame and means related to Ps 22 from some Mesopotamian and Mediterranean lands. It presents examples of the means of forsakenness/abandonment, taunt speech, nakedness, and feast/meal and the values of patronage, kinship/family, and trust coming from these places.

Forsakenness/Abandonment

The word *forsake* connotes that a relationship has existed between two parties. The relationship between the parties is so dear. When this dearest relationship breaks due to the breaching of the oath by one of the parties, the ensuing consequence is the forsaking of the offendee by the aggrieved party. The following examples shows the gods forsaking the kings or the people under their realm.

A piece of Akkadian text known as *Ludlul Bēl Nēmeqi*,[6] from an ancient wisdom literature sometimes called Babylonian Job, speaks of a person forsaken or abandoned by his/her gods and friends. The text dates back to around mid to late 1st millennium BC. The text relates the hero's, named Shubshi-meshre-shakkan,[7] simple prayer of about "four hundred to five hundred lines"[8] written on four tablets. The tablets contain a hymn of praise; the description of the hero's near-death situation in a lament form; the appearance of beings sent by Marduk, the Babylonian god; and the recounting of his restoration and deliverance from suffering. The text ends with the singing of praise towards Marduk.[9]

Louis E. Newman states that "this composition presents the plaint of one Shubshi-meshre-shakkan, whose protecting god and goddess have abandoned him, leaving him prey to illness and evil omens, while his former friends gleefully anticipate his death. In this text, Shubshi-meshre-shakkan was sick, mocked, and rejected."[10] The interesting claim of Shubshi-meshre-shakkan is that he "is a pious man who faithfully performs his acts of devotion."[11] Yet in spite of his piety, he still experienced suffering and pain. Noting that the god Marduk is angry with him, he believed that his personal deities abandoned him. He thought that he might have committed sin inadvertently so that he needed to appease them. Eventually, Marduk sent someone to deliver him from all his malady and suffering and restore him to health.[12]

Another instance of a king being forsaken is about the Assyrian epic known as Tukulti-Ninurta I (1233–1197 BCE). The epic records the prayer of Tukulti-Ninurta I to Shamash, the god of judgement. It legitimizes and celebrates "the destruction of Babylon by the Assyrian king Tukulti-Ninurta I."[13] The record indicates the reason for

Tukulti-Ninurta I's conquer of the Babylonian king Kastiliash IV. It portrays the Babylonian king as "the breaker of oaths and the violator of the parity-treaty that had been the basis of the relations between Assyria and Babylon since the time of the kings' fathers."[14] Because he broke the treaty, the god Marduk abandoned Kastiliash, as Tukulti-Ninurta I claims in the epic.

The situation portrayed in the examples indicates that the gods may abandon the people who trust in them. The reasons may be that they have committed sin or have broken the treaty with the gods. Those who are abandoned are put to shame.[15] Conversely, In the case of the victors over those who are abandoned by the gods, honor comes to them.

Forsakenness in the OT is used with inanimate objects, with persons as object, and with abstracts as objects.[16] For persons, "this sort of turning away or separation also generates juridical, economic, political, and emotional considerations."[17] For personal relationship, it can refer to abandoning a wife or husband which may result in divorce.[18] Some instances of forsakenness/abandonment happen between God and human beings, where God forsakes or abandons humanity because of sin and other reasons. In some cases, humanity appeals to God to not abandon him/her and hopes that God establishes a relationship with him/her again.[19] When the word is used with Yahweh or God as the subject and humanity as the object, it suggests two things: God/Yahweh promises never to leave humanity (Gen 28:15) and God/Yahweh abandons his relationship with humanity (Ps 22:2).

The word *forsaken* where God and humanity are directly involved appears thirty-three times in the OT. An example of this occurrence is God's relationship with Jacob. In Gen 28:15, God promised that he would never abandon Jacob, who ran away from his family for fear of his life, until he returned to the land of Canaan. In the Mediterranean perspective, separation from the family brings shame to the person detached. By bringing back Jacob to Canaan (Gen 30:25–35:29) from his exile in Paddan-Aram (27:41–30:24), God indeed restored Jacob's honor. Also, the restoration of Jacob's relationship with his brother who had accepted him well brought him honor. The exchanging and receiving of presents are the culmination of the acceptance to the family (33:4–11).

oneself and one's family."[73] The influence of patronage comes from the Roman world where the term "patronage is borrowed from."[74] Raymond Westbrook illustrates that the patron is part of the "powerful aristocrat who gathered around him [patron] loyal followers, known as clienteles."[75] The patron receives more honor if he/she gathers more number of clienteles and if he/she provides more benefaction.[76] Anselm Hagedorn, Crook, and Eric Clark Stewart point that "the greater the benefactions and the number of clients, the more honour one achieved."[77]

During the Roman period, a big gulf existed between the rich and the poor. The indifference of the rich, especially in the Greek society, towards their obligation to the poor, widows, or orphans in their own society ran deep.[78] By negligence of their obligations, in essence, the rich shamed the poor. Consequently, they lost their honorable status in society. Although having wealth was an advantage, it did not actualize patronage. Wealth was not the sole basis for the actualization of patronage. The status of the person in society was also an important matter.[79]

At the early stages of the united monarchy of Israel, in fact even during the time of the judges, only a few owned lands and properties.[80] In an economy in which a fraction of the society owns a vast number of wealth, the majority are poor and in need of assistance. In order to protect and ensure the well-being of the poor families, the patronage system is necessary.[81] The patron, the socially superior person in the relationship, is willing to provide materials and goods in exchange for "honor, loyalty and service that the clients would provide."[82] Also, the patron provides the client access to protection, honor, and material benefits.[83] The patron-client relationship is viewed as reciprocal. The client swears "allegiance to the patron and the patron"[84] swears to protect the client. It forges mutual loyalty and personal connection which form the bond between the patron and the client.[85] Importantly, the bond between them is a personal one.

The client, who is socially dependent upon the patron, looks for a person of a better status to be his/her own benefactor. In exchange for the goods and materials given, the clients "grant the patrons honor as their benefactors."[86] Hobbs stresses that the patron gains honor through the widespread knowledge that he can sustain a large body of clients or retainers through his "generosity," and clients gain honor by being associated with such figure. The breaking of this bond by one or the other results in shaming the opposite partner.... Failure to maintain one's clients through provision of protection results in shaming for both.[87]

Reciprocity is a crucial element in patronage. The client must reciprocate the favor given by the patron. "Goods, entertainment, and advancement"[88] are kinds of favor extended by the patron to the client. In turn, the client honors the patron by remaining loyal and doing the utmost service to and for the patron.[89] The favor may be obtained by the petitioner or gained by personal initiative.[90] The client must publicize the favor and express gratitude for the benefits he/she has received. The client's act elevates the patron's reputation or honor.[91]

An important note must be taken in order to understand the basic features of patron-client relationships as enumerated by Neyrey. (a) The relationship is asymmetrical. (b) It is unconditional, which means that the son will most likely always receive the inheritance. (c) There is also a strong personal obligation involving the importance of loyalty or faithfulness. The strong protects the weak, and the weak entrusts himself/herself to the strong. (d) It is entered voluntarily. (e) It has an element of favoritism. (f) It involves reciprocity, an exchange of services for goods or the other way around. (g) It has a "kingship glaze."[92] The patron becomes a parent to the client. (h) The patron and the client both give and receive honor.[93]

One of the positive qualities of patronage is the "quality of kinship or family feeling."[94] God is the father and the people are his children. He is "the ultimate patron, or benefactor, of all God's children. As patron, God gives people life and shows favor to them in numerous ways. Humans reciprocate by obeying God's commandments, showing God gratitude and praise, and in turn acting as patrons to others who need favors."[95]

Patronage in the ancient Near East. The Amarna letters illustrate the patron-client relationship. A Canaanite scribe wrote letters to a pharaoh, assuming a client relationship with pharaoh. The scribe asserted in those letters that the pharaohs served as patrons and the Canaanites as their clients.[96] The idea that pharaohs are patrons and the people are clients also occurs in Palestine and Syria. In those places, people believe that the pharaohs were their protectors. They had not engaged in honoring other gods; rather, they remained faithful to the pharaoh alone. However, the pharaoh did not accept such an arrangement. He considered the kings of Palestine and Syria as his workers and has the authority to sack them at anytime he wanted.[97]

Mark R. Sneed mentions that patron terms like *my lord, my father, your son,* or *your servant* were used by the scribes to address the pharaohs.[98] Lemche explains that

> Pharaoh's understanding of political relations was therefore impersonal and state oriented: the petty kings were Egyptian officials employed by Pharaoh to carry out his orders and decrees; they were not to act on their own behalf. Loyalty to Pharaoh therefore meant being true to the orders given to you, not the more comprehensive feeling among people from Syria and Palestine of personal allegiance and loyalty.[99]

In the ANE, a certain deity may be identified with a certain nation. Some deities may also be "associated with specific places, rather than nations, or with tribal groups, even with households."[100] They function as patron or matron gods. Kings or nations attribute their success to certain patron gods. An example of the success stories on patron gods helping a king is "The Tale of Sinuhe." Sinuhe was a Palestinian exile to Egypt who believed in one of the patron gods of Egypt. He attributed his prosperity and protection to this god while being in exile in Egypt. Other nations also choose their own patron gods and rely on them as those who can provide their good.[101]

Patronage in Israel. Lemche and Hobbs hold that the system of politics of Israel was patronage in nature. Simkins cites examples of patronage in the Israelite system. Saul serves as a patron by providing gifts of vineyards and fields including appointments of military rank to David, who assumes to be the client. David in turn shows his loyalty to Saul by recognizing him as father and sparing his life twice. In turn, Saul recognizes that relationship by addressing David as his son (1 Sam 24:11, 26:17-25). At the time David ran away from Saul, the king of Gath served as David's patron king.[102] Other examples abound in the OT such as Elisha calling Elijah father (2 Kgs 2:12), Naaman's servants calling him the same way (5:13),[103] and Ahaz submitting himself to Tiglathpileser as his servant and son (16:5–9).[104]

Sneed also explains that the people of Israel consider God as the superpatron. God rewards the loyalty and obedience of his clients, the pious and the wise. The rewards are long life and prosperity. The disobedient, the foolish, and the wicked bring shame to his name. They will receive retribution such as sickness, poverty, and death.[105]

Lemche adds that in Syria and Palestine, people believe that the almighty God is their patron. The Egyptians believe that he is the ultimate ruler of the kingdom. This God provides security and welfare to his people, not as king but as a patron. The clients can switch to better patrons who can provide their needs if they are dissatisfied with their current patrons.[106]

It is also to be noted that the patronage system, although dyadic in nature, can be developed into "a socio-political pyramidal network,"[107] as Pfoh puts it. The ladder in this network begins with the poor. The poor climbs up to the patron, the broker, until he/she reaches the pinnacle of the higher patron. In the case of Israel, the king serves as a patron of the people of Israel. He also serves as the mediator or broker between the people and God, the higher patron or superpatron.[108]

Kinship/Family

Kinship[109] is significant in the preservation of honor. Belonging to a family or kindred means adherence to family expectations and standards. This means that the shame of one member in the family affects the whole, destroying the family solidarity and honor.[110] The value of the family depends on the honor rating of the community. To gain more honor, the family has to climb the honor ladder. Every member is expected to preserve the honor and contribute to the accumulation of it.[111]

The honor and shame of the family are not personal matters. They are always bound up with groups or with the family. Importantly, the members of the group try to remain part of the group or the family. Losing membership in the family means loss of honor which leads to shame. The shame the person experiences can be "loss of face before persons," failure to reach "an ideal or public exposure," "embarrassment by society," "fear of social rejection," and "humiliation"[112] to name some. The promise of exclusion and inclusion is part of the social control of the shame-based society.[113]

Shame is a corporate matter which inherently has a relational dimension. The case for this matter shatters the relational aspect of the sense of belongingness. The experience of shame originated in the garden of Eden with the first man and woman. Their shame shattered the trusting relationship. The broken relationship led to loneliness and estrangement of an individual from the group or family. Estrangement can only be overcome when the "original unity is restored."[114]

Some background from the ANE may be appropriate in this regard. Narratives and depictions of shame from the group and family relationship is also prevalent in the ANE context. DeSilva points out that one of the responsibilities of kinship is to hide the shame of the kin. Instead of parading the "failings of a person's family members,"[115] the kin has to cover up or hide the failures to shield him/her "from public exposure and shame."[116]

Sarah J. Dille points out the importance of having honorable ancestors and being part of it. She states, "Kinship is a source of honor if one has honorable ancestors. Being the offspring of Abraham (Isa. 41.8; 51.2f) or Jacob (45.25; 48.1) confers honor to the descendants."[117] The presentation of the genealogies is an important component of honor and shame cultures. To be part of the genealogy or to trace one's root in the genealogy provides honor.[118] Robin Stockitt states, "By recording a person's lineage one can find a place for that person within communities over time and in space. A genealogy is a coded message about the claim that the person has to status, rank, or power."[119] Records of genealogies are well-attested in the OT.[120]

The natural kinship bond in ancient Israel is indicated by father-son relationships. Yahweh serving as the father and Israel as the son is an example of this bond.[121] Deuteronomy 8:5–6 talks about the father's responsibility to correct his son. The relationship between father and son figuratively refers to God as the father of the people of Israel.[122] This bond should be maintained in order to keep either party from shame. The OT shows some examples of estrangement from family.[123] Earthly parents, father and mother, can forsake or abandon their children. In contrast, God as the divine father never does the same (Ps 27:9–10).[124]

Trust

The fundamental human value of trust is an important aspect of developing a strong relationship. Trust is tied with the notion of commitment—the making and the keeping of promises, oaths, or vows. A trustworthy person is honorable. However, the person who cannot be trusted is dishonorable. The Westerners understand trust in a completely different way from the honor and shame culture. In the Western world, "truth, honesty, right and wrong, guilt and innocence"[125] are foremost. In the contrary, in honor and shame cultures, the truth is concealed rather than expose the criminal behavior. In the Islam world, divulging the crime is "impolite, disrespectful, uncivil, or discourteous: one cannot trust a dishonorable person."[126]

As any other aspect in the honor and shame culture, dishonor must be avenged, especially that shame has been done. Honor is restored by shunning or, to the extreme, murdering the person. Moreover, Western societies hold to the notion of individualism while honor-shame cultures focus on the communal facet, giving importance to the honor of the lineage, family, and/or community. What may be common to both is the understanding that trust is a social good.[127]

Trust is also a distinct factor in the patron-client relationship. It means that a patron has to provide security and essentially the needs of the client. A patron ought to have unquestioned integrity for clients to trust him/her down to the ground. Jackson Wu states, "A basic obligation of patrons was to show themselves faithful or reliable such that clients could trust them. In response to a patron's faithfulness, a client was expected to show loyalty."[128] A trust relationship develops between the patron and the client through the patron's provision to the client and the client performing services to the patron. The reciprocation between them breeds honesty and reliability which strengthens trust. The one who reciprocates is "worthy of at least minimal trust."[129]

Robert L. Oprisko indicates that trustworthiness is more than being loyal. A person who is trusted must show oneself trustworthy. That person must be willing to risk one's own reputation to show solidarity with others. Also, one's actions should strengthen one's reliability "to form or deepen"[130] one's relationship with others. In other words, trust is formed between persons who are in close relationship. Distrust is also higher towards someone considered as an outsider or foreigner. Hospitality is an important aspect of resolving distrust.[131] One may be included or excluded by the extension of hospitality.

Trust is not confined within human relationships alone. It is also evident in the relationship between God and the people of Israel. The surrounding nations also believe and trust in their pantheon gods. One of the members of the pantheon of the gods is Baal. Baal is a Semitic deity in the "Canaanite pantheon, or company of gods."[132] Baalim, the plural form of Baal, own the land and have control over it, including the increase of crops, fruits, and cattle. The Canaanites think that these gods make "the land, animals, and people fertile."[133] A farmer may trust in them and may become dependent on their generosity and favor. Human sexual acts are performed as acts of worship in order to prompt these gods to make the land, animals, and people fertile.

The trustworthiness of the gods was supported by the words imputed upon them. Jimmy Jack McBee Roberts, on statements supporting the reliability of the gods, states, "Thus we read of Enlil 'whose word cannot be changed, whose reliable consent cannot be transgressed.' We read of Shamash, 'whose yes remains yes, whose no, no,' and 'whose positive answer no god can change.' Similar comments are made about Ninurta, Marduk, and numerous other gods and goddesses."[134]

An older Egyptian literary work known as the "The Tale of Sinuhe" notably speaks about Sinuhe's reverence towards the gods of Egypt. The story indicates the only one patron deity he worshipped. This god was his protector and support while in exile in Egypt. Although he mentioned other gods, Sinuhe put his trust on this particular patron god, primarily for his mercy and power. Notably, he expressed thanks to this god after he had defeated the chief of Retenu. He recognized the protection and the prosperity this god gave while he was in exile in a foreign land. The tale indicates that it had been a practice in Egypt and most probably in the surrounding nations of Canaan to trust in the deities of the pantheon the people honor.[135]

In the ANE, the names of different gods were placed on the newborn child's mouth. The expressing of the names of the gods indicated the invocation of the person's trust in the particular deity mentioned. The people trust a particular deity because of the deity's unique characteristics, such as being a watcher, a provider, or a protector.[136]

In his later inscription inscribed during the third campaign against Syro-Palestine, Sennacherib recorded his trust in the god Ashur. "(Trusting) in the aid of Ashur, my lord, I fought with them and brought about their defeat. The Egyptian charioteers and princes, together with the charioteers of the Ethiopian king, my hands took alive in the midst of battle."[137] Another inscription records Sennacherib's prayer stating his trust in his great gods who aided him in his victory over his enemy. "The great gods, Ashur, Sin, Shamash, Marduk, Nabu, Nergal, Ishtar of Nineveh, Ishtar of Arbela, the gods in whom I trust, they came to my aid."[138] These inscriptions seem to indicate that the continuing trust in different gods by kings or ordinary persons has been a practice in the ANE. They seem to point out that those who trust in their gods never seem to be disappointed but rather helped and aided by the gods.

Baal worship influenced the Israelite religious worship during the time of judges (Judg 3:7), becoming widespread during Ahab's time of the divided kingdom of Israel (1 Kgs 16:31–33), which also infiltrated the Judean kingdom (1 Chr 28:1–2). It became so deep-seated in Israelite worship that they were willing to trust in any of the Canaanite pantheons to provide them security, protection, provision, and promises. For the people of Israel, trusting in these gods was an act of directly affronting Yahweh, who claimed to be the only God and without anyone else above him (Jer 2:14–19).[139] In Israelite history, the question of whether the gods can be trusted has a negative answer. Can the gods fulfill their promises? No, the gods are "too many, too fickle, too limited, and too devious."[140] Trusting in these gods results in devastation and impotence.[141] Only in God who created the world should the people of God put their trust for he is worthy (Isa 40:12–31).[142]

Trust in God is one of the themes in the OT. The wisdom of Proverbs calls for trust in God rather than in one's own understanding (Prov 3:5). Those who trust in God experience peace (Isa 26:3), direction (Prov 3:6), security (Ps 112:7), and righteousness and justice (Ps 37:4–6). Most importantly, they will not experience forsakenness/ abandonment from God (Ps 9:10) but they will be blanketed by God's providence, strength, protection, and help (Ps 28:7).

Feast/Meal

Feasting is an important means of honor and shame. Feasting may be a banquet or just a sense of feasting. A feast/meal is an important means of communication in the honor and shame society, especially when someone is invited. The message conveyed depends on the type of banquet done, either ceremonial or ritual. Malina defines ceremonial feast as "a banquet in which the inviter and the invited celebrate their mutual solidarity, their belonging to each other, their oneness."[143] Also, he defines ritual festive meal as "one that marks some individual or group transition or transformation, held to give honor to those undergoing the important social change."[144] Feasting marks an important transition in the life of a person or group.

The purposes of a meal are to create social equality and bonding, heighten social stratification, and strengthen the social accountability among those who take part in the meal. At the table, guests are ranked according to the quality and quantity of food served to them. One has to strictly observe the rank and status in the dinner party to strengthen the stability of the state. One has to know his/her rank and place and must be content with that.[145]

The Jews believed that eating either unites people with God or separates them from God (Isa 55:1–3). "Food is the most common gift in Scripture. It is given to relatives, acquaintances, kings, and prophets.

Table fellowship is synonymous with fellowship in all aspects of life."[146] On the other hand, people's refusal to eat together severs their relationship (1 Sam 20:34). Those who do not eat or drink together have no obligation to each other and may even become enemies. "The worst kind of traitor is the traitor with whom one has shared food (Ps 41:9, Obad 7)."[147]

A century ago, W. R. Smith noted that commensality among Semitic peoples was thought of "as confirming or even as constituting kinship in a very real sense."[148] The story of Esau and Jacob competing over Isaac's blessing with food illustrates this. Joachim Jeremias affirms this close connection. He states, "In Judaism in particular, table-fellowship means fellowship before God, for the eating of a piece of broken bread by everyone who shares in the meal brings out the fact that they all have a share in the blessing which the master of the house had spoken over the unbroken bread."[149] Meals occupy an important place in the kinship of the Hebrew people. Reta Halteman Finger states that "sharing bread or salt bound one to another in a special way."[150]

Deliverance in the Mediterranean and Mesopotamian Contexts

This section presents how deliverance works in the context of the selected Mediterranean and Mesopotamian nations. In relation to forsakenness and abandonment, shame comes upon the kings who break their oath with their gods. Breaking of the covenant will mean abandonment from the gods, thus relegating them to shame. However, the faithful to their oath with the gods find honor, for which the gods remain with them.

Taunt speech has the purpose of shaming a person. Part of it is gossip, although it can either uplift or destroy an individual. The reason for taunting is the failure to preserve the integral honor of the family or group. The Egyptians has a unique response to taunt speech and its derivates. The response is the concept of truth, judgment, and righteousness. A person who holds this principle cannot hurt others, thereby avoids attributing shame upon them. Another counteraction is positive gossip—the spread of good reports about a person. The purpose of positive gossip differs from taunts or negative gossip but to preserve the honor and integrity of the individual.

Nakedness is one of the reasons for shame. A person forced naked is diminished to a lowly status. Captors stripping naked their captives to humiliate them, poverty, and ill fortune are reasons for nakedness. The Egyptians have a way of restoring the nakedness of an individual. They do good by clothing the naked and feeding the hungry. The act of dressing a person from nakedness is an act of deliverance from shame. It also renders double honor, first to the one clothed from nakedness because it restores his/her dignity and second to the one who provides the clothing because it gives him/her pride. Being better clothed or dressed means acquiring honor and status.

In the issue of patronage, a person in distress and malady is in a state of shame. Restoration from shame can come from someone of higher status who lends support, aid, and help. To reciprocate the help, the restored should serve and remain loyal to the patron. A patron-client relationship then is established.

As for kings, they rely on patron gods to provide them protection, prosperity, and victory over their enemies. However, they have to keep the oath they established with their gods in order to maintain the relationship. Only by faithfully abiding in the oath can they guarantee the good the gods can give to them.

Trust is an important matter in deliverance. The kings who trust in the gods are confident that they will receive favor from them. In going to war, they enslave and capture their enemies without having the feeling of shame towards them. Subduing their enemies brings honor upon themselves. Conversely, the subdued ones are put to shame by the physical and emotional malady inflicted upon them by their enemies. The victors claim honor for themselves but attribute all their success to their patron gods.

The examples this paper mentions indicate that the patron-client relationship between the kings and the gods, trust, and forsakenness/abandonment interconnect with deliverance and the avoidance of shame. The value of kinship/family provides deliverance also for members. As long as one remains in the family, he/she remains honorable. Anyone who breaks the trusting relationship is estranged and put to shame. The estranged one must make amends, adhere to the family ideals of right, and try to preserve family unity in the family before the restoration of honor.

Feast or gathering for a meal is a means toward the value of kinship/family that provides deliverance. The estranged person's restoration to the family's fellowship may be through an invitation to a meal by the family or the community. The one restored to the community acquires honor. The freedom to have table fellowship with the invitees removes the feeling of shame of estrangement, abandonment, and disgust.

Summary

I mentioned that the David, the king of Israel, is the probable author of Ps 22. David wrote this psalm around the 10th century BC when Israel had already settled in the land of Canaan. Since it was written during this period, the writing of the psalm may have been influenced by Israel's close cultural kinship with the ANE.

In this regard, I discussed in this section the values and means in some Mediterranean and Mesopotamian contexts that may have influenced the writing of the psalm. Patronage, a value that forges a relationship between a patron and a client, has been a common practice in these areas. Although Israel's politics had been transformed into a monarchical system in the 10th century BC, the patronage system was still clearly in place. The king serves as the patron who provides security, protection, and provision while the people serve as the clients who, in turn, reciprocate loyalty and service to the patron. Israel recognized God as their superpatron. The other nations mentioned have their own superpatron gods.

The means of forsakenness/abandonment also existed during those times. Some records show that the gods forsake or abandon the nations, especially the kings, because of their sins. The people or the king have to appease the gods for the restoration of their relationship. Those forsaken or abandoned are shamed but the victorious are honored by the gods. God forsakes or abandons the people of Israel because of their sins and disobedience, leaving them in a state of shame. Yet, he promises the people of Israel that he will restore his relationship with them and will never leave them again.

The value of kinship/family is also prevalent among the nations and of Israel. The sense of belongingness is important in this value. One has to be a member of the family in order to receive honor. Estrangement from the family leads to shame. Honor can only be restored upon a person's unity with the kinship or the family. The value of trust is important in the honor and shame culture. A person can only be called trustworthy when he/she is loyal to the group. Loyalty to the group is a means of trust. Conversely, in the patron-client relationship, trust comes when a patron shows faithfulness and reliability to the client by fulfilling his/her obligations as a patron. Reciprocally, trust is shown by the client through his/her loyal service to the patron.

Taunt speech is a means of communication. The taunt speeches—insult, mockery, and scorn—known as challenge are used as a social control to put a person to shame. To avoid shame, the person must react to taunt speech through more insult. The reaction to the challenge is a riposte. In addition, making someone naked is a way of shaming and humiliating that person. Thus, nakedness becomes a condition of shame. In order to restore honor, the naked person must be dressed.

Feast or sharing of a meal is a means for the restoration of honor. Refusal to partake in the meal indicates a traitorous attitude and severance of a relationship. Partaking of a meal, especially in the ritual feasts, marks a significant transition in the life of a person from shame to honor. The background reveals that the abovementioned values and means existed in the specific Mediterranean and Mesopotamian lands considered. These values and means may have directly or indirectly influenced the values and means as reflected in David's composition of Ps 22. The next chapter shows that these values and means are present in Ps 22. It looks into the terms or concepts that reflect these values and means.

---

[1] Pablo Alberto Deiros, "Cultura," *Diccionario Hispano-Americano de La Misión* 120.

[2] Deiros, "Cultura," 120.

[3] Ronald S. Hendel states, "Recent research has demonstrated that culture and ethnicity are more matters of belief and custom than they are proof of common descent. In the memorable title of one such study, nations or ethnic groups are 'imagined communities,' imagined into existence by those who believe in the

group and participate in social interactions. In the case of ancient Israel, the imagination that flows into the construction of a cultural identity is, at least in part, preserved for us in the biblical portrayal of Israel's origins. The most important of these imaginative constructs are stories of the Exodus-Sinai-Wanderings period, related in the books of Exodus through Deuteronomy." Ronald S. Hendel, "Israel among the Nations: Biblical Culture in the Ancient Near East," in *Cultures of the Jews: A New History*, ed. David Biale (New York: Schocken Books, 2002), 47; Ronald S. Hendel, *Remembering Abraham: Culture, Memory, and History in the Hebrew Bible* (Oxford: Oxford University Press, 2005), 7.

[4] Alfred Louis Kroeber, "What Anthropology Is About," in *Readings for a History of Anthropological Theory*, ed. Paul A. Erickson and Liam Donat Murphy, 5th ed. (Toronto: University of Toronto Press, 2017), 136.

[5] Ibid.

[6] *ANET*, s.v. "Ludlul Bēl Nēmeqi."

[7] Bill T. Arnold and Bryan E. Beyer, eds., *Readings from the Ancient Near East: Primary Sources for Old Testament Study*, Encountering Biblical Studies (Grand Rapids: Baker Academic, 2002), 177.

[8] Patricia Vesely, *Friendship and Virtue Ethics in the Book of Job* (Cambridge: Cambridge University Press, 2019), 99.

[9] Carol A. Newsom, *The Book of Job: A Contest of Moral Imaginations* (Oxford: Oxford University Press, 2009), 74.

[10] Louis E. Newman, ללמד ולמד: *Studies in Jewish Education and Judaica in Honor of Louis Newman*, ed. Alexander M. Shapiro and Burton I. Cohen (New York: Ktav, 1984), 159; Julian Jaynes, *The Origin of Consciousness in the Breakdown of the Bicameral Mind* (Boston: Houghton Mifflin, 1990), 225.

[11] Clyde E. Fant and Mitchell G. Reddish, *Lost Treasures of the Bible: Understanding the Bible through Archaeological Artifacts in World Museums* (Grand Rapids: Eerdmans, 2008), 262.

[12] Alan Lenzi, "The Curious Case of Failed Revelation in Ludlul Bēl Nēmeqi: A New Suggestion for the Poem's Scholarly Purpose," in *Mediating between Heaven and Earth: Communication with the Divine in the Ancient Near East*, ed. C. L. Crouch, Jonathan Stökl, and Anna Elise Zernecke (New York: Bloomsbury, 2012), 48. See also Benjamin Read Foster, *Before the Muses: Archaic, Classical, Mature*, 2nd ed. (Bethesda, MD: CDL, 1996), 1:307; *ANET*, s.v. "Ludlul Bēl Nēmeqi"; John L. McLaughlin, *The Ancient Near East: An Essential Guide* (Nashville: Abingdon, 2012), 13–14; Roland Edmund Murphy, *Introduction to the Wisdom Literature of the Old Testament* (Collegeville, MN: Liturgical Press, 1965), 24.

[13] Christoph O. Schroeder, *History, Justice, and the Agency of God: A Hermeneutical and Exegetical Investigation on Isaiah and Psalms* (Leiden: Brill, 2001), 147.

[14] Ibid.

[15] Peter Partner, *God of Battles: Holy Wars of Christianity and Islam* (New York: HarperCollins, 1998), 1.

[16] Erhard Gerstenberger, "עָזַב," *TDOT* 10:586–87.

[17] Ibid., 586.

[18] *HALOT*, s.v. "עָזַב."

[19] *DCH* 6, s.v. "עָזַב"; *Kohlenberger/Mounce Concise Hebrew-Aramaic Dictionary of the Old Testament* 1, s.v. "עָזַב"; Gerstenberger, *TDOT* 10:586.

[20] 1 Kgs 8:57; Isa 41:17; Pss 9:10; 27:9, 10; 37:28, 33; 94:14.

[21] Deut 31:17; 2 Chr 32:31; Jer 12:7–8; Lam 5:19–20; Ezek 8:12, 9:9.

[22] Mark McVann, "Communicativeness (Mouth-Ears)," in *Handbook of Biblical Social Values*, ed. J. J. Pilch and Bruce J. Malina, updated ed. (Peabody, MA: Hendrickson, 2000), 26.

[23] Ibid., 25–26.

[24] Lawrence M. Wills, *Not God's People: Insiders and Outsiders in the Biblical World* (Lanham, MD: Rowman & Littlefield, 2008), 71.

[25] McVann, "Communicativeness (Mouth-Ears)," 27.

[26] Lyn M. Bechtel, "Shame as a Sanction of Social Control in Biblical Israel: Judicial, Political, and Social Shaming," *JSOT* 16.49 (1991): 72.

[27] Xuan Huong Thi Pham, *Mourning in the Ancient Near East and the Hebrew Bible*, JSOTSup 302 (Sheffield: Sheffield Academic, 1999), 73. See also Bechtel, "Shame as a Sanction," 72.

[28] Richard L. Rohrbaugh, *The New Testament in Cross-Cultural Perspective* (Eugene, OR: Cascade, 2007), 129.

[29] Ibid.

[30] Ibid.

[31] Joseph Plevnik, "Honor/Shame," in *Biblical Social Values and Their Meaning: A Handbook*, ed. J. J. Pilch and Bruce J. Malina (Peabody, MA: Hendrickson, 1993), 100. Petri Merenlahti states that in the honor and shame contexts, "honor guaranteed people the position in which they were born." Petri Merenlahti, *A Smaller God: On the Divinely Human Nature of Biblical Literature* (Eugene, OR: Cascade, 2015), 39. These people do not need to move up the ladder in the society. However, when publicly challenged, they need to acquire the honor. He states that "the challenge could be positive—someone would bestow a gift on you, or pay you a compliment—or negative, like an insult or taunt." Ibid. The challenge must be imperatively responded "like an honorable person should." Ibid. Failure to do so means increasing the honor of the other party at one's own failure. The public determines whether the response is "any good." Ibid.

[32] Victor H. Matthews, "Honor and Shame in Gender-Related Legal Situations in the Hebrew Bible," in *Gender and Law in the Hebrew Bible and the Ancient Near East*, ed. Victor H. Matthews, Bernard M. Levinson, and Tikva Frymer-Kensky (Sheffield: Sheffield Academic, 2009), 98.

33 Ibid., 98–99.

34 Tikva Frymer-Kensky, "Gender and Law: An Introduction," in *Gender and Law in the Hebrew Bible and the Ancient Near East*, ed. Victor H. Matthews, Bernard M. Levinson, and Tikva Frymer-Kensky (Sheffield: Sheffield Academic, 2004), 20.

35 2 Kgs 19:21–23, 1 Chr 30:10, Isa 37:23–24, Zeph 2:8.

36 Pss 39:9, 79:4, 89:51, 123:4.

37 Geoffrey P. Miller, "Verbal Feud in the Hebrew Bible: Judges 3:12–30 and 19–21," *JNES* 55.2 (1996): 108.

38 Geoffrey P. Miller, "A Riposte Form in the Song of Deborah," in *Gender and Law in the Hebrew Bible and the Ancient Near East*, ed. Victor H. Matthews, Bernard M. Levinson, and Tikva Frymer-Kensky, JSOTSup 262 (Sheffield: Sheffield Academic, 1998), 121.

39 "Akkadian Myths and Epics: The Creation Epic," trans. E. A. Speiser (*ANET*, 66–67).

40 See also Glenn Stanfield Holland, *Gods in the Desert: Religions of the Ancient Near East* (Lanham, MD: Rowman & Littlefield, 2009), 125.

41 A. D. Smelik Klaas, "Ma'at," *DDD* 534.

42 Ma'at is an Egyptian goddess who personifies truth and justice and "the cosmic force of harmony and stability." J. I. Packer, Merrill C. Tenney, and William White, eds., *Illustrated Manners and Customs of the Bible* (Nashville: Nelson, 1997), 91. A suggestion persists that she corresponds to the lady of wisdom in the Bible. A. D. Smelik Klaas strongly rejects the idea. See Klaas, "Ma'at," 535.

43 Maulana Karenga, *Maat, the Moral Ideal in Ancient Egypt: A Study in Classical African Ethics*, African Studies: History, Politics, Economics, Culture (New York: Routledge, 2004), 358–60.

44 Gale A. Yee, *Poor Banished Children of Eve: Woman as Evil in the Hebrew Bible* (Minneapolis: Augsburg Fortress, 2003), 74.

45 James Montgomery Boice, *Genesis: Creation and Fall, Genesis 1–11; An Expositional Commentary* (Grand Rapids: Baker Books, 2006), 1:147.

46 See Waltke and Yu, *Old Testament Theology*, 263.

47 Joel Sanchez, "Honor and Shame in the Ancient Near East," *Crucified Life Ministries*, 12 December 2015, para. 10, http://crucifiedlifemin.com/auto-draft-2/.

48 Jonathan K. Crane, "Shameful Ambivalences: Dimensions of Rabbinic Shame," *AJSR* 35.1 (2011): 63, https://doi.org/10.1017/S0364009411000031.

49 Paul R. Raabe, *Obadiah: A New Translation with Introduction and Commentary*, ed. William Foxwell Albright and David Noel Freedman, AB 24D (New York: Doubleday, 1996), 170. Raabe points out that the case in Obadiah is ironical. Edom was covered and clothed with the garment of shame. The irony is that the person put to shame is not covered by clothing. Instead, the person is forced or coerced to be undressed or naked before others into shame. Pham explains that

the Hebrew words "ערוה and ערום, usually translated 'nakedness' and 'naked' refer to two different kinds of nakedness. They can describe a state of complete nakedness (e.g. Gen 2:25; 3:10; Hos 2:11), or they can mean 'poorly clothed' (e.g. Deut 28:48; Isa 58:7; Ezek 18:7)." Pham, *Mourning*, 74. In the context of Jer 8:9, Pham points out that the nakedness of Jerusalem is not complete nakedness. Jerusalem is girt with a sackcloth from hip down but her chest is laid bare "for beating as a mourning practice." Ibid. He also emphasizes that exposure of one's body, as in Lam 1:8 and the story of Noah in Gen 9:20–27, is a nakedness "which brings great shame." Ibid., 14.

50 Julia Asher-Greve and Deborah Sweeney, "On Nakedness, Nudity, and Gender in Egyptian and Mesopotamian Art," in *Images and Gender: Contributions to the Hermeneutics of Reading Ancient Art*, ed. Silvia Schroer (London: Academic Press, 2006), 113.

51 An Egyptian stele depicts the Canaanite goddess Qedeshet standing naked on the back of a lion. Beside her is Reshef, the Canaanite warrior god. On her left is Min-Amun-Ra who functions as the god of fertility and male potency. The worship of Canaanite gods shows the impact of Egyptian rule in the Levant sometime between 1292 and 1069 BC. It must be noted, though, that depiction of nakedness in this Egyptian iconography as a show of honor points more on gods rather than human beings. James Blake Weiner, "Interview: Nudity in the Ancient World," *Ancient History Encyclopedia*, 18 December 2018, https://www.ancient.eu/article/1295/interview-nudity-in-the-ancient-world/.

52 "Setna Khaemuas and the Mummies," trans. Robert Kriech Ritner (William Kelly Simpson, ed., *The Literature of Ancient Egypt: An Anthology of Stories, Instructions, Stelae, Autobiographies, and Poetry*, 3rd ed. [New Haven: Yale University Press, 2003], 466).

53 Asher-Greve and Sweeney, "On Nakedness," 113.

54 "Tomb relief from Saqqara," (Prentice Duell, *The Mastaba of Mereruka: By the Sakkarah Expedition* [Chicago: University of Chicago Press, 1938], plate 37).

55 Ibid. Neyrey notes that when a man shows his nakedness by aggressively exposing his penis or buttocks to somebody else, "such a display is a claim of power and superiority, for masculine strength is symbolized by the penis." Jerome H. Neyrey, "Nudity," in *Handbook of Biblical Social Values*, ed. J. J. Pilch and Bruce J. Malina (Peabody, MA: Hendrickson, 1993), 121. In the case of Setna, it was not a cause of aggression because he already covered his penis with a clay pot by the time Pharaoh passed by and stopped to inform him of the welfare of his family. Joshua J. Mark, "The Tales of Prince Setna," *Ancient History Encyclopedia*, 2 May 2017, https://www.ancient.eu/article/1054/the-tales-of-prince-setna/.

56 Elizabeth Bloch-Smith, "Acculturating Gender Roles: Goddess Images as Conveyors of Culture in Ancient Israel," in *Image, Text, Exegesis: Iconographic*

Interpretation and the Hebrew Bible, ed. Izaak J. de Hulster et al. (London: T&T Clark, 2015), 2. The goddess Inanna/Ishtar is depicted in the Uruk vase as nude. In human form, she is considered as the goddess of sexual love. She is also depicted in other arts as wearing a robe with weapons on her shoulders. Asher-Greve and Sweeney, "On Nakedness," 126. Ogden Goelet mentions that the Egyptian gods who are naked may symbolize fertility, especially for the old ones, but childhood, youth, and innocence for the gods associated with children. Ogden Goelet, "Nudity in Ancient Egypt," *Source* 12.2 (1993): 22–23.

[57] Bloch-Smith, "Acculturating Gender Roles," 2.

[58] Ibid.

[59] A Middle Babylonian text from Ḫana and a text from Nuzi record of a woman divorced and stripped naked by her husband because of adultery. The purpose of stripping her naked is to humiliate and shame her. Another Nuzi text relates that a woman who would divorce her husband must be sent forth naked. This is to shame her and to ensure that she would not have any economic security. Nuzi was a city in the kingdom of Arrapha. It did not have its own king but had its own military components. It was probably destroyed by the Assyrians at around 1350 BCE. Goelet holds that in all periods of the Egyptian domination, captives were paraded naked in order to humiliate them. Goelet, "Nudity in Ancient Egypt," 20.

[60] Bechtel, "Shame as a Sanction," 64.

[61] Ibid. Bechtel explains how the captors humiliate their captives. She says, "Humiliating captive warriors lowered them and their nation to an inferior position and raised up the victors in status. Consequently, captive warriors or kings were made to walk naked, to grovel in the dust abjectly, or to feel helpless and defenseless in order to 'put them down' into a humiliating position and to lower their status." Ibid., 64–65. Asher-Greve and Sweeney also mention that stripping someone of his/her clothing is a way of degrading that person especially before the enemies. Asher-Greve and Sweeney, "On Nakedness," 113.

[62] Crane, "Shameful Ambivalences," 84.

[63] Asher-Greve and Sweeney indicate that the involuntary stripping of clothing trespasses personal boundaries. The trespassing is related to what Crane mentions regarding the injury afflicted on the dignity of a person. Sociologically, a naked man belongs to the bottom of the social scale for reasons of indebtedness or for neglect in providing necessities. Asher-Greve and Sweeney, "On Nakedness," 114. Such a one is an object of shame in the community and viewed negatively, according to Alicia J. Batten. The return of clothing to a person means restoration of his/her dignity. Alicia J. Batten, "Clothing and Adornment," *BTB* 40.3 (2010): 149, https://doi.org/10.1177/0146107910375547.

[64] Asher-Greve and Sweeney, "On Nakedness," 151.

[65] Ibid.

[66] Ibid.

[67] John A. Bailey, "Initiation and the Primal Woman in Gilgamesh and Genesis 2–3," *JBL* 89.2 (1970): 145, https://doi.org/10.2307/3263044. See also Claus Westermann, *Genesis 1–11* (Neukirchen-Vluyn: Neukirchener Verlag, 1974), 653.

[68] David A. deSilva, "Patronage," *DNTB* 766.

[69] E. Randolph Richards and Brandon J. O'Brien, *Misreading Scripture with Western Eyes: Removing Cultural Blinders to Better Understand the Bible* (Downers Grove, IL: InterVarsity Press, 2012), 103.

[70] Ronald A. Simkins, "Patronage and the Political Economy of Monarchic Israel," *Semeia* 87 (1999): 128.

[71] Emanuel Pfoh, *The Emergence of Israel in Ancient Palestine: Historical and Anthropological Perspectives* (London: Routledge, 2016), 86.

[72] Ibid.

[73] deSilva, "Patronage," 766.

[74] Raymond Westbrook, "Patronage in the Ancient Near East," *JESHO* 48.2 (2005): 210.

[75] Ibid.

[76] Nathan Nzyoka Joshua mentions that the system of benefaction works in "conjunction with other coexistent social systems, especially in the G-R [Greco-Roman] household and Jewish kinship systems." Nathan Nzyoka Joshua, *Benefaction and Patronage in Leadership: A Socio-Historical Exegesis of the Pastoral Epistles* (Carlisle, Cumbria: Langham, 2018), Google book, ch. 1, "1.1 General Introduction," para. 6.

[77] Anselm C. Hagedorn, Zeba A. Crook, and Eric Clark Stewart, *In Other Words: Essays on Social Science Methods and the New Testament in Honor of Jerome H. Neyrey* (Sheffield: Sheffield Phoenix, 2007), 56.

[78] The practice of neglecting the poor was true among the Christian believers. Daniel L. Balch points that by neglecting the poor, the ruling elite treated them unjustly and with contempt, especially that they denied them the provision of food only the rich can afford. He adds that Luke attacks this attitude of the wealthy and instructs them to modify their beliefs. Daniel L. Balch, "Rich and Poor, Proud and Humble in Luke-Acts," in *The Social World of the First Christians: Essays in Honor of Wayne A. Meeks*, ed. L. Michael White and O. Larry Yarbrough (Minneapolis: Augsburg Fortress, 1995), 214–15.

[79] Pfoh, *Emergence of Israel*, 123; Phebe Lowell Bowditch, *Horace and the Gift Economy of Patronage* (Berkeley: University of California Press, 2001), 42.

[80] Settlement in the land of Canaan during the Iron Age was on the highlands. Matthews describes that settlement then was "rather harsh and filled with work necessary for simple survival." Victor H. Matthews, *The History of Bronze and Iron Age Israel* (Oxford: Oxford University Press, 2018), 87. Their economy was "of agriculture combined with the management of sheep, goats, and cattle." Ibid. See also Larry G. Herr, "Archaeological Sources for the History of

Palestine: The Iron Age 2 Period; Emerging Nations," *BA* 60.3 (1997): 125, https://doi.org/10.2307/3210608; Norman K. Gottwald, "The Participation of Free Agrarians in the Introduction of Monarchy to Ancient Israel: An Application of H. A. Landsberger's Framework for the Analysis of Peasant Movements," in *Social Scientific Criticism of the Hebrew Bible and Its Social World: The Israelite Monarchy*, ed. Norman K. Gottwald (Missoula, MT: Scholars Press, 1986), 88–89.

[81] Bowditch, *Horace*, 42. See also David A. deSilva, *An Introduction to the New Testament: Contexts, Methods and Ministry Formation*, 2nd ed. (Downers Grove, IL: InterVarsity Press, 2018), 100; David A. deSilva, *Perseverance in Gratitude: A Socio-Rhetorical Commentary on the Epistle to the Hebrews* (Grand Rapids: Eerdmans, 2000), 60; David A. deSilva, *4 Maccabees* (Sheffield: Sheffield Academic, 1998), 127–28. The patronage system is an asymmetrical relationship indicating a difference of status where one party, the patron (master or benefactor), provides something to which the other party, the client (slave or beneficiary), "does not have access." Bowditch, *Horace*, 42. See also Richard P. Saller, *Personal Patronage under the Early Empire* (Cambridge: Cambridge University Press, 2002), 1. Niels Peter Lemche adds that the patronage organization is vertical. The patron is on top of the echelon of the society, members of the leading lineage, while the clients belong to the ordinary persons and families, the lower classes in the society. He also mentions that the patronage system can be found in all levels of society, even in Mesopotamia. Niels Peter Lemche, "From Patronage Society to Patronage Society," in *The Origins of the Ancient Israelite States*, ed. Volkmar Fritz and Philip R. Davies (Sheffield: Sheffield Academic, 1996), 109; Niels Peter Lemche and E. F. Maniscalco, *Prelude to Israel's Past: Background and Beginning of Israelite History and Identity* (Peabody, MA: Hendrickson, 1998), 102.

[82] deSilva, "Patronage," 766. See also A. Sue Russell, *In the World but Not of the World: The Liminal Life of Pre-Constantine Christian Communities* (Eugene, OR: Wipf & Stock, 2019), 163.

[83] Ronald A. Piper, "Glory, Honor and Patronage in the Fourth Gospel: Understanding the 'Doxa' Given to Disciples in John 17," in *Social Scientific Models for Interpreting the Bible: Essays by the Context Group in Honor of Bruce J. Malina*, ed. J. J. Pilch (Leiden: Brill, 2001), 294.

[84] Lemche, "From Patronage Society," 111.

[85] deSilva, "Patronage," 767. The patrons are "asked to provide money, grain, employment or land." Ibid. They are also sought for the "professional or social advancement" they can provide. Ibid.

[86] Craig S. Keener, *The IVP Bible Background Commentary: New Testament*, 2nd ed. (Downers Grove, IL: InterVarsity, 2014), 784. There are some examples of clients not giving back due honor to their patrons. During the 1st century AD at the time of Paul, some Pauline churches "did not award honors to their

benefactors, a practice that may have caused patrons to feel slighted." John S. Kloppenborg, "Greco-Roman Thiasoi, the Ekklēsia at Corinth, and Conflict Management," in *Redescribing Paul and the Corinthians*, ed. Ron Cameron and Merrill P. Miller (Atlanta: Society of Biblical Literature, 2011), 213.

[87] T. Raymond Hobbs, "Reflections on Honor, Shame, and Covenant Relations," *JBL* 116.3 (1997): 501–2.

[88] David A. deSilva, "Exchanging Favor for Wrath: Apostasy in Hebrews and Patron-Client Relationships," *JBL* 115.1 (1996): 92.

[89] Marshall Sahlins, *Stone Age Economics* (Chicago: Aldine, 1972), 195.

[90] J. J. Pilch, *A Cultural Handbook to the Bible* (Grand Rapids: Eerdmans, 2012), 165.

[91] deSilva, "Exchanging Favor," 92.

[92] Jerome H. Neyrey, *Render to God: New Testament Understandings of the Divine* (Minneapolis: Augsburg Fortress, 2004), 250.

[93] Ibid., 250–51; Pfoh, *Emergence of Israel*, 122–24.

[94] Bruce J. Malina, "Patronage," in *Handbook of Biblical Social Values*, ed. J. J. Pilch and Bruce J. Malina, 3rd ed. (Eugene, OR: Wipf & Stock, 2016), 131.

[95] Reta Halteman Finger, *Of Widows and Meals: Communal Meals in the Book of Acts* (Grand Rapids: Eerdmans, 2007), 127.

[96] Mark R. Sneed, *The Social World of the Sages: An Introduction to Israelite and Jewish Wisdom Literature* (Minneapolis: Augsburg Fortress, 2015), 278.

[97] Lemche, "From Patronage Society," 113.

[98] See "The Amarna Letters from Canaan," (Shlomo Izre'el, *CANE* [Peabody, MA: Hendrickson], 4:2413, 2417.

[99] Lemche, "From Patronage Society," 113. Lemche explains that the political system of the Egyptians is more likely to be like the modern concept of states.

[100] Daniel I. Block, *The Gods of the Nations: A Study in Ancient Near Eastern National Theology* (Eugene, OR: Wipf & Stock, 2013), 73.

[101] Holland, *Gods in the Desert*, 95. See also "The Story of Sinuhe," (*ANET*, 18–22).

[102] Jonathan Kirsch, *King David: The Real Life of the Man Who Ruled Israel* (New York: Random House, 2009), 114; Barbara Green, *David's Capacity for Compassion: A Literary-Hermeneutical Study of 1–2 Samuel* (London: Bloomsbury, 2017), 122.

[103] Based on the patron-client relationship, Naaman serves as the patron of his servants. He provides for the benefit of his servants, yet he requires reciprocal support from them. See Malina, "Patronage," 133.

[104] Simkins, "Patronage," 128. Simkins points out that "the suzerain-vassal relationship was an expression of patronage" such as the case of the Tiglathpileser and Ahaz relationship. Ibid.

[105] Sneed, *Social World*, 278–79.

[106] Lemche, "From Patronage Society," 113–14.

[107] Pfoh, *Emergence of Israel*, 124.

[108] Ibid.

[109] J. David Schloen holds that during the monarchical period, kingship did not replace kinship. In fact, he states that "the emergence of monarchy in Israel in the 10th-century B.C. entailed a reconstruction and territorial expansion of smaller-scale kin-based modes of organization." J. David Schloen, *The House of the Father as Fact and Symbol: Patrimonialism in Ugarit and the Ancient Near East*, Studies in the Archaeology and History of the Levant 2 (Winona Lake, IN: Eisenbrauns, 2001), 360. See also Lawrence E. Stager, "Forging an Identity: The Emergence of Ancient Israel," in *The Oxford History of the Biblical World*, ed. Michael D. Coogan (New York: Oxford University Press, 2001), 149–51.

[110] Malina, *New Testament World*, 40.

[111] Jeanne Choy Tate, *Something Greater: Culture, Family, and Community as Living Story* (Eugene, OR: Wipf & Stock, 2013), 54.

[112] J. J. Pilch, *Introducing the Cultural Context of the Old Testament* (New York: Paulist, 1991), 1:66.

[113] Partner, *God of Battles*, 69.

[114] Dietrich Bonhoeffer, *Ethics*, ed. Clifford J. Green, trans. Reinhard Krauss et al., Dietrich Bonhoeffer Works 6 (Minneapolis: Augsburg Fortress, 2005), 306.

[115] DeSilva, *Honor, Patronage, Kinship*, 171.

[116] Robin Stockitt, *Restoring the Shamed: Towards a Theology of Shame* (Eugene, OR: Cascade, 2012), E-book edition, ch. 3, "Architecture, Shame and Division," para. 2.

[117] Sarah J. Dille, "Honor Restored: Honor, Shame, and God as Redeeming Kinsman in Second Isaiah," in *Relating to the Text: Interdisciplinary and Form-Critical Insights on the Bible*, ed. Timothy J. Sandoval, Carleen Mandolfo, and Martin J. Buss (New York: T&T Clark, 2003), 234.

[118] Kenneth C. Hanson and Douglas E. Oakman note the different purposes of genealogy. They state that "one's genealogy may be used to establish religious purity, rights to political leadership, inheritance rights, marriage eligibility, and ethnic connections." Kenneth C. Hanson and Douglas E. Oakman, *Palestine in the Time of Jesus: Social Structures and Social Conflicts* (Minneapolis: Augsburg Fortress, 2008), 27. As stated above, genealogies are important in the honor and shame cultures.

[119] Stockitt, *Restoring the Shamed*, E-book edition, ch. 3, "Belonging, Shame and Kinship," para. 1.

[120] Examples of the genealogies in the OT are found in Gen 5, 10, 45; Exod 6:14–27; Num 26:2–51; 1 Chr 6–9; Ezra 2, 10; Neh 7, 11.

[121] Exod 4:22, Isa 63:16, Jer 31:9, Hos 11:1.

[122] Stefan C. Reif holds that "kings and other leaders, as well as gods, were known as 'father.'" Stefan C. Reif, "The Fathership of God in Early Rabbinic

Literature," in *Family and Kinship in the Deuterocanonical and Cognate Literature*, ed. Angelo Passaro (Berlin: de Gruyter, 2013), 505.

123 Ps 69:8, Isa 1:4, Ezek 14:5, Mal 4:6.

124 This psalm speaks about the psalmist's complaint that his parents had forsaken him. As should be expected in the kinship relationship, the parents or family members must support the one in trouble. In his situation, the psalmist's affiliation with them is already severed. His rejection is a form of shame. The restoration of the kinship relationship seems far from being repaired. In exchange for that severed family relationship, he puts his confidence in God, who now becomes his parent, to take him as part of God's family. He now belongs to a no ordinary family and status, a part of God's great family of the living (v. 13), an honor not given to evildoers. In addition, the benefit of being a member of God's family includes protection against the enemies who are false witnesses and violent (vv. 12–13). To reciprocate, the psalmist proclaims the goodness of the Lord and calls others to wait upon him (vv. 13–14).

125 Keith E. Swartley, *Encountering the World of Islam* (Downers Grove, IL: InterVarsity Press, 2014), 119.

126 Ibid. In the Muslim world, trust is part of one's religious commitment. Muslims believe that "God is, that he reveals himself, and that he cares for mankind." Ibid., 88.

127 Piotr Sztompka, *Trust: A Sociological Theory* (Cambridge: Cambridge University Press, 1999), 102; Sissela Bok, *Lying: Moral Choice in Public and Private Life* (New York: Vintage Books, 2011), 26; Amy Plantinga-Pauw, *Proverbs and Ecclesiastes: A Theological Commentary on the Bible* (Louisville: Westminster John Knox, 2015), 67.

128 Jackson Wu, *Reading Romans with Eastern Eyes: Honor and Shame in Paul's Message and Mission* (Downers Grove, IL: InterVarsity Press, 2019), 78. See also Neyrey, *Honor and Shame*, 113; deSilva, *Introduction*, 106.

129 David Gilmore, ed., *Honor and Shame and the Unity of the Mediterranean* (Washington, DC: American Anthropological Association, 1987), 95.

130 Robert L. Oprisko, *Honor: A Phenomenology* (New York: Routledge, 2012), E-book edition, ch. 10, "Building Trust," para. 6.

131 Bruce J. Malina, "Hospitality," in *Handbook of Biblical Social Values*, ed. J. J. Pilch and Bruce J. Malina, 3rd ed. (Eugene, OR: Wipf & Stock, 2016), 96–99.

132 J. D. Douglas and Merrill C. Tenney, "Baal (Deity)," *Zondervan Illustrated Bible Dictionary* 149. See also Kevin Green, "Baal," *Zondervan All-in-One Bible Reference Guide* 93.

133 K. Green, "Baal," 93. See also Marianne Race and Laurie Brink, *In This Place: Reflections on the Land of the Gospels for the Liturgical Cycles* (Eugene, OR: Wipf & Stock, 2008), 8.

134 Jimmy Jack McBee Roberts, *The Bible and the Ancient Near East: Collected Essays* (Winona Lake, IN: Eisenbrauns, 2002), 124. See also Julia M. O'Brien,

Hosea, ed. Gail R. O'Day and David L. Petersen, Theological Bible Commentary (Louisville: Westminster John Knox, 2009), 261.

[135] Holland, *Gods in the Desert*, 95. See also R. B. Parkinson, *The Tale of Sinuhe* (Oxford: Oxford University Press, 2009); R. B. Parkinson, *The Tale of Sinuhe and Other Ancient Egyptian Poems, 1940–1640 BC* (Oxford: Oxford University Press, 1998), 21–53.

[136] Ichiro Nakata, "Popular Concerns Reflected in Old Babylonian Mari Theophoric Personal Names," in *Official Cult and Popular Religion in the Ancient Near East: Papers of the First Colloquium on the Ancient Near East; The City and Its Life, Held at the Middle Eastern Culture Center in Japan (Mitaka, Tokyo, March 20–22, 1992)*, ed. Eiko Matsushima (Heidelberg: Winter, 1993), 118; Jack M. Sasson, ed., *Civilizations of the Ancient Near East* (Peabody, MA: Hendrickson, 2000), 4:2361.

[137] Daniel David Luckenbill, *Ancient Records of Assyria and Babylonia* (Santa Barbara, CA: Greenwood, 1927), 1:240. See also Sa-Moon Kang, *Divine War in the Old Testament and in the Ancient Near East* (Berlin: de Gruyter, 2011), 18. Sa-Moon Kang indicated in his book how the divine intervention happened in the military events. In these events, the kings called for the aid of their gods and indicated their trust in the gods they worship. Kang, *Divine War*, 17.

[138] Kang, *Divine War*, 18. See also Luckenbill, *Ancient Records*, 1:240.

[139] J. Andrew Dearman, *Jeremiah, Lamentations* (Grand Rapids: Zondervan, 2011), 60.

[140] Roberts, *The Bible*, 131.

[141] Michael Sadgrove, *I Will Trust in You: A Companion to the Evening Psalms* (London: Society of Promoting Christian Knowledge, 2012), E-book edition, ch. 23, "Maker and Deliverer," para. 7. In the ANE, trusting in the deities was a common practice. At the time of his accession, Essarhadon, the king of Assyria, reveals his belief in the counsel of the gods in regard to the affairs of his kingdom. He points out that the constant counsel of the gods towards him led him to trust in them. He states, "In good time there came upon me favorable signs in heaven and on earth. With the message of ecstatic, the instructions of gods and goddess(es), they regularly and repeatedly caused (my) heart to trust." Andrew Knapp, *Royal Apologetic in the Ancient Near East*, WAWSup 4 (Atlanta: SBL Press, 2015), 316.

[142] Waltke and Yu, *Old Testament Theology*, 204.

[143] Bruce J. Malina, "Feast," in *Handbook of Biblical Social Values*, ed. J. J. Pilch and Bruce J. Malina, 3rd ed. (Eugene, OR: Wipf & Stock, 2016), 76.

[144] Ibid.

[145] Finger, *Of Widows and Meals*, 176.

[146] Ibid. The examples of texts about table fellowship are the following: Gen 14:18–20; 26:26–31; 29:22, 27–28; 31:44–46, 51–54; Josh 9:3–15; Judg 9:26–28; 2 Sam 3:20; 9:7, 10–11; Prov 15:17, 17:1.

[147] Ibid., 177.

[148] W. R. Smith, *Lectures on the Religion of the Semites, First Series: The Fundamental Institutions* (Edinburgh: Black, 1889), 177; Finger, *Of Widows and Meals*, 176.

[149] Joachim Jeremias, *The Proclamation of Jesus*, The New Testament Theology (New York: Scribner's Sons, 1971), 115.

[150] Finger, *Of Widows and Meals*, 178.

CHAPTER 2

LITERARY BACKGROUND OF PSALM 22

Some Psalms scholars indicate that the values of patronage, kinship/family, and trust and the means of forsakenness/abandonment, taunt speech, nakedness, and feast/meal appear in Ps 22.[1] The previous chapter already dealt with these values and means from the context of some Mediterranean and Mesopotamian nations. It shows that the same values and means found in Ps 22 appear in these places as well. On this premise, the present chapter explores the occurrences of these values and means within Ps 22. It proceeds with the literary and linguistic analyses of Ps 22 to elaborate on the terms, phrases, and literary features that relates with the values and means under study. The investigations cover the textual, syntactic, and grammatical aspects of some selected terms and passages linked with the values and means mentioned.

The Literary and Linguistic Contexts of Psalm 22

This section looks at the literary and linguistic contexts of Ps 22. The literary analysis aims to present the probable themes evident in this psalm that has a connotation of the values and means of interest in this study. The structure outlines and displays the patterns found in it. The linguistic analysis explores the form and genre of the psalm.

Themes of Psalm 22

The themes of God as savior and king, deliverance, and trust seem to appear in Ps 22. The theme God as savior and king encompasses the whole of this psalm. This section discusses these themes briefly.

The themes occurring in Ps 22 build on the theme God as the savior and the king. The name אֵל, "God" (vv. 2, 3, 11),[2] connotes God as the savior (v. 2) and king (v. 4). The psalmist, at the outset, cries to God for salvation from his agony (vv. 2, 3). God himself delivers and rescues the ancestors of the psalmist (v. 5). God saves the psalmist from his distress (v. 22) and the afflicted from their affliction (v. 24). God is savior, deliverer, rescuer, and helper. His acts on behalf of his people provides honor to them.

The psalmist's declaration that is יִשְׂרָאֵל יוֹשֵׁב תְּהִלּוֹת, "enthroned upon the praises of Israel" supports the theme of God as king. Also, the name יִשְׂרָאֵל, "God contends" (vv. 4, 24),[3] indicates that God is a warrior king. He is not just an ordinary king but a victorious warrior and fighter.[4] Verse 28 (29) asserts, "For kinship belongs to the LORD, and he rules the nations" (ESV, emphasis original).

Four terms appear in this psalm to indicate the theme of deliverance: יָשַׁע, "help, save"[5] (vv. 2, 22[2x]); פלט, "deliver, rescue, escape"[6] (vv. 5, 9[2x]); מָלַט, "to save someone"[7]; and עזר, "help, assist"[8] (vv. 12, 20[2x]). The psalmist desires that God saves; delivers; lets him flee; and helps him from rejection, physical sickness, and enemies. These deliverance terms are related to the theme of trust.

The terms בטח, "trust" (vv. 5, 6, 10[4x])[9] and גלל, "commit, trust"[10] (v. 9[1x]) exhibit the theme of trust. The subject of this trust are the fathers.[11] The fathers' trust in God resulted in their deliverance, and God kept them from shame. This psalm also highlights the psalmist's confidence in God. Since his birth, he never faltered in trusting God. Although his enemies challenged his trust, he remains dedicated and trustful in him.

Form and Genre of Psalm 22

The book of Psalms, no longer thought as isolated works compiled in a slipshod manner, is a canonical whole with "overarching patterns and themes"[12] connecting smaller groups of psalms. It is indeed "a collection of Hebrew prayers and hymns ... addressed to God or express truth about God in song."[13] The book of Psalms has five divisions: Book 1 (Pss 1–41), Book 2 (Pss 42–72), Book 3 (Pss 73–89), Book 4 (Pss 90–106), Book 5 (Pss 107–150).[14]

Nancy L. DeClaissé-Walford observes that out of the forty-one psalms in Book 1, twenty-seven are laments. She notes that the psalms in this section belong or are attributed to David, except Pss 1–2. These psalms are interconnected. Also, she argues that Pss 22, 23, and 24 form a unit based on the Nahal Hever Psalms scroll (5/6 HevPs), which preserves portions of the psalms "grouped together in succession amid Pss 7–14, 18, and then 25, 29, and 31."[15] The groupings allow the sequence reading for these psalms. Trust in God is the common theme of these three psalms.[16]

Davidson supports the interconnectedness of the three psalms but focuses on the theme of messianic trilogy. He holds that each psalm focuses on the ministry of Jesus. Psalm 22 prefigures the death of Jesus Christ on the cross. Psalm 23 focuses on Jesus as the real shepherd. Psalm 24 pictures Jesus as victoriously walking in the heavenly sanctuary at the time of the "inauguration of Zion as the dwelling place of God on earth."[17]

Psalm 22, an individual lament psalm, has two sections: the lament and the praise.[18] Prayer and hymn permeate both sections. Parallelisms and metaphors also pervade the psalm. The psalmist, believed to be David, directs his prayer of lament to God.[19] He expresses his disappointment about God's seeming distance and failure to hear his prayer and complaints and see his struggles with the attacks of the enemies and their corresponding effects on his social, emotional, and physical well-being. For these reasons, he also prays for help from the Lord, whom he believes is the helper, deliverer, and savior. The prayer ends not in despair but in a statement that God hears and delivers. The ending of the prayer serves as a transition from the lament to the praise.[20]

The psalmist's praise follows the statement of deliverance. It is a hymn with vows to praise the Lord among his congregation and a call to all others to do the same and worship him. It also contains an affirmation that God does not turn his face away but instead, he listens and hears the cries of the afflicted in their affliction. The praise includes a communal meal for the afflicted and a universal worship scene involving all nations of the earth. The worship recognizes the rulership of Yahweh, whom people serve. The praise ends with the affirmation that God does righteous deeds all the time.

David wrote Ps 22 at the time of his distress and persecution under Saul who threatened him with death. He wrote this psalm to encourage himself in the Lord. The psalm became part of the psalms compiled for liturgical use to serve as an encouragement to those who may experience distress and threat from their enemies.[21]

Structure of Psalm 22

Psalm 22 is a psalm of lament with praise. Like other lament psalms, it contains two parts: the lament and the praise. The typical division of the lament that some scholars present has three parts: complaint against God (vv. 2–12), complaint against enemies (vv. 13–19), and call for deliverance (vv. 20–22).[22] The complaint against God centers on God's abandonment of the psalmist in his ordeals. Ironically, the covenant God, who promises protection and security, abandons his client at the time of peril. The complaint against the enemies has multiple facets: the people's mockery and insult against the psalmist and his emotional and physical sickness due to life threats from his enemies who are out to destroy him. The call for deliverance ensues because of his enemies. He trusts that God can help, deliver, and save him from his tribulations. The lament concludes with the prayer of confidence for eventual deliverance.

The praise part has three sections formed in a chiasm: the psalmist's call to praise (vv. 23–24) paired with the people's praise (vv. 30–32), the reason to praise (vv. 25, 28–29), and the acts of praising and feasting (vv. 26–27). The psalmist declares praise towards God because he delivers his people from suffering, and he willingly listens to the cry of his suffering people. He vows to praise Yahweh among the congregation and urges others to do so. The gathering of the distressed and well-to-do comes with a festive meal and worship of Yahweh. The psalmist also acknowledges Yahweh's sovereignty over the earth and calls the people to do the same. In response, people serve and worship him. Even the future generations will know his righteous deeds.[23]

However, this paper presents Ps 22's structure with a focus on deliverance, honor, and shame. The lament section of the psalm seems to vividly show the three divisions. The praise section focuses more on the deliverance and honor. The general structure of Ps 22 below shows an alternative division of the lament and praise with focus on deliverance, claim to honor, and shame under the enemies.

The lament. The lament has three divisions. The first division focuses on deliverance: I, failure of deliverance; I', call for deliverance; and I", success of deliverance. The word רָחוֹק, "far"[24] (vv. 2, 12, 20) and the terms for deliverance (salvation, help, rescue, and answer) connect these sections. I and I" form an inclusio of the lament because of the presence of the words רָחוֹק (vv. 2, 20); יְשׁוּעָה, "help, salvation,"[25] "deliverance,"[26] "victory"[27] or יָשַׁע, "to save, to deliver, to be victorious"[28] (vv. 2, 22); and עָנָה, "to answer"[29] (vv. 3, 22). The second division, II and II', shows the claim for honor (vv. 4–6, 10–11). The third division, III and III', marks the shame under the enemies (vv. 7–9, 13–19).

The I section (vv. 2–3) forms a synthetic parallelism,[30] which highlights rejection, as indicated in A and A'. The parallel terms for rejection are עֲזַבְתָּנִי, "You forsake me" and לֹא תַעֲנֶה, "You have not answered." B and B' indicate the far distance of salvation, רָחוֹק מִישׁוּעָתִי, "far from my salvation," and the elusiveness of rest, לֹא־דוּמִיָּה, "no rest."

The II section (vv. 4–6) is the first of two expressions to the claim for honor. It is a staircase parallelism[31] that begins with praise, trust, and confidence which lead to deliverance and climax in freedom from shame. A declares God's glory through the expression of praise. B, B', B", and B"' reveal trust and confidence towards God. C, C', and C"' confirm God's deliverance that climaxes in freedom from shame.

The III section (vv. 7–9) narrates the shame the psalter experiences under the enemies. This section shows a staircase parallelism. The first staircase is the parallel A and A'. It is the expression of the psalmist of his worthlessness, being a disgrace, and a disdain of the people. The next staircase is the synthetic parallel B, B', and B" which indicate the taunting and mockery of the enemies. C climaxes the staircase which shows the direct quotation of the enemies' mockery. The object of the challenge is to destroy the psalmist's honor and Yahweh's credibility to rescue those who trust in him, especially the psalmist, from their predicament.[32]

The II' section (vv. 10–11) is the second claim for honor. It is an inverted parallelism. The parallel A and A' indicate God as the progenitor, an adoptive father of the psalmist from his birth. In both instances, God is directly addressed as אַתָּה, "you." B parallels B' and both indicate that the mother's provision of security and care is a manifestation of God's care.

The I' section (v. 12) is a progression of the previous section. This section builds on God's protective and caring nature. To call God for deliverance is apt here. A is a call on God not to be far for two reasons: B, trouble is near and B', no one can help.

The III' section (vv. 13–19) is the second of the two expressions of shame under the enemies. It provides the reason for the call for deliverance. The structure creates an A and A' and B and B' synthetic parallelism. A describes the enemies and their aggression. B discloses the effect of the assault on the emotions of the psalmist. A' repeats A with added identification and attack of the enemies. B' describes the impact of the attack the enemies inflicted on his physique. Also, it marks the enemies' final blow against the psalmist.

The phrase סְבָבוּנִי, "they surround me" and the synonymous phrases כִּתְּרוּנִי, "they enclosed me" and הִקִּיפוּנִי, "they encompass me" connect A and A'. The use of animal imagery to describe the enemies shows the power and fierceness of the enemies. The word עַצְמוֹתָי, "my bones" connects B and B'. The bones signify the psalmist's wholeness of being, the enemies' target of attack.

The I" section (vv. 20–22) indicates the success of the deliverance. This section serves as the climax of the lament part. It forms a climactic parallelism progressing into a series of volition. A calls for the closing of the distance between God and the psalmist. B calls for the hastening of the coming of the help. C calls for the deliverance of the psalmist's only life from the power of the enemies to kill, illustrated as a sword. D calls for victory over the strength of the enemies, described figuratively as the jaws of the lion. E culminates the section with the eventual answer to his cry for deliverance from the enemies, again described as the horns of the oxen.

The praise. The praise section forms another chiasm. A indicates that the psalmist vows to praise the Lord and calls others to do the same. A' indicates that the future generations will also honor the Lord. Both A and A' focus on congregational praise and worship of the Lord. In A, the subject of praise and worship is the psalmist and the generation of

Israel. In A', the subject of praise and worship extends to the rich, to all those who are dying, and to the coming generation. The word זֶרַע, "seed"[33] connects A and A'. In A, the seed refers to the seed of Jacob, כָּל־זֶרַע יַעֲקֹב. In A', the seed extends beyond the people of Israel to לְדּוֹר, "to *the coming* generation, family." B and B' show the reason for praising God. Two words that link this section are סתר, "to hide, conceal"[34] and שׁוּב, "to turn back, return."[35] B shows that the afflicted worship the Lord because the Lord did not turn his attention away from the outcast. B' indicates that the Lord is the ruler of the earth and the universe. Because the Lord is the ruler, the families return to worship him. C is the center of praise. The psalmist vows to praise the Lord; even those who seek him will do the same. The praise includes feasting with those who are afflicted. To see the condensed version of the presentation above, a general structure of Ps 22 is presented below.

---

[1] See Chapter 1 for the references.

[2] This paper follows the *BHS* verse distribution.

[3] See also G. Gerleman, "יִשְׂרָאֵל," *TLOT* 2:581.

[4] W. D. Tucker Jr. and Jamie A. Grant, *Psalms*, NIVAC (Grand Rapids: Zondervan, 2018), 2: E-book edition, Psalm 98, "Participating in Noisy Worship (98:4-6)," para. 2; Peter C. Craigie, *The Book of Deuteronomy*, NICOT (Grand Rapids: Eerdmans, 1976), 65.

[5] BDB, s.v. "יְשׁוּעָה"; *HALOT*, s.v. "יְשׁוּעָה"; *DBLH*, s.v. "יְשׁוּעָה."

[6] BDB, s.v. "פָּלַט"; *HALOT*, s.v. "פָּלַט"; *DBLH*, s.v. "פָּלַט."

[7] *HALOT*, s.v. "מָלַט."

[8] BDB, s.v. "עָזַר"; *HALOT*, s.v. "עָזַר"; *DBLH*, s.v. "עָזַר."

[9] BDB, s.v. "בָּטַח"; *HALOT*, s.v. "בָּזָה"; *DBLH*, s.v. "בָּטַח."

[10] *DBLH*, s.v. "גָּלַל."

[11] The fathers may refer specifically to the people of Israel who were delivered and rescued from their bondage in Egypt.

[12] Osborne, *Hermeneutical Spiral*, 222. Gunkel and Mowinckel propose the methodology of reading and interpreting the Psalms individually. But Brevard S. Childs questions the canonical shaping of the Psalms and at the same time opens a new methodology of reading and interpreting the Psalms. His student, Gerald Henry Wilson, proposed different techniques of interpreting the Psalms and concludes that the collection of psalms was "the result of a purposeful, editorial activity which sought to impart a meaningful arrangement which encompassed the whole." Gerald Henry Wilson, *The Editing of the Hebrew*

Psalter, SBLDS 76 (Chico, CA: Scholars Press, 1985), 199. See also H. Gunkel, *The Psalms: A Form-Critical Introduction* (Philadelphia: Fortress, 1967), 5; W. D. Tucker Jr., "Psalms 1, Book Of," *Dictionary of the Old Testament: Wisdom, Poetry and Writings* 581; Brevard S. Childs, *Introduction to the Old Testament as Scripture* (Philadelphia: Fortress, 1979), 511–13.

[13] Gordon D. Fee and Douglas K. Stuart, *How to Read the Bible for All Its Worth: A Guide to Understanding the Bible* (Grand Rapids: Zondervan, 2009), 205.

[14] R. K. Harrison, *Introduction to the Old Testament with a Comprehensive Review of Old Testament Studies and a Special Supplement on the Apocrypha* (Grand Rapids: Eerdmans, 1973), 986. Waltke divides the psalm differently. See Bruce K. Waltke, "Psalms, Theology Of," *NIDOTTE* 4:1100–1103.

[15] Nancy L. Declaissé-Walford, "An Intertextual Reading of Psalms 22, 23, and 24," in *The Book of Psalms: Composition and Reception*, ed. Peter W. Flint and Patrick D. Miller (Leiden: Brill, 2005), 139, https://doi.org/10.1163/9789047414797_009.

[16] Ibid., 142–43.

[17] Richard M. Davidson, "Psalms 22, 23, and 24: A Messianic Trilogy?" (paper presented at the ETS Annual Meeting of the Old Testament Psalms Session, San Diego, CA, 20 November 2019), 2.

[18] "Introduction" [Psalm 22], *SDABC*, ed. Francis D. Nichol, rev. ed. (Washington, DC: Review & Herald, 1976), 3:682. C. Briggs and E. Briggs consider this psalm as a lament with five strophes. Briggs and Briggs, *The Book of Psalms*, 188.

[19] James L. Mays considers Ps 22, as a whole, as a "prayer for help." He noted that its "basic purpose" is in the petition of the psalmist to God to deliver him from "life-threatening trouble." James L. Mays, *Psalms*, ed. James L. Mays, IBC (Atlanta: John Knox, 1994), 106. He outlines the troubles of the psalmists as "God's providential care is missing (vv. 1–2); others reject (vv. 6–8) and attack him (vv. 12–13, 16–18); and the needy one experiences the loss of life power (vv. 14–15). The prayer asserts trust in the LORD (vv. 3–5, 9–10)." Ibid., 105.

[20] "Introduction," *SDABC*, 3:682.

[21] Mays denies that the voice heard in this psalm is any "particular historical person at a certain time but one individual case of the typical." Mays, *Psalms*, 105.

[22] Robert G. Bratcher and William David Reybum suggest that the lament part of Ps 22 "may be divided into three parts, each of which contains a desperate plea for help, joined to an affirmation of faith and praise (verses 1–5, 6–11, 12–21)." Bratcher and Reyburn, *Book of Psalms*, 212. This paper adapts three divisions of the psalm which focus on the two subjects of complaints referring to God and the enemies and the eventual call for deliverance.

[23] Jennie R. Ebeling, "Gatekeeper," *EDB* 484.

[24] BDB, s.v. "רָחֹק."

[25] *HALOT*, s.v. "יְשׁוּעָה."

[26] BDB, s.v. "יְשׁוּעָה."

[27] *DBLH*, s.v. "יְשׁוּעָה."

[28] John E. Hartley, "יָשַׁע," *TWOT* 1:414; BDB, s.v. "יָשַׁע"; *DCH* 4, s.v. "יָשַׁע."

[29] BDB, s.v. "עָנָה"; *GHCLOT*, s.v. "עָנָה"; *HALOT*, s.v. "עָנָה."

[30] Grant R. Osborne defines synthetic or step parallelism as referring "to a development of thought in which the second line adds ideas to the first." Grant R. Osborne, *The Hermeneutical Spiral: A Comprehensive Introduction to Biblical Interpretation*, rev. and expanded 2nd ed. (Downers Grove, IL: InterVarsity Press, 2010), 227–28.

[31] The staircase parallelism, known also as climactic parallelism, shows that the second phrase repeats the units of the first phrase while progressing the thought. See an illustration of the staircase parallelism in William W. Klein, Craig L. Blomberg, and Robert L. Hubbard Jr., *Introduction to Biblical Interpretation*, rev. and exp. ed. (Nashville: Nelson, 2004), 297–98; Packer, Tenney, and White, *Illustrated Manners*, 367; Philip P. Jenson, *New Bible Commentary: Twenty-First Century Edition*, ed. D. A. Carson et al., 4th ed. (Leicester: Inter-Varsity Press, 1994), "Staircase parallelism," para. 1.

[32] Ebeling, "Gatekeeper," 484.

[33] BDB, s.v. "זֶרַע"; *HALOT*, s.v. "זֶרַע."

[34] BDB, s.v. "סָתַר"; *LALHB*, s.v. "סָתַר."

[35] BDB, s.v. "שׁוּב"; *LALHB*, s.v. "שׁוּב."

CHAPTER 3

HONOR AND SHAME PASSAGES IN PSALM 22

This section looks at the passages from which the means of forsakenness/ abandonment, taunt speech, nakedness, and feast/meal and the values of patronage, kinship/family, and trust come. It is presented into two categories: shame and honor. Each section of the values or means reviews the textual criticism of pertinent passages and analyzes the grammar and the syntax, the interpretation, and the shame and honor implications and presents a summary.

The section on shame deals with how David went through the shameful experience. The next section discusses David's honor sources to cover his shame. The next chapter presents his expected deliverance to remove his shame and restore his honor.

Shame

This section presents the means of forsakenness/abandonment, taunt speech, and nakedness. The terms and phrases in the selected verses disclose the occurrence of the means for shame in Ps 22. Also, how David went through these shame experiences is the primary concern of this section.

Forsakenness/abandonment. Verses 2–3 deal with the means of forsakenness/ abandonment. The breaking of the patronage relationship causes the psalmist's abandonment. As explained below, patronage is a relationship between the patron and

Structure of Psalm 22

Superscript: A psalm belonging to David (v. 1)
Lament
I. Failure of deliverance (vv. 2–3)
  A Rejection (עֲזַבְתָּנִי)
    B Farness of salvation (רָחוֹק מִישׁוּעָתִי; v. 2)
  A' Rejection (רָחוֹק מִישׁוּעָתִי)
    B No rest (v. 3)
  II. Claim for honor (vv. 4–6)
    A Honor due God (יִשְׂרָאֵל תְּהִלּוֹת; v. 4)
      B' The fathers trusted (בָּטַח)
        C God delivered them (פָּלַט; v. 5b)
      B" The fathers cried for help (זָעַק)
        C' God rescued them (מָלַט; v. 5c)
      B''' The fathers trusted (בָּטַח)
        C''' They were not ashamed (לֹא־בוֹשׁוּ; v. 5d)
    III. Shame under enemies (vv. 7–9)
      A Feeling of worthlessness (v. 7a)
      A' Disgraced and despised by people (v. 7b)
        B Enemies taunt (v. 8a)
        B' Enemies mock with lips (v. 8b)
        B''' Enemies mock with head (v. 8c)
          C Enemies' statement of mockery (v. 9)
  II.' Claim for honor (vv. 10–11)
    A God is progenitor (v. 10a)
      B Psalmist placed on mother's trust (v. 10b)
      B' Psalmist placed in God's care (v. 11a)
    A' God as progenitor (v. 11)
I'. Call for deliverance (v. 12)
  A Call not to be far (אַל־תִּרְחַק; v. 12a)
    B Trouble is near (צָרָה קְרוֹבָה; v. 12b)
    B' No one to help (אֵין עוֹזֵר; v. 12c)
    III'. Shame under enemies (vv. 13–19)
      A Enemies' aggression (סְבָבוּנִי, כִּתְּרוּנִי; vv. 13–14)
        B Physical and emotional malady (עַצְמוֹתַי; vv. 15–16)

A' Enemies' aggression (סְבָבוּנִי, הִקִּיפוּנִי; v. 17)
B' Physical malady (עַצְמוֹתָי; vv. 18–19)
I". Success of deliverance (vv. 20–22)
A Call not to be far (אַל־תִּרְחָק; v. 20a)
B Call for help (לְעֶזְרָתִי חוּשָׁה; v. 20b)
C Call for deliverance (הַצִּילָה; v. 21)
D Call for salvation (הוֹשִׁיעֵנִי; v. 22a)
E Statement of deliverance (עֲנִיתָנִי; v. 22b)
Praise
A Call to praise (כָּל־זֶרַע יַעֲקֹב; vv. 23–24)
B Reason to praise (לֹא־הִסְתִּיר; v. 25)
C Praise and feasting (vv. 26–27)
B' Reason to praise (יָשֻׁבוּ; vv. 28–29)
A' People's praise (לַדּוֹר; vv. 30–32)

client, where the patron provides for the client's needs while the client remains loyal to the patron. The term עֲזַבְתָּנִי, from the root עָזַב, displays the means of forsakenness/abandonment. Other words such as מַעֲנֶה and דוּמִיָּה with their respective negation (לֹא) intensify the forsakenness/abandonment.

Textual criticism. In v. 2, the LXX adds the phrase πρόσχες μοι. It is a verbal clause directly appealing to God. The verbal clause seems to complete the "far/near" merism in vv. 2 and 12 to form an inclusio.[1] The translation may be like this: "Please urgently come near me!"[2] Although this may be probable, the Hebrew text stills supersedes the Greek text because it seems that the translators added this clause for a better understanding of the passage.

Besides, the LXX interestingly translates the word שַׁאֲגָתִי into των παραπτωματων μου, "from my transgressions."[3] This rendering of the LXX is probably an assumption of the translators based on the word עָזַב. עָזַב appears in contexts where sin and transgression are prominent.[4] However, in Ps 22, it is unlikely since there is no hint in the psalm that the psalmist breaks any of the stipulations in the covenant relationship.

Lexical analysis. In v. 2, the word עָזַב, "to abandon, leave, forsake,"[5] the stem of עֲזַבְתָּנִי, carries the idea of shame in the Akkadian and the Ethiopic derivatives.[6] The sense of the word means to refuse to accept or acknowledge something and conceived of as leaving it behind or forsaking it.[7] Here, God is the subject of abandonment, and the psalmist is the object.[8]

The term מִישׁוּעָתִי, "away from my salvation" is a verbal noun with preposition מִן. It comes from יְשׁוּעָה which has a wide range of meanings such as "help, salvation,"[9] "welfare, deliverance, prosperity, safety and security,"[10] "health,"[11] and "victory."[12] Here, the word *salvation* is used but does not undervalue the other meanings attached to the word יְשׁוּעָה.

In v. 2, the word שַׁאֲגָתִי appears. The stem שְׁאָגָה means two things: (a) the "scream" of a person challenged[13] and (b) the "loud deep and rumbling cry of the lion."[14] The context of this psalm associates שְׁאָגָה with (a) the petitioner's expression of the intensity of the lament (v. 2) and (b) the roaring of the hostile powers, adversaries, and enemies who desire to devour and destroy the psalmist (v. 13).[15]

The word תַעֲנֶה (v. 3)—from עָנָה, "to reply, answer"[16]—is closely related to the means of forsakenness/abandonment. In this context, the sense of the word refers to an action, a response to a signal or request. Verbal dialogue is not expected but rather a reaction for "beneficial sense."[17]

The word דוּמִיָּה means "silence, repose,"[18] or "rest."[19] Relative to one's relationship with God, it means "the silent expectation of divine aid, confidence placed in God."[20] The sense of "rest" indicates a "relief from trouble with an implication of being in a right relationship to God."[21] The psalmist complains about the absence of the divine aid that results in "no rest or relief from his situation"[22] (v. 3).

Grammatical and syntactical analysis. This section presents the syntactical analysis of the passage. After the direct address in v. 2, the psalmist expresses a series of complaints. The interrogative לָמָה, "why" marks the complaints. God is the one addressed in the complaints, as specified through the use of the second person suffix.

The first complaint is לָמָה עֲזַבְתָּנִי, "Why have you forsaken me?" The second complaint is רָחוֹק מִישׁוּעָתִי, "far from my salvation." The word רָחוֹק intensifies the distance of the supposed act of salvation from the petitioner, מִישׁוּעָתִי. The preposition מִן emphasizes the moving away of יְשׁוּעָה from the psalmist.[23] The third complaint is the construct דִּבְרֵי

שַׁאֲגָתִי, "words of my groanings." The interrogative לָמֶה fills in the ellipsis in the second and third complaints.

Verse 3 begins with another direct address, the vocative אֱלֹהַי, "my God." The psalmist addresses God in the first person to emphasize the relationship existing between them. The psalmist continues with two more complaints stated in plain statements of facts about God's seeming inattentiveness to his complaints.

Structure and translation. This section presents the structure and translation of vv. 2–3. In v. 2, A is the direct address, the B's present the interrogative of the complaint, the C's state the reasons for the complaint, and the D's refer to the recipient of the cause for complaints. In v. 3, A is the direct address. The B's indicate the call. The C's show the result of the call. The D's point to the object of the result of the call.

> **A** My God! My God!
>   **B** Why have you
>   **C** forsaken
>   **D** me?
>   **B'** *Why are you*
>   **C'** far from saving
>   **D'** me?
>   **B"** *Why are you*
>   **C"** *far from the* words of my groanings? (v. 2)
> **A** Oh, my God!
>   **B** I cry by day
>   **C** but there is no answer
>   **D** *for me!*
>   **B'** *I cry* by night
>   **C'** but *there is* no rest
>   **D'** for me. (v. 3, ESV, emphasis mine)

Interpretation. After addressing God directly, David then presents his complaints to him on matters of his relationship with him. He questions his perceived[24] forsakenness and abandonment by God.[25] The question seems to indicate that the psalmist's relationship with God was very close before the complaint. The turn of events left the psalmist bewildered because of the separation. The psalmist wonders why God refused to acknowledge their established relationship and is willing to forsake the covenant relationship. The psalmist is groping for an answer to this particular situation but seems to find none. The immediate response to his question does not seem to be imminent.

In Deut 31, when Yahweh is the subject and man is the object of abandonment, two things may be noted. (a) Yahweh promises the people of Israel that he will not leave neither forsake them (vv. 6, 8). The promise includes his "eternal presence and protection on the nation as a whole."[26] Yahweh serves as their leader and help.[27] His abiding presence upon Israel will give them victory against the people of Canaan (v. 3). For this, Yahweh ascribes honor to Israel.

(b) God forsakes Israel because of their idolatry (v. 17). Israel turns to other gods to worship and serve them,[28] which was tantamount to abandonment of their covenant with Yahweh. Because they first abandon Yahweh, in return Yahweh abandons them. The abandonment will bring disasters and sufferings to Israel (v. 17).[29] Israel will be put to shame, as the prophet Jeremiah says: "All [Israel] who forsake you [Yahweh] shall be put to shame" (Jer 17:13).

Confession of sin and genuine repentance avert God's chastisement against the people (Judg 10:10, 12:10; Ezra 9:10). As a result, God will raise a deliverer to lead the people from their oppressors (Judg 2:16–18). The effect of subduing the enemies are peace and prosperity. Yahweh warns the people that they should no longer forsake him lest a repeat of the horrible.[30] Because of his grace, Yahweh reconciles humanity back to him.

Yet the psalmist's complaints seem to denote that his relationship is right with God. He has done nothing careless against him. His falling out of favor appears to have no apparent reason at all. His abandonment implies his loss of economic prosperity, emotional support, and reliable help.

In spite of the abandonment, the psalmist continues to seek God for his salvation. He holds that God is the only source of deliverance.[31] Yet, his deliverance moves farther away (v. 2). Job seems to experience like David's in Ps 22. Job feels that God hates him, [32] וַיִּשְׂטְמֵנִי "and he hated me." To be hated means to be detached from the group, which is tantamount to shame. God's hatred and God as an assailant increase the intensity of Job's suffering (vv. 6–14).[33] In addition, God's allies, "his friends" (kinship group), open their mouth in derision (Job 16:9)[34] and scorn him (v. 20). For this reason, Job complains about the intensity of his sufferings.

Yet, Job believes that he has a witness in heaven, a vindicator/an advocate (Job 16:19), as his agent to "help him to settle his dispute, to secure *the right of a man with God*"[35] (cf. v. 21a). Unlike Daniel (10:13–14), the hostile enemy—Satan (Job 1:6–2:9)—was not revealed to Job. Yet like Daniel, Job has an advocate, God himself, who will restore Job's honor in the midst of his suffering (42:10–17). Robert L. Alden marks that the work of the advocate is just like that of the Messiah who shall vindicate the cause of the poor and afflicted of the earth (Isa 11:4).[36] In the case of Ps 22, David seeks no advocate except God to deliver him from his abandonment.

Indeed, Job was delivered from his predicament. He was restored into the fellowship of Yahweh and his friends. Yahweh's restoration of Job's prosperity means that his state of being poor materially ended. Also, Yahweh restored him to health and, most importantly, into his fellowship. In celebration of his restoration, Job had a festive meal in his own home, inviting his kin (Job 42:11). The fellowship meal shows Job's restoration into the community and kinship fellowship has been re-established.[37]

In spite of Job's experience, Scriptures also provide ample pieces of evidence of God giving deliverance and salvation to individuals (Gen 49:18, Exod 15:2) and God's people (Exod 14:3, Isa 33:2). The deliverance they prayed for is primarily from external evils with emphasis on spiritual ideas.[38] Also, the salvation they ask for offers different benefits.

James Swanson states two significant understandings of יְשׁוּעָה, "salvation": (a) "to be in a state of freedom from danger"[39] and (b) "deliverance in a religious sense."[40] The first one indicates physical salvation, where the physical body is preserved from harm or unpleasantness. An example of this kind of salvation[41] is the physical removal of the people of Israel from Egypt by the power of God's presence with them (Exod 14:13). Moses praises God for this particular marvelous deed so that he exclaims, "The Lord is my strength and my song, and he has become my salvation [וַיְהִי־לִי לִישׁוּעָה]" (Exod 15:2, ESV).

The second sense of salvation refers to a spiritual sense.[42] This salvation is deliverance from sin or evil. David once called out to the Lord to save him from harm and place him on higher ground where sin could not reach him. He states, "But I am afflicted and in pain; let your salvation [יְשׁוּעָתְךָ], O God, set me on high!" (Ps 69:30, ESV). His sin brought him down to disgrace. Yet, Yahweh's salvation placed him on a high status.[43] In Yahweh, David's shame turns into honor.

A third sense may imply welfare and prosperity.[44] It is also linked with honor. The loss of יְשׁוּעָה means the loss of honor. The situation of Job describes this sense of יְשׁוּעָה in line with prosperity and calamity. Prosperity means (1) God's friendship with him and its benefits (29:2–5a); (2) the presence of his children around him (v. 5b); (3) the respect of princes and nobles to him (vv. 7–11); (4) his patronage towards the poor, orphans, dying, widows, blind, lame, and needy (vv. 12–16); and (5) his honorable status as chief and king (v. 25). These all indicate that Job is exalted and noble. Job lost this status as the calamity struck him. He became a laughingstock (30:1), byword (v. 9), detestable (v. 10), and shameful (v. 11). He lost his nobility[45] and prosperity. He states, "My honor is pursued as by the wind, and my prosperity [יְשֻׁעָתִי] has passed away like a cloud" (Job 30:15, ESV).[46]

In the context of Ps 22, it seems that the sense of deliverance from sin or evil is unlikely. Words that may indicate the psalmist's committal of sin or that sin bothers the psalmist is unclear.[47] The most likely salvation is his physical removal from harm or unpleasantness and his state of being. Some expressions on the state of being are evident in the psalm.

The psalmist desires God's salvation. The distance of his salvation intensifies his abandonment. It includes the separation of his welfare, good health, and security. The psalmist seems to be holistically vulnerable. Amidst his distress, God has not relieved him of his troubles nor acted favorably toward him. God has not lent his ears toward his intense groanings. Without deliverance from God, he remains in a state of shame.

The superlative repetition of the interrogative "why" means the complete and total shaming of the psalmist. The psalmist expects that the answer to his petition comes as an act to alleviate his situation. He expects Yahweh to vouchsafe him through his help and deliverance.[48] The far distance of his salvation complements his abandonment, and God does not hear his groanings. To make matters worse, the answer to his calls and rest eludes him. These sealed his abandonment.

The psalmist is forsaken and shamed. He wonders why no action has taken place for the restoration of his honor. He has all the questions, but the answer and the act of God to relieve him from his situation remain elusive. His predicament and restoration of his relationship with God is far from being resolved.

Honor and shame implication. In the honor and shame concept, the lineal hierarchical relationship attributes an identity towards the members of the family or kinship. Embeddedness in the group or group alliance is vital in maintaining honor and status.[49] For the psalmist, he has a relationship with God, a "vertical dyadic"[50] relationship. In the vertical dyadic relationship, the patron has the power to provide protection, salvation, and rest to the client. The psalmist gets his honor from this relationship.

However, God's relationship with the psalmist is problematic. God has not exercised his power to subdue the enemies of the psalmist to enhance his dyadic relationship with him. Instead, he abandons the psalmist, eventually breaking the attachment and the bond between them. The abandonment disgraces the psalmist. The psalmist is without a protector of his honor. He is vulnerably unprotected and prone to the attacks and ridicule of the enemies. The estrangement and fall from favor from the mighty One—God—led to his illness, suffering, and adversity.

Summary. This section indicates that the relationship between God/Yahweh and the psalmist was broken. The fractured relationship led to God's denial of the psalmist's salvation and deliverance, even ignoring his cries of distress, resulting to restlessness. God, as the patron, is no longer obligated to respond favorably to the client's request and give relief to his/her troubled situation. The psalmist questions the reason for God's/Yahweh's abandonment of him but does not have any answer as of the meantime. The abandonment brought him utter shame and opened the way for his enemies to shame him.

Nakedness. This section deals with the psalmist's predicament under the attacks of his enemies (vv. 17–19). It explores the enemies' ways to bring him to a shameful status. The eventual forceful removal of his garments and clothing is the ultimate act to put him in total shame.

In the OT, nakedness is associated with shame, and clothing is associated with honor.[51] In the beginning, nakedness did not elicit shame.[52] As Kenneth A. Mathews puts it, the nakedness of Adam and Eve symbolized their oblivion to evil.[53] L. E. P. Erith aptly indicates that "innocence knows no shame, which comes from consciousness of sin."[54]

When Adam and Eve discovered they were naked following their sin, both felt shame in the presence of each other.[55] "Shame in the presence of nakedness is ... a result of sin"[56] (Gen 3:7). Harvey Newcomb states that "the immediate discovery of their nakedness, by our first parents, after their disobedience, is probably intended to show the nakedness and shame which sin has brought upon our souls."[57] The man and the woman sewed fig leaves and loincloths to hide their shame and nakedness (Gen 3:7). However, the covering they made was not enough to cover their shame and nakedness. God's provision of covering was the only solution to their nakedness and shame (Gen 3:21).

John Skinner describes the change Adam and Eve saw as a "new sense of shame."[58] William David Reyburn and Euan McGregor Fry appropriately defines shame as the "painful consciousness of having done or thought something that is recognized as wrong or unacceptable; it is generally most intense in the presence of other people."[59] Also, they state that "the realization of nakedness leads to the realization of a relational brokenness in their relationship with God and with each other."[60] With this situation, Adam and Eve became aware of their unworthiness to face God.[61]

The realization led Adam and Eve to sew fig leaves to cover their shame. The sewed coverings were inadequate because it did not remove their shame. Dan Lé correctly states that nakedness is unpleasant, and it needs some defense.[62] The severe result of the "shameful state of nakedness results in curses and expulsion."[63] Consequently, God confirms the inadequacy of the human expedience[64] by making for them "garments of skin and clothed them" (v. 21). God's act of making a garment is "salvific in character."[65] God covers Adam and Eve with clothes of skin, indicating the change of their status from curse. The clothing hid their nakedness and covered their shame.[66]

The Scriptures and the ANE, in terms of war, picture nakedness as a means to humiliate the war captives further while marching towards captivity. This shame of nakedness is "the shame of defeat and enslavement."[67] Sheila Bridge states that "nakedness is almost always a symbol of shame, reserved for the destitute, the conquered or the deranged."[68]

In common situations, a person who has clothing is more honorable than the person naked. In the honor and shame context, "clothing signals a claim to honor in terms of gender, role, and status."[69] In short, nakedness means "emptiness, vulnerability, and shame."[70] Clothing means "protection and wealth."[71] Also, it is a "constant and pervasive symbol of dignity and authority."[72]

Textual criticism. The textual variant appears in the translation of Aquila and Symmachus of the Hebrew word כְּלָבִים, "dogs" with θηραταί, "to seek, endeavor"[73] (v. 17). Aquila, Theodotion, and Jerome had the vocalization of כְּלָבִים, *kĕlābîm*, as *kallābîm*, "hunters."[74] Aquila and Symmachus based their translation on the alternative vocalization.[75] In the Egyptian language, *tsm* is a common term for "hunting dog."[76] In the ANE, "hunting dogs" are "correspondingly rare."[77] In Psalms, the meaning of the term כֶּלֶב is "dog." In four occurrences in Psalms (22:17, 20; 59:7, 15), the term appears as a metaphor of enemies who oppress and have that hateful activity against the psalmist.[78] In Ps 22, the more appropriate translation for כְּלָבִים is "dogs" rather than "hunters."

Another textual variant that appears in the text is the word כָּאֲרָ. However, this paper does not give a detailed discussion of this textual variant for reasons that some scholars have already discussed this matter lengthily.[79] What it adheres to is the MT rendition כָּאֲרִי, "like a lion" rather than the LXX Greek translation ὤρυξαν, "they pierced."[80]

Lexical analysis. The two words directly linked with nakedness are בְגָדַי from בֶּגֶד, "clothing, covering"[81] and לְבוּשִׁי from לְבוּשׁ, "garment"[82] (v. 19). The term בֶּגֶד refers to a "garment, clothing, raiment, robe of any kind, from the filthy clothing of the leper to the holy robes of the high priest, the simplest covering of the poor as well as the costly raiment of the rich and noble."[83] It can also refer to a cloak, "a specific outer piece of clothing."[84] The original meaning of the verb form means "to clothe, to cover, to veil."[85] To remove the clothing of an individual means to reveal the nakedness of the person.

The word לְבוּשׁ comes from the same semantic range as בֶּגֶד. It refers to a "common garb or priestly or royal robe, *of a* male or female."[86] It can also refer to the garment worn by a warrior or worshippers, servants, mourners.[87] The style of clothing determines the social status of a person. Figuratively, it refers to "the state of being of a person or their character."[88]

The verbs used for the distribution of the clothing and the garment are (a) יְחַלְּקוּ from חָלַק, "divide," "separate into portions," "distribute," and "divide and scatter"[89] and (b) יַפִּילוּ from נָפַל, "to fall."[90] On some rare occasions, חָלַק means "'division' of stolen property,"[91] which portrays a war-like situation where the victorious enemy divides the spoils from the fallen foe.[92] The *hiphil* of נָפַל means "to cast a lot,"[93] with particular use of the word גּוֹרָל, "lot."[94]

Grammatical and syntactical analysis. The passage under this strophe is in vv. 17–18. The relative causal conjunction כִּי, "for"[95] marks the transition from the previous strophe, vv. 13–16. This present strophe, vv. 17–18, indicates the reasons for the psalmist's physical and emotional sickness (vv. 13–16). What follows are four lines of "they" and "I" description of the psalmist's attackers and his assessment of his condition.

The first line (v. 17) comprises three cola. In the first two cola, the persistent perfective[96] verbs סְבָבוּנִי and הִקִּיפוּנִי appear. They indicate that the enemies persistently laid siege of the psa8lmist. These synonymous verbs fill in the ellipsis in the third colon.

The second line (v. 18a) has a quatrain of five verbal clauses.[97] The first clause shifts the subject from "they" to "I." The focus is on the psalmist, who states his present condition.[98] The second clause shifts to the subject from "I" to "they" (v. 18b). The focus turns to the enemies who continually humiliate the psalmist. The third clause "has in view the initial and continuing phases within the internal temporal structure of past situation."[99] The past condition points to the event when the psalmist was taunted and ridiculed by the hostile party (v. 8). The fourth clause, a simple resultative non-perfective clause, indicates that the acts of the enemies to stare and gloat has a resulting action, that is "they apportioned my garments." The fifth clause, the causative non-perfective clause, indicates that the action begins at the same time as the speaking.

Structure. The structure for v. 16 is a split synonymous and synthetic parallelism. The first and second cola are synonymous, but the third colon becomes synthetic since it adds information to the previous two cola. The illustration of the structure looks like this:

A Transition statement (v. 16a)
  B Enemies encircle the psalmist (v. 16a)
  B' Enemies encircle the psalmist (v. 16b)
    C Enemies pierce the psalmist's hands and feet (v. 16c)

The structure of v. 17 is an inverse of the structure of v. 16. The first colon seems to be out of joint, but it is the antecedent of the second and third cola in this verse. The structure is a synthetic parallelism between the first and second cola. The second and third cola create a synonymous parallelism. The structure is illustrated below:

A Psalmist's total suffering (v. 17a)
  B Enemies stare at him (v. 17b)
  B' Enemies gloat over him (v. 17c)

The structure of v. 18 is a synonymous parallelism or a chiasm indicating the total submission of the psalmist to his enemies. The ultimate goal of the building is to humiliate the psalmist by forcibly removing his garments.

A Garments of psalmist apportioned
  B Enemies apportion psalmist's garments
A' Garments up for casting lots

Text and translation. This section presents the Hebrew text and the working translation.

Hebrew Text		Working Translation
כִּי סְבָבוּנִי כְּלָבִים עֲדַת מְרֵעִים		For dogs surround me.
הִקִּיפוּנִי כָּאֲרִי יָדַי וְרַגְלָי:	17	Evildoers go around me. Like a lion [they mauled] my hands and my feet.
אֲסַפֵּר כָּל־עַצְמוֹתָי הֵמָּה יַבִּיטוּ		I count all my bones. They
יִרְאוּ־בִי:	18	stare at me. They gloat over me.
יְחַלְּקוּ בְגָדַי לָהֶם וְעַל־לְבוּשִׁי יַפִּילוּ		They apportioned my
גוֹרָל:	19	clothing for them. And upon my garments, they cast lots.

Interpretation. The passage (vv. 17–19) dealt with in this section draws attention to the final attack of the enemies to humiliate the psalmist. The enemies' attack started with taunting (vv. 7–8), then surrounding and encircling (vv. 13–14, 17a), physical assault (v. 17b), and staring and gloating over the emaciated condition of the psalmist (v. 18). The enemies' ultimate act to humiliate the psalmist is stripping[100] his inner clothing and outer garment. The enemies divide their spoils through the casting of lots (v. 19). The attack of the enemy is methodical. The enemies reduced him to nothing.

The physical and emotional condition of the psalmist is a result of the assault of the enemies. The three parallel images describe the three conditions. The common point of this condition is the psalmist's total humiliation and approach to death (vv. 15–16).[101] The enemies attack the very life of the psalmist.

The figurative expression "poured out like water" (v. 15a) describes that the psalmist's strength is spent out. He is completely exhausted and utterly weak.[102] Lamentations 2:11 seems to be a parallel expression of the psalm: "My bowels are poured out like water." The context of this passage shows that the life of the lamenter is "ebbing away."[103] However, a similar expression in 2 Sam 14:14, "we are spilled like water," indicates not just the loss of strength or ebbing away of life but a death sentence.

The expression "poured out like water" situates the psalmist at the brink of death.

The parallel expression "all my bones are out of joint" (v. 15b) indicates defeat or death. The literal rendering of this expression is "all my bones are separated/scattered from one another." The scattering of bones in a war zone is typical. In the context of Ps 53:4, God scatters the bones of the enemies of his people. Bones scattered parallels shame. The image of scattered bones, especially on the battlefield, is definitive of "utter defeat and hopelessness."[104] It may also refer to extreme fear. Such was the countenance of Belshazzar when the judgment of God came upon him. Though he did not understand the meaning of the text written on the wall at that time, he realized it was a time of defeat and death sentence for him (Dan 5:6, 30). As the previous expression, the psalmist is in a situation of inevitable defeat and death.

Another expression used by the psalmist to describe his situation is the parallel colon: "My heart becomes like wax; it has melted within my bowels" (v. 15c). The heart (לֵב) is the center of human existence. It refers to the "vital, affective, noetic, and voluntative"[105] aspects of a person. The melting of heart seems to "describe the fear evoked by enemies who are waiting and watching for death to come."[106] The psalmist is incapable of launching a counterattack against the enemies because fear affected his whole existence. He "has lost all courage and hope."[107] Nahum uses a pictorial language to describe Nineveh's indescribable horror[108] amid God's judgment. One of the expressions he used is "hearts melt" (Nah 2:11), synonymous with the psalmist's "heart ... melted." T. Laesch captures this picture well:

> The heart of the people [Nineveh], their spirit, once so fearless, so proud, so indomitable, now is melted like wax. Alarm, fear, terror, consternation, black despair grip them. No longer can they form any plan of resistance; their knees tremble; sickening anguish, nauseating horror grips their loins. Their faces "gather blackness," assume the livid, ashen color of people frightened to death.[109]

Aside from the melting of the heart, the psalmist declares that his strength is dried up (v. 16a). He compares it with the potsherd, a piece of broken earthenware, "proverbially for anything of no value."[110] Strength may refer to "the economic and military resources"[111] of the psalmist. It may also refer to human strength and power. Strength and might enable the fighters and warriors to go to battle (Josh 14:11). Failure of force in fighting means defeat. Thus, when the psalmist "complains his strength has vanished,"[112] he describes that his military might and strength for battle has crumbled to pieces. Yet a cliché indicates that man shall not prevail by his power. What matters is God's help (1 Sam 2:9).

The psalmist further describes his inability to protect himself verbally. In a figurative expression, he states, "my tongue sticks to my jaws" (v. 16). The phrase "their tongue stuck to the roof of their mouth" appear in Job 29:10, Ps 137:4, Ezek 3:26, and Lam 4:4. The phrase indicates the inability to speak or refrain from speaking, except for Lamentations, where it means "thirst." In Job, the expression means that the big or the important men in the town became silent and stopped talking.[113] The silence of these honorific men ascribes higher esteem and honor to Job. A person speaking is made honorable by the one who is kept silent.

In Ezekiel, God silenced the prophet to prevent him from rebuking the people of Jerusalem. The prophet's silence is one of judgment. It brought humiliation to the people of Jerusalem. The judgment would bring Jerusalem to captivity that would eventually put them to shame (Ezek 3:27).

Psalm 137 reflects the humiliation the Israelite captives endured in the land of Babylon. In Ps 137, the exiles are taunted by their captors to sing of their homeland, the glorious Zion, but they could not sing (v. 3).[114] They are bitterly humiliated. Also, a conscious refusal to remember Jerusalem elicits a curse on their "skillful hand and voice."[115] Here, the one placed under the curse of being unable to speak is in a shameful status. The same humiliation seems to reflect the psalmist's disgrace in Ps 22.

The last line of the psalmist's description of his physical and emotional sickness takes a twist. The subject changes from the third person, referring to the psalmist himself, to the second person, referring to Yahweh. All other occurrences of the second person in this psalm refer to Yahweh (vv. 1–5, 10–11, 20, 26, 28), who is supposed to be the deliverer of the psalmist.

However, the statement of the psalmist occurring at the last line of this section seems to indicate that Yahweh colludes with the psalmist's adversary to place him down[116] to the dust of death, וְלַעֲפַר־מָוֶת (v. 16b). The dust of death may represent a lowly position or humiliation.[117] This psalm's context seems to suggest that the dust of death refers to the place of the grave[118] or tomb and "the netherworld."[119] The occurrence of the word מָוֶת, referring to the dead person,[120] appears to support this idea. The last line indicates that the end of all the psalmist's predicament leads to the grave where the dead are. To simply put it, death is his end.

The systematic assault of the enemies against the psalmist shows them surrounding and encircling, staring, and gloating, and eventually dividing and casting lots with his garments (vv. 17–19). The passage describes the enemies as dogs, evildoers, and like a lion (v. 17). The parallel passage typifies the enemies as many young bulls and bulls of Bashan and like a tearing and roaring lion (vv. 13–14). A young bull is known for its ferocity and strength[121] and wildness.[122] The metaphor bulls of Bashan emphasizes the state of being well-nourished. Bulls may refer to warriors or "may also function as a metaphorical designation for leaders (cf. Isa 10:13; ... Ps 68:30)."[123] The lion represents an "unmatched power and majesty"[124] or a valiant warrior. In the OT, dogs are "often wild, scavenger animal[s] that ran in packs"[125] with a "very negative image, representing the despised, the unclean, or the enemy waiting to devour."[126] In this psalm, the ferocious animals mentioned refer to the hostile enemies drawing up battle formation, waiting to pounce on the psalmist. The enemies, in a sense, are durable, ferocious, wild, capable, and fearless warriors. They lay siege, enclose, encircle, and bound him to seal his way of escape. This event seems to suggest the psalmist's eventual capture.

Another physical malady with which the psalmist describes himself is as if he is dead. The expression "I can count all my bones" (v. 18a, ESV) means that the psalmist is at the full measure of his sufferings. Like his previous statement, "all my bones are separated," this situation describes defeat and death. With his condition, the enemies look and gloat over his case. The enemies' first look is a look of triumph with a sense of delight. Psalm 92:12 captures that sense of pleasure: "My eyes look with delight on [the downfall of] my enemies"[127] (Helmer Ringgren's translation). Paired with it is the look of hate, mockery, and gloating. The enemies looked upon him "with malicious satisfaction at [his] sufferings."[128]

The psalmist also indicates the apportioning and casting of lots of his garments. Some examples in the OT define the status of an individual according to the בֶּגֶד, "garment/clothing" he/she wears. The removal and the putting on of a garment may signify a change in the person's status (1 Kgs 21:27). The OT provides ample examples of garment change which indicate a change of status, from shame to honor. Pharaoh changed Joseph's clothing with a garment reflecting the honor Pharaoh ascribed to him to become the second highest-ranking official in Egypt (Gen 41:42). The priestly garments given to Aaron and his sons indicate their holy status (Exod 29:21).[129]

The OT provides examples of removal or change of garment as a sign of a change of status. Kenneth A. Mathews holds that Tamar's taking off of her widow's clothing and putting it back again "exhibited the depths of her humiliation."[130] Two views exist as to the meaning of Tamar's wearing a veil to disguise herself. (a) The veil accentuated Tamar's attractiveness, thus signifying an "elevated status (cf. Isa 3:18–23)."[131] (b) It was a typical costume of a prostitute.[132] However, the text simply states that she was thought of and described as a prostitute (Exod 38:14, 21). Most probably, she might have adopted a posture of a prostitute to make her appear as one (Gen 38:14–19).[133] The description that Tamar was a prostitute reduced her to someone who had "no claim of social legitimacy."[134] Her apparel signaled her status, from shame to shame.[135]

Lé also indicates that nakedness and clothing are divided into three basic categories: "(1) literal nakedness (natural vulnerability, simplicity and emptiness), (2) adulterous nakedness (sinful and sexual), and (3) judgmental nakedness (shameful and judgmental)."[136] The first category is linked "not with sex but with poverty, vulnerability and humiliation (e.g., Job 22:6; Is 58:7)."[137]

In his rhetoric, Eliphaz the Temanite accused Job of unnecessarily keeping "the clothing of debtors as deposits on loans, even to the point of leaving them naked. Exodus 22:26[25] required such pledged clothing be returned by sundown (cf. Deut 24:6, 17; Eze 18:12)."[138] He insinuated that terror and darkness came upon Job because he afflicted the vulnerable and defenseless. This act of leaving others naked is an act of oppression.

God has an injunction in order to prevent people from going naked. In detailing true fasting, he enjoins his people to meet the needs of the marginalized, care for them, and provide them welfare. Clothing is one way of meeting the needs of the naked (Isa 58:6–7). A relationship is also formed in covering nakedness. On the contrary, neglecting or exposing people to nakedness terminates relationships.[139]

In the experience of Jerusalem, these three categories of nakedness and clothing occur. First, nakedness is used as a metaphor for her wretched condition (Ezek 16:8). Jerusalem is described as an abandoned child. She has not received the care necessary to "promote general health and well-being for newborn children."[140] When he sees her in this condition, Yahweh has compassion for her and rescues her.[141] By the power of God's word, she recovers and is revived[142] from her despicable state until she "flourish[es] like a plant of the field" (v. 7). At the age of maturity, Yahweh claims her as his bride (v. 8), making her beauty "royal, resplendent, and internationally acclaimed."[143] Jerusalem's status changes from a shameful state of being unloved and neglected to an honorific state of royalty.

The description of Jerusalem above seems to refer to Israel's wretched condition when they were in bondage and oppressed in Egypt (Exod 1). God then delivered them, out of bondage and rescued them into the wilderness. He poured out his provisions and took care of them there (Deut 32:10–14). In the wilderness, God made a covenant with them promising to be Israel's God[144] (Exod 19:1–8; 20:5). He faithfully fulfilled his covenant promises by providing providential care to the people of Israel. He also brought them home to the land of Canaan (Exod 6:8, Deut 9:1, Judg 2:1).

Second, nakedness refers to Jerusalem's practice of adulterous nakedness. Yahweh's story of love towards Jerusalem should have been reciprocated by the same kind of love. Instead, Jerusalem abused her royal status by shifting her allegiance away from Yahweh to the gods of her lovers. Lamar Eugene Cooper Sr. summarizes Ezekiel's description of Jerusalem's whoring that led her to exile: "pride (v. 15a), spiritual prostitution (vv. 15b–19), materialistic idolatry (vv. 16–19), human sacrifices (vv. 20–21), forgetting God (v. 22), propagating her prostitution (vv. 23–25), trusting relations with pagan nations (vv. 26–29), and a weak will that cast off all moral restraints (vv. 30–34)."[145] These acts are specified as Jerusalem's nakedness uncovered in whorings with lovers and child sacrifice to her idols (v. 36).

Third, nakedness refers to the judgment God imposed upon Jerusalem. Because of her unfaithfulness, Israel is punished. Yahweh uncovers her nakedness before her international lovers (v. 37). Leslie C. Allen points out the legal aspect of this judgment. He states: "The public exposure of the naked body was a symbolic act of legal punishment for adulterers: it reversed the husband's provision of clothing (v. 10) and took away the wife's married identity."[146]

Yahweh's uncovering of Jerusalem's nakedness reveals her vulnerability, defenseless, and helplessness. Yahweh uses Israel's lovers—literally the Egyptians, Assyrians, and Babylonians—to conquer and vanquish Israel (vv. 22, 36–37). The nations mentioned become the "example of the justice and judgment of God."[147] Jerusalem is eventually conquered by the military might Babylon as Yahweh's retribution for her unfaithfulness. The uncovering of her nakedness means the forfeiture of "all the perquisites of royal rank given by the God of Israel."[148] She is back to her shameful status as she was when Yahweh first found her. She becomes an object of reproach and everyone around despise her (v. 57).

Yahweh also pronounced a similar judgment to Babylon in a taunt song saying, "Your nakedness shall be uncovered, and your disgrace shall be seen" (Isa 47:3). Eventually, Babylon fell under Cyrus, the king of Greece. Its idols, including their worshippers, were taken into captivity with no one to rescue them.[149] Babylon's demise was God's judgment and vengeance on behalf of his people Israel whom Babylon took captive (Dan 1:1). From a glorious and honorific kingdom, Babylon was reduced to an insignificant one.

Yahweh, however, does not leave Jerusalem totally destitute forever. After Jerusalem suffers her punishment (Ezek 16:58), Yahweh, in his mercy and grace, establishes a new covenant with her. He is going to restore her honor again (e.g., her royal status, vv. 8–14) including those who are of lesser status compared to Jerusalem (vv. 61–63). Yahweh indeed covers the nakedness of Jerusalem and restores her as the apple of his eye (Deut 32:10, Zech 2:8).

Other examples of humiliating others by rendering them naked from the ANE also occurs. An example of this is the stripping of a wife naked because of adultery. The reason for the judgment is her "severe infringement on her husband's rights."[150] The husband terminates his "economical 'contract'"[151] by "disrobing of her clothes, and leave the responsibility to take care of her needs and vulnerability."[152]

The same occurrence can also be seen in the OT. Ezekiel records God's stripping Israel of her clothing, baring her nakedness as a consequence of her sleeping with the enemy (Ezek 16:36–40, 23:26–31). Adultery is a capital crime that entails punishment.[153] If a woman is caught in harlotry, she is punished by "tearing off the clothes, public humiliation in nakedness, public trial, public stoning in death, dismemberment of the body, and burning of the house."[154] This law is recorded in Lev 20:10–12 and Deut 22:22.

Some examples of humiliating the captives occur also in the OT. The princes of Tyre removed their princely garments as a sign of their downfall and destruction. Metaphorically, "they will be clothed with terror both at the economic and physical prospects of their fiefdoms"[155] (see also Ezek 26:16). Seeing Tyre's condition, her allies would be singing a funeral dirge to indicate the contrast of "her present condition with her former glory."[156]

David also took garments as spoils from the enemies to humiliate them during his military campaigns. When David and his men attacked and raided the Geshurites, the Girzites, and the Amalekites, they killed the men and women alike and took their animal spoils, including their garments (1 Sam 27:8–9). David defeated his enemies soundly and turned over all the spoils of war to his men. By turning over the garments and spoils of war to his men, he ensured their allegiance and he would be installed by them as their king.[157] His enemies' defeat was his honor but the enemies' shame.

The synonymous word of בֶּגֶד, which is לְבוּשׁ, "garment/clothing" is related to honor and shame. In Job, people hoard garments to keep up their high social status. They may keep their riches but will lose all their wealth overnight (Job 27:16–19). The loss of their riches may send them to a lowly status of shame. Others are naked without clothing and eventually perish for lack of it (Job 24:7, 10; 31:19). In the book of Esther, clothing a person with a robe is a way of giving honor to that person. Such is the example of Mordecai, who was honored by the king of Persia (Esth 6:11).

The involuntary apportioning and casting of lots for the psalmist's garments is the ultimate act of the enemy to reduce him to shame. The enemies' apportioning of the psalmist's garments implies that he is made naked. He is stripped of his honor and reduced to shame.

Honor and shame implication. The picture of the enemies surrounding the psalmist is indicative of being captured. Eventually, the psalmist is devastated and defeated. The enemies receive all the honor for successfully defeating the psalmist, thereby putting the psalmist to shame. The enemies triumphantly inflict a reversal of the status. The psalmist's place is among the dead in the graves.

The psalmist, as a vanquished foe, becomes powerless. The hostile party challenges his honor by their taunt, scorn, and mockery (vv. 7–9). He has to do a riposte to defend his honor. Yet, his predicament makes him unable to speak. His inability to speak renders him inutile to do a riposte. He fails to defend himself, so he shrinks to a status of shame.

The clothing a person wears is indicative of his/her status in society. It shows the personal level of wealth. The rich wear costly apparel, while the poor wear garments symbolic of their financial capacity. At least a person has an inner and outer garment to remain a human being, a person still having an honor. The forcible removal of clothing has the intention of shaming the person. The enemies forcefully strip the psalmist naked, thus reversing his status to shame. The psalmist needs Yahweh to deliver him from this shameful situation.

Summary. This section focuses on the systematic attack of the enemies against the psalmist and their success in bringing him defeat and captivity. The animal pictures depict the enemies as bulls, dogs, and lion. The enemies are powerful, aggressive, capable, and valiant. They carefully implement warfare tactics by closing in on him and eventually capturing him.

In contrast, the psalmist is powerless, hopeless, incapable of launching a counter-attack, defeated, and eventually put on the brink of death. He is torn, speechless, mauled, and naked. His defeat victoriously honors the enemies. His captivity brings him to shame.

Taunt speech. Taunt is an "utterance or composition designed to denigrate its object."[158] The remark can be an insult, mock, or ridicule. The tone of speech affects mockery, taunting, or sarcasm. Its purpose is to provoke anger, slander, or wound a person.[159] Burke O. Long describes taunting as "a battle of words between opponents."[160] The utterances insinuate a person, group, or thing as inferior to another.[161] The taunting also shows that "a person has been shamefully reduced to a lower social position in his or her own eyes and in the eyes of the community."[162]

In the OT, taunting occurs "as a collective action inflicted by a group on another group or individual."[163] Its occurrences are often found in Psalms, the Prophets, and some accounts in the narratives (i.e., 1 Sam 17:8–10, 44).[164] In Ps 22:6–9, David presents his condition in the society and his enemies' action to inflict shame on his status. He stresses his shameful personal situation in a metaphoric and figurative language. He also accentuates the enemies' behavior and taunts speeches to impute shame upon him. The enemies' taunt speeches are חֶרְפָּה, בָּזָה, and לַעַג. The acts of sarcasm that accompany such taunt speeches are בְּשָׂפָה יַפְטִירוּ and יָנִיעוּ רֹאשׁ.

Textual criticism. The textual variant in v. 8 appears in the Syr. and the Vulg. translations. The Syr. and Vulg. translations may not affect the translation nor the interpretation of the text. The previous section discusses the textual variant in v. 9 relating to the word גֹּל.

Lexical analysis. In v. 7, the word תּוֹלַעַת, "worm, grub"[165] appears to set the tone of the shameful condition of the psalmist. The metaphorical meaning of this word is a "small insignificant, powerless creature"[166] in contrast to the small yet powerful and destructive creature that destroys anything along its way.[167] The term וְלֹא־אִישׁ, "and not a man" is used synonymously with תּוֹלַעַת. The word אִישׁ primarily connotes "man as an individual," involving both man and woman. In the OT, humanity has no ordinary status because he/she possesses "great individual worth."[168] Thus, וְלֹא־אִישׁ could mean that the psalmist is not a man of worth but a defeated warrior in battle.

The first word relating to taunt speeches is חֶרְפָּה, "taunt,"[169] "reproach,"[170] "scorn, contempt."[171] חֶרְפָּה is synonymous with "disgrace and shame."[172] Taunting involves verbal abuse with aggression. When used in the sense of contempt, the word becomes the opposite of the *piel* כָּבוֹד, which implies treating someone as important or giving someone honor.[173] The psalmist's suffering and humiliation[174] and his loyalty to Yahweh may be the subject of reproach in Ps 22.

The next word describing taunt is בָּזָה, "despise, regard with contempt."[175] In the Palestinian background, the act is done by raising "the head loftily and disdainfully."[176] The sense of this word indicates that the subject is "looked down on with disdain and possibly hatred."[177] The root בָּזָה in the old Babylonian is *buzzu'u*(m) or *buzzûm*, which means "to treat wickedly, unrighteously."[178] In other instances, it means "abhor"[179] (Egyptian), which includes the sound of loathing and disapproving conduct.[180]

Before they verbally abuse the psalmist, the taunters look upon him with hostility. The term רָאִי (cf. v. 18) does not refer to the simple seeing, but it connotes a careful and conspicuous use of "the perception of sight to view objects and make judgments based on the perceptions"[181] in a hostile manner. Remarkably, this antagonistic look is the direct opposite of regarding or treating someone "with consideration, respect, and esteem."[182]

The hostile look is accompanied by mocking or derision. The Hebrew word for mock or deride is לָעַג[183] The sense of the word is "to treat with contempt ... verbally,"[184] especially the enemy. The term "refers to disclaiming people, deriding them, despising them to their faces, ridiculing them.... It indicates strongly attacking and accusing people's position and words."[185] The semantic range of לָעַג includes the two previous words חֶרְפָּה and בָּזָה.

Along with these three words are "typical gestures of mockery" evident in Ps 22 such as יַפְטִירוּ בְשָׂפָה, "make a wry mouth, pull a face" and יָנִיעוּ רֹאשׁ, "they wag their heads."[186] In the OT, the natural object of mockery is human enemies. In this psalm's context, the subject is the enemies of the psalmist.[187]

The following terms are the acts of God's deliverance mentioned by the enemies to taunt the psalmist. The word פָּלַט appears in this passage again (vv. 5, 9a).[188] For emphasis' sake, the essence of this word indicates deliverance from hostility—either from persons, oppression, or distress—to a secure and safe place. Another synonymous word with פָּלַט is יַצִּילֵהוּ from נָצַל, "snatch away, deliver"[189] (v. 9b). The *hiphil* נָצַל has the definition "to snatch, to deliver anyone from danger; with an acc. [accusative] of pers. [person]."[190] It "indicates removal or liberation from all types of restrictions."[191] The OT use of this word with the divine as the subject indicates "Israel's expectation that Yahweh will free the people and individuals from various types of distress and will deliver them from threats."[192] The term חָפֵץ, "delight in, have pleasure in"[193] has Yahweh as the subject. The word indicates that Yahweh "takes a high degree of pleasure, or mental satisfaction in"[194] the psalmist, which also includes his protection and preservation.

Grammatical and syntactical analysis. The strophe on taunt speeches is composed of three lines (vv. 7–9). It describes the shameful situation of the psalmist, the taunt speeches, and the actual speech spoken by the enemies against the psalmist. It also contrasts the suffering and humiliation of the psalmist with the statement of facts describing the honor the fathers received from God through his acts of deliverance and sparing them from any shameful situation (vv. 5–6).

The first line (v. 7) of the strophe is a bicolon. The first colon is composed of a concrete non-verbal clause and an attributive adjectival phrase that describes the psalmist's sociological status. The second colon is composed of two predicative adjectival phrases to define further the subject's complicated situation inflicted by the people's adverse attitude towards the psalmist.

The second line (v. 8) is composed of a tricolon. Each succeeding colon intensifies the act of taunting. The connotation of totality for כָּל implies that all those around the psalmist are his adversaries. The qualifier active fientive participle *rōʾay* is used substantively as the *nomen agentis*[195] of the taunting. The parts of the body used are the vocal cord, mouth, and head.

The third line (v. 9) is a bicolon, a direct quotation of the taunts of the enemy emphasizing the superiority complex of the taunters towards the psalmist, whom they consider as inferior in status. The subject of the first colon is the psalmist and the direct object is Yahweh. The second colon shifts the order. The shift indicates that the topic of taunting is the psalmist and Yahweh. In the second colon, the causal fientive perfective clause follows the causative jussive.[196] Still, the subject of the causative jussive and fientive perfective is Yahweh.

Structure. Verses 7–9 form a staircase parallelism. A indicates the psalmist's poor appraisal of himself. B states the people's verbal abuse and his familial relations' look of disdain toward him, which intensify his poor evaluation of himself. C heightens A and B by the enemies insulting rhetoric.

> **A** Psalmist's appraisal of himself (v. 7)
>   **B** Verbal abuse and look of disdain by detractors (v. 8)
>   **C** Enemies' insulting rhetoric (v. 9)

Text and translation. This section presents the Hebrew text and the working translation.

Hebrew Text		Working Translation
וְאָנֹכִי תוֹלַעַת וְלֹא־אִישׁ חֶרְפַּת אָדָם וּבְזוּי עָם:	7	I am a worm and not a man; *I am* a reproach of man and despised by people.
כָּל־רֹאַי יַלְעִגוּ לִי יַפְטִירוּ בְשָׂפָה יָנִיעוּ רֹאשׁ:	8	All who sees me mocks me. They despise with their lips. They shook *with their* heads.
גֹּל אֶל־יְהוָה יְפַלְּטֵהוּ יַצִּילֵהוּ כִּי חָפֵץ בּוֹ:	9	Commit unto the Lord! Let him rescue him indeed! Let him deliver him for he delighted in him.

Interpretation. In this passage (vv. 7–9), David directs God's attention towards his humiliation and shame. In the previous verses (vv. 5–6), he alludes to the honor the fathers received from God. His description of his lowly suffering directly contrasts the highly honorable state of the fathers. The psalmist becomes the subject of taunting because of his shameful status. He faces an enemy who does not fear to make him the subject of scorn, contempt, and mockery.

In v. 7, he metaphorically describes himself as a worm: small, insignificant, and powerless. That depiction of a human as a worm is especially significant in the book of Job. Bildad's discourse indicates that humanity is both a maggot and a worm (Job 25:6). It may be a statement referring to decay and death. Also, it may be an "extreme depiction that seems to deny human worth and dignity as God-given."[197] Job's response is an affirmation to Bildad's discourse. A man/woman who is powerless and emasculated is helpless and has no salvation (26:1). Concerning David's situation, his status as a worm means that (a) he has no worth and dignity as a man and (b) he anticipates death as the end of all his suffering and humiliation. In short, David accedes that he is the most despicable person. In the same manner, Israel as a nation finds itself in the same picture of shame under the oppression of its enemies. It is called a worm (Isa 41:14), distressed and afflicted by the attacks of the nations surrounding it. For its deliverance from the status of shame, it can trust Yahweh, the Redeemer, to help it overcome its enemies.

In contrast, man, referring to the whole of humanity inclusive of the male and female genders, has a special place in God's creation. Job's inquiry on God indicates that Yahweh places man in so high an honor and thoughtful care.[198] Also, in his question, he underscores God's thinking highly of man so much that he sets his heart on him when man is, in fact, insignificant. He notes, too, that God continues to intervene in man's affairs so that Job challenges God to quit stepping in in his activities and just leave him alone (Job 17:17–18). "In Psalms 8:5 the psalmist asks the same question in an attitude of praise and marvel at God's gracious care of his creatures."[199] David, the psalmist of Ps 8, purposefully mentions God's concern for humanity. He highlights the high status of humanity as God's crowning act of creation.[200]

Two more descriptions of humiliation intensify the psalmist's situation. First, the hostile party is the man himself. Man refers to the whole of humanity. Every member of the community joins in aggressive verbal abuse to shame the psalmist. In the OT, a person is reproached because of famine and hunger (Joel 2:19); destruction of property (Neh 2:17); physical, emotional, and spiritual distress (Ps 31:10–12); iniquities (79:4, 8–9); and God's wrath and rejection (Ps 44:9, 13; Jer 42:18) or in behalf of God's people (Isa 49:7). In this present psalm, the psalmist becomes a byword probably because God rejects him (Ps 22:2) and of his emotional distress (v. 7a) which causes his physical and mental ailment (vv. 15–16). At this point, he is on the brink of defeat. He is about to be in a state of total shame.

Second, there is an unexpected change of hostile group who goes against the psalmist. His kin becomes his antagonist. They are supposed to alleviate his shameful situation. Instead, they look down on him with disdain and hatred. The psalmist himself acknowledges that his family rejected and treated him with contempt. The antagonism means that he has lost his honor because he has become a total outcast in his family. As an outcast in the family, his shame is complete.

In v. 9, the hostile party makes a rhetoric, encouraging the psalmist to trust in Yahweh. But the rhetoric has a hint of sarcasm and insult. The enemies seem to assert superior status and their honorable state over the psalmist. The psalmist's declaration of his poor state mentioned in the previous passages (vv. 7–8) builds the foundation of the sarcasm.

Also, the enemies challenge the psalmist's loyalty towards Yahweh. They command him to trust and put his confidence upon him. Surprisingly, in this psalm, the hostile party, rather than the psalmist, mentions the name of Yahweh first. Of the six occurrences of the term Yahweh in this particular psalm, the first appearance is in v. 9. Interestingly, Yahweh is described by this hostile party as someone who can be trusted, who saves, rescues, and regards the psalmist with esteem. Delighting in or regarding someone with esteem means that a certain person has established a strong affinity with somebody in whom he/she delights. The person who delights is willing to be and to do anything for that somebody. By doing so, he/she provides honor to the person in whom he/she delights.

The attributes of Yahweh mentioned by the enemies reflect that Yahweh is a faithful patron and father. With these descriptions of who Yahweh is, the enemies seem to encourage the psalmist to put his full confidence on Yahweh for Yahweh can deliver him from them, snatch him out of danger, and assure him of protection and preservation. They seem to imply that Yahweh is willing to do all these for the psalmist. Yet, with all the seemingly good intentions of the enemies, they indeed desire to destroy the psalmist. Their intentions become evident in the ensuing verses (vv. 12–13, 16–18).

The taunts and rhetoric of the hostile party—those who mock him, humanity, and his kinship group—are in actuality a form of challenge upon the psalmist. In the social values of the Mediterranean, the "people engage many times daily in a game of 'push and shove.' The game relates to honor, the value of this culture. The pushing and shoving are attempts to besmirch the honor of the other in some compelling ways. Specialists give this game a technical name: challenge and riposte."[201] As long as the psalmist cannot answer the challenge to defend his honor through a riposte, he remains in absolute shame.

In this challenge, a twist to the subject of taunting develops. The hostile party also taunts Yahweh's ability to rescue and to deliver the psalmist, in whom he delights. They seem to encourage the psalmist to place his full confidence in Yahweh but in actuality, the encouragement has a hint of sarcasm. The sarcasm indicates that Yahweh cannot be trusted because he cannot save, rescue, and provide security and protection; neither can he restore the psalmist's honor. The insult is directed first to the psalmist and second to Yahweh.

The psalmist responds to the challenge by asserting that Yahweh is dependable and reliable. Instead of shoving back, he affirms Yahweh's trustworthiness through his claims that Yahweh is his progenitor (vv. 10–11). Also, in contrast to humanity's hostility towards him, Yahweh acts as his adoptive father who takes care of him through his mother's protection and care. By being accepted into the kinship relationship of Yahweh, the psalmist's honor is restored.

Honor and shame implication. The words "worm and not man" used by the psalmist to describe himself indicates his shameful social status. These descriptions suggest that he is insignificant and does not belong to the society of humanity. From the biblical perspective, his status as a worm is an antithesis to the honorific state God placed upon man. Also, the term "not a man" is a status of defeat. In honor and shame parlance, a person "who defeats another gains or enhances honor."[202] A defeated person is shamed.

The psalmist's separation from society and state of defeat seems to be the basis of the taunting words of humanity and his kin. The terms *reproach* and *despise* are shame and dishonor terms which humanity and the kin uses to taunt the psalmist. The psalmist's honor supposedly comes from his group affiliation. However, humanity dishonors him with their verbal abuse. The contemptuous attitude of the family/kin of the psalmist fortifies his shameful status. In an honor and shame society, the honor of a person is dependent upon the attribution by his group affiliation or his family/kin. However, neither of these groups attribute honor to the psalmist. Instead, they affirm his shameful status.

The taunters' act of seeing is no ordinary scrutiny but rather a perusal to ridicule the psalmist. It is in opposition to treating someone with respect. Respect is related to honor. The taunters' primary objective to scrutinize the psalmist is to cast shame upon him rather than pay him respect. Their taunt speech challenges the psalmist's loyalty and trust in Yahweh. Indirectly, they challenge Yahweh's ability to deliver and to save the psalmist, including Yahweh's attachment to the psalmist. They challenge both the psalmist's and Yahweh's honor. Yahweh and the psalmist's failure to pose a riposte to the challenge means their defeat. "To be defeated is to be dishonored, to be reduced to shame, to become a nonentity, and therefore to be in the condition of life most despicable in the eyes of the vast majority."[203]

Summary. In vv. 7–9, the psalmist describes himself in the most despicable situation. He faces taunts from the people and his family. He becomes the subject of hostile scrutiny and mockery by those who see him. His detractors' hostile behavior includes the use of the voice, the lip, and the head to taunt him. The detractors add a taunting speech to insult both the psalmist and Yahweh, in whom he puts his trust. The taunt speech is a challenge by the detractors awaiting a riposte from the psalmist.

The psalmist's despicable situation reduces him to a shameful state. Being taunted by the people and by his own family indicates his separation from group affiliation and places him in a dishonorable state. The challenge of the hostile party in the form of a taunting speech indicates that he is basically in a state of defeat, a shame indeed. He needs to rise and do a riposte to defend his honor. Instead of directly challenging the enemies, he turns to Yahweh and calls for help. The next section discusses the values and means illustrating the origin of the psalmist's honor.

Honor

This section discusses the values of patronage, family/kinship, trust and the means of feast/meal. These values and means are the sources or ways for the psalmist's restoration of honor. The section that follows this explains the role of deliverance for the restoration of the psalmist's honor.

Patronage. The value of patronage is a system of benefaction where a wealthy benefactor, known as a patron, provides "material goods and financial support to a 'client' in exchange for various services and loyalty."[204] The patron grants "protection, favors, justice, or any form of assistance."[205] Terms relating to patronage occurring in different passages in Ps 22 are אֵלִי, "my God"; אֱלֹהַי, "my God" (vv. 2–3, 11); and יְהוָה, "Yahweh" (vv. 9, 20, 24, 27, 28). The terms מִישׁוּעָתִי, "my salvation" and תַעֲנֶה, "you answered" also indicate the action of the patron.

Textual criticism. This section compares the Greek and Hebrew texts of v. 4. In the first clause, the Greek states συ δε εν αγιοις κατοικεις. The prepositional phrase εν αγιοις functions as a dative of place.[206] The Hebrew adjective קָדוֹשׁ functions as an attributive predicate which modifies the אַתָּה. The second clause in Hebrew is corresponded in Greek as an adjectival noun phrase ὁ ἔπαινος Ισραηλ. The Hebrew has a verbal adjective participial clause[207] יוֹשֵׁב תְּהִלּוֹת יִשְׂרָאֵל.

The Greek εν αγιοις refers to God's dwelling place—the temple or the sanctuary. The Hebrew counterpart קָדוֹשׁ attributes holiness to God. The second clause of the Greek describes God as "the praise of Israel." The Hebrew indicates "the praises of Israel" as the dwelling place of God. The Greek translation is "you (yourself) dwell in the sanctuary, the praise of Israel." The Hebrew translation is "you are holy. [You] are dwelling on the praises of Israel." The LXX seems to interpret the text rather than translate the Hebrew text in correspondence. The Hebrew text remains preferred here because of the importance of God's attribute of holiness.

Lexical analysis. The terms אֵלִי, אֱלֹהַי, and יְהוָה identify the patron of the psalmist. The vocative אֵלִי, "my God"[208] comes from the word אֵל, "God, god"[209] which may refer to a foreign deity or Israel's chief deity,[210] "the only and true God of Israel."[211] For Israel, God's name is יְהוָה, "Yahweh."[212] יְהוָה is Israel's deliverer from their distress. The parallel term [213]אֱלֹהַי, "my God" (v. 3) from the word אֱלֹהִים, "God, gods"[214] refers to יְהוָה as the psalmist's personal God. As a divine being, he has attributes such as greatness, might, power, and high status[215] which qualify him to be the psalmist's patron.

The following terms in v. 4 relate to the characteristic of God. The term קָדוֹשׁ, "holy, sacred"[216] carries the idea of being "apart, ... separate from human infirmity, impurity, and sin."[217] The verb of this term denotes the aspect of honor attributed to one's sacredness.[218] When God or Yahweh is the subject of this term, it indicates the characteristic as par excellence. As a patron, God's holiness means that he will never fail to fulfill his duty as a patron.

The term יוֹשֵׁב comes from יָשַׁב, "sit, remain, dwell."[219] The appearance of this term in this psalm carries an honorific theme. It means to "sit on the throne, be enthroned."[220] Only a king or an honorable person can sit enthroned. In this psalm, God carries the honorific title of being exalted.

The other term in the passage is תְּהִלּוֹת from תְּהִלָּה, "praise, song of praise."[221] It refers to God's honorific status which puts him in a state or quality of being widely honored or acclaimed by the people of Israel.[222] In the OT, the object of praise is Yahweh alone. The people of Israel praise God for being a faithful patron. God brings Israel out of bondage, shows them many wondrous acts, and sends them to the promised land (Deut 10:21). The psalmist urges all people to praise God because he is holy (Ps 99:3). Attached to his holiness is justice, salvation, righteousness, and faithfulness.[223]

The word יִשְׂרָאֵל is a "west Semitic proper name."[224] This name also ascribes an honorific status to God. The name Israel is explained as "for you have striven with God and with men, and have prevailed" (Gen 32:28). Yahweh first gave the name to Jacob after Jacob strove and contended with God and yet prevailed (Gen 32:22–32). His children became known later as "the sons of Israel" (42:5). Then, the "sons of Israel" came to be known as a larger group (49:16, 28).[225] Eventually, this name became a designation of God's people, a religious entity.[226]

Grammatical and syntactical analysis. The passage in v. 2 is composed of a direct address, one verb clause, and two verbless clauses. The two verbless clauses seem to preserve the rhythm of the verse. Verse 3 contains a direct address, two verb clauses, and two verbless clauses with a prepositional phrase. Verse 4 comprises two verbless clauses. Verse 20 comprises a direct address and two verb clauses.

The passage in v. 2 begins with the direct address אֵלִי repeated twice. The repetition of אֵלִי indicates an emphasis[227] on the urgency of the call. The direct address emphasizes a sense of ownership or belongingness, which means that a relationship does exist between God and the psalmist. God is the psalmist's personal God. The term אֵלִי may be translated correctly as "my God." The clauses that follow state the case of his call on God. In v. 3, the psalmist uses an alternative vocative אֱלֹהַי, which also functions like the vocative אֵלִי.[228]

Yahweh, the name of God, appears in vv. 9 and 27 as a datival accusative. It is the name in whom the subject, the psalmist, puts his trust. In v. 20, it functions as a vocative. The psalmist now directs his address to Yahweh. In v. 24, the name Yahweh appears as an adverbial genitive[229] יִרְאֵי יְהוָה, "fear of Yahweh." The adverbial genitive implies that someone fears Yahweh. In v. 29, it functions as a genitive of ownership.

In v. 4, the passage begins with the second person independent personal pronoun אַתָּה, "you, your, yourself"[230] which functions as a subjective nominative surrogating for the antecedent nouns[231] אֵלִי, אֱלֹהַי, and יְהוָה (vv. 4, 10, 11, 20). In vv. 4, 10, and 11, אַתָּה functions as the subject in the verbless clauses. In v. 20, it functions as a direct address pointing to Yahweh.

The adjective קָדוֹשׁ modifies אַתָּה, whose antecedent is God. It functions as a predicative adjective asserting God's holiness. The parting of the first two clauses ends with this word. The translation of the phrase וְאַתָּה קָדוֹשׁ is "you are holy."

The term יוֹשֵׁב from יָשַׁב marks the next clause. It is a kind of orientational metaphor that "represents an abstract concept in terms of spatial orientation."[232] The participle יוֹשֵׁב, "enthroned" is conceptualized as a high position of honor in a kingly space. God is the subject of the passage.

The other terms in the passage are in the construct state, תְּהִלּוֹת יִשְׂרָאֵל, "praise of Israel."תְּהִלּוֹת is the construct translated with the genitive case "praises of." The word יִשְׂרָאֵל is the *status absolutus* in the genitival relationship. It functions as a genitive of agency,[233] which means that יִשְׂרָאֵל does the action of the verbal noun תְּהִלָּה.

Structure. The structure of vv. 2–3 and 20 is synthetic parallelism also known as "complementary parallelism."[234] The sets of lines in this parallelism grow or expand and complement or supplement the thought of the first line. The structure below illustrates this parallelism.

In v. 2, the structure shows the intensity of the petitioner's cry against God's refusal to provide him salvation and give him attention. In v. 3, the second line, supplementing the first line, shows the ill effects of the hostility of God towards the psalmist. It shows God's failure to act upon the psalmist's cry for deliverance. In v. 4, the tone changes to a positive one, indicating two complementing characteristics of God. In v. 20, the psalmist addresses God directly. The first clause addresses his need for defense from enemies and the second clause intensifies it with a cry for help.

> v. 2: A Direct address
> > B Complains about the abandonment
> > > C Complains about the distance of salvation
> > > > D Complains about the distance of the answer to his pain
> v. 3: A Direct address
> > B Cry but no answer
> > B' Cry but no respite
> v. 4: A Interjection
> > B God is holy
> > B' God is worthy of praise
> v. 20: A Direct address
> > B Cry for defense
> > B' Cry for help

Text and translation. This section presents the Hebrew text and the working translation.

Hebrew Text		Working Translation
אֵלִי אֵלִי לָמָה עֲזַבְתָּנִי רָחוֹק מִישׁוּעָתִי דִּבְרֵי שַׁאֲגָתִי׃	2	My God! My God! Why have you forsaken me? *Why are you* far from saving me? *Why are you far from the* words of my groanings?
אֱלֹהַי אֶקְרָא יוֹמָם וְלֹא תַעֲנֶה וְלַיְלָה וְלֹא־דוּמִיָּה לִי	3	Oh, my God! I cry by day, but you did not answer *me*! *I cry* by night, but *there is* no rest for me!
וְאַתָּה קָדוֹשׁ יוֹשֵׁב תְּהִלּוֹת יִשְׂרָאֵל׃	4	Yet you are holy! [You] are dwelling on the praises of Israel!
וְאַתָּה יְהוָה אַל־תִּרְחָק אֱיָלוּתִי לְעֶזְרָתִי חוּשָׁה׃	20	But you, Oh Lord, Do not be far from my defense! Make haste to help me!

Interpretation. The psalmist opens his petition with the address towards God. He addresses him as "my God" as a basis to approach him with his lament, complaints, and requests. At the outset, the psalmist recognizes that God is the creator and his very own divine patron. In the OT, the occurrences of the first person attached to the name אֵל and אֱלֹהִים indicate that the speaker treats God as a very personal, dear, and treasured possession. Moses, Ethan the Ezrahite, Daniel, and the afflicted treat him as such.

Other personalities in the OT call God as אֵלִי. When Moses uses the expression "my God," he seems to claim that God is personal to him, indicating their saving relationship (Exod 15:2). The saving God he serves is the same God whom his ancestors serve (3:6, 15). Also, Yahweh, the warrior king who fights for his people's salvation and deliverance from oppression, is Moses's God. As a covenant God, he pledges to take care of them and ensure their welfare and safety. By acting so, he assumes the role of a patron deity.[235]

When the psalmist calls on God as "my God," it seems likely that he has the experience of Moses in mind. In six other psalms, David calls God "my God." He thinks of God as his deliverer, a warrior who will alleviate his distress and remove the grips of his enemies. He states, "The LORD is my rock and my fortress and my deliverer, my God, my rock, in whom I take refuge, my shield, and the horn of my salvation, my stronghold" (Ps 18:3, ESV). God is his help (63:7), king (68:24), father and rock of salvation (89:27), deliverer, guard, and judge (140:2, 5, 12–13).

His repetition of the vocative "my God" implies the degree of his relationship with Yahweh.[236] Their relationship is strong and unwavering. The first bond is between a creator and a creature. As a creator, he secures, provides, and sustains his creation. The second bond is between a patron and a client. Yahweh as a patron protects, saves, rescues, gives health, and recreates. He redeems the psalmist and overthrows his foes. His stance towards his people never changes. As a faithful patron, he accomplishes all of these on behalf of his client. In response, the psalmist reciprocates Yahweh with his eventual offering of praise and honor.[237]

Also, the repetition of the vocative indicates the urgency of the call which is ignited by the psalmist's afflictions. The psalmist's cry is out of his desperate situation.[238] He tries to compel God to function as a real patron. His complaints is directed towards God to make him aware of his present situation and his expectation of God as a patron.

The patrons have multifaceted social functions.[239] As "powerful individuals who controlled resources,"[240] they are "expected to use their positions to hand out favors to inferiors," the clients.[241] The favors may depend on the "needs or desires of the petitioner."[242] They may be resources such as land, money, influence, or food.[243] They also include "protection, debt relief,"[244] or brokering access to another patron.[245]

The psalmist needs salvation, help, and rest from his shameful situation. He recognizes God as his only divine patron. His statement that God is holy indicates God's attribute of holiness that sets him apart, distinct, and incomparable to other gods. God's holiness is in contrast with the gods who compete against one another to gain the allegiance of more followers.[246] God is distinct compared to those gods, for he saves without humans needing to appease him, unlike the gods who require works from humans to earn their favor to act.[247] God's acts are for humanity's goodwill, but the acts of the gods for humanity are narcissistic.[248] "God is reliable to save Israel and will ultimately do so."[249]

Vital to the holiness of God is his immutability. Because his ways are all pure, he fulfills all his promises. He always hears and answers the pleas of those who cry to him. God never fails his people. God is great and is faithful to deliver his people.[250] In God's presence, the psalmist is covered with holy awe, "fearful respect, and utter dependence"[251] on God's overpowering and awful presence. Exodus 15:11 succinctly expresses this thought: "Who is like you, O LORD, among the gods? Who is like you, majestic in holiness, awesome in glorious deeds, doing wonders?" (emphasis is from ESV).

Jerry Bridges indicates that God's "holiness is the perfection of all His other attributes: His power is holy power; His mercy is holy mercy; His wisdom is holy wisdom. It is His holiness more than any other attribute that makes Him worthy of our praise."[252] Because of these attributes, God expects his people to acknowledge his holiness and demands that they also be holy (Lev 20:20; cf. 11:44–45, 19:2, 21:8). Humanity has to recognize his/her need for a savior and deliverer. He/she must be less confident in his/her abilities and self-sufficiency. The recognition of one's frailty is holiness.[253]

To add depth to God's honor, the psalmist recognizes God's sovereignty over Israel. Israel's praise is an acclamation of God's honorific status. A holy and sovereign God can be trusted. Although he has not received any answer to his complaints, the psalmist knows that God hears and answers cries. He believes that God will favorably act on his behalf. In response to God's beneficent acts, he intends to honor and praise God. God is worthy of praise, honor, and respect because of his acts of deliverance upon God's faithful people (vv. 5–6).

In Psalms, God appears as a warrior king several times. He reigns forever and administers justice (Ps 45:6). He beats his enemies (v. 5). His kingdom was from long ago (55:19, 74:12). He is a warrior who rescues and protects his petitioners (55:18) yet humiliates the petitioners' enemies (v. 19). He rules all the earth (47:3). He is Yahweh.[254]

Yahweh also established a covenant with Israel, a suzerainty treaty. In the case of the Exodus, Yahweh was the suzerain and Israel the vassal.[255] The stipulations in this treaty were "oath-bound obligations or as covenant order of life."[256] In this covenant, Yahweh "pledged his love and protection to Israel and expected their loyalty to his laws in return."[257] The treaty involved Israel swearing an "oath fidelity to God."[258] It also formalized Yahweh's relationship with the people of Israel.[259] In this relationship, God functioned as a benefactor to provided assistance continually to the beneficiaries—Israel. The beneficiaries shall singularly remain "loyal to ... and offer services to the Patron."[260]

When God gives his name Yahweh to the people of Israel, he reveals his nature and his character. Yahweh means "who 'causes to be' or 'brings into being.'"[261] Attached to his name is his unchangeableness, his continued and faithful presence with his people (Exod 3:12, 15; 6:2, 4).[262] He is "actively present to redeem his people and overthrow his foes."[263] He is a "gracious, covenant-keeping God of Israel (cf. Exod 6:2–8)."[264]

In the later experiences of the people of Israel, "Daniel referred to him as the One 'who keeps his covenant of love with all who love him and obey his commands'"[265] (Dan 9:4). In this covenant relationship, Yahweh is bound to Israel and Israel to him. To maintain that relationship and Yahweh as their God, Israel must be like him.[266] As long as they remain faithful to the covenant, Yahweh will fulfill his part.[267] He will continue to fight on behalf of them as a divine warrior. Failure to keep the covenant means judgments "by means of wars from foreign invaders."[268]

Thompson summarizes Yahweh's character succinctly.

> He is the giver of life and one who brings death. He is a god of war and peace.... But most important to the biblical tradition, Yahweh is the god of the covenant. Yahweh created, maintains, and sustains the natural world, which includes humanity. There are covenants with Noah which include the natural world, with the patriarchs, with Moses and the people, Aaron and Phinehas and the priesthood, David and the royal house,

and others. No matter what the origin of the name or the non-Israelite nature of his epithets, Yahweh had chosen Israel to be his people and had entered into covenants with them. This fact is the central theme of the OT.[269]

Also, Mark S. Smith notes the similarities between El and Yahweh. Both "exhibit a similar compassionate disposition toward humanity."[270] Both act as a father, merciful and gracious, progenitor of humanity, healer, and the divine patron of Israel. The people of Israel recognize that El and Yahweh are the same and one God (Exod 8:10; Deut 4:35, 39; 32:39).

With this picture of God, the psalmist David has all the reasons to send his petition to God. He asks God why he is forsaken but still petitions to save him from his physical dilemma and his foes. Always, he can trust God to fulfill his side of the covenant.

Honor and shame implication. When the psalmist calls on God and his name Yahweh, he places himself before the presence of an honorific being, someone set apart and unlike anyone else. Yahweh is God of the covenant relationship. As both parties hold on to the covenant, honor is preserved. The dissolution of the bond leads to shame. Yet, Yahweh, as a patron, remains faithful to his side of the covenant. He honors his client by serving as a savior, protector, deliverer, and creator. When he addresses God, the psalmist seems to be in a state of shame. He needs to address God to claim the patron's honor.

Summary. The psalmist addresses God with the words אֵלִי, אֱלֹהָי, and יְהוָה. He recognizes God as his patron who can rescue, save, and provide health to him. He comes before the honorific God asking to alleviate his shameful state and restore him to honor. He understands that God will always accept his side of the covenant. Also, God/Yahweh is as an honorific patron who faithfully fulfills his obligation as a patron.

Family/kinship. Family-centeredness or kinship is a social institution "that serves as the means for bringing new human beings into existence and then nurturing them for a lifetime."[271] Kinship members are husband, wife, mother, father, brother, sister, parent, grandparent, cousin, son-in-law.[272] The value objects of the kinship relationship are "self, others, nature, space, and the All (God)."[273] The psalmist clarifies that he belongs to a kinship group where God is the progenitor and he is the product of the group. This section considers the kinship/family value and the terms related to the assertion of kinship membership.

In the shame and honor context, the family relations ascribe identity to an individual. In other words, a person is known according to his/her kinship relationships.[274] A person can maintain or elevate his/her social status through his/her family. The family honor may also be attributed to the individual as long as he/she remains loyal to the family relationship.

In the lament of the psalmist, he invokes his social status through his ties with his family. He claims that what is due to his family members is also due to him. The term אֲבֹתֵינוּ is a component of family relationship which the psalmist uses to connect himself with the family. This section explores the terms that are connected with the value of kinship/family, their importance in the preservation of honor, and deliverance.

The verbs בָּטַח and זָעַק indicate the fathers' acts to indicate trust and the call for help to God. For the fathers' acts, God attributes to them favor and honor. Some examples of the occurrences of these two verbs are discussed in this section.

Textual criticism. This section takes into account the textual variant that appears in vv. 10–11. The spelling מִבְטַחִי found in the Targum, the LXX, and the Samaritan Pentateuch does not follow the paradigm of the Hebrew conjugation. The scribe probably shortened the word מַבְטִיחִי into מִבְטַחִי. The *hiphil* participle has the correct morphology rather than the presentation of other versions. The MT text is the most probable.

The Targum, LXX, and the Samaritan Pentateuch translations render the phrase עַל־שְׁדֵי as מִשְׁדִי. The translations dropped the independent preposition עַל and changed the preposition to the inseparable preposition לֹ. מִן. עַל functions as a simple locational preposition "upon, on, over."[275] The locational preposition מִן "describes the place where a thing or person originated or the direction where a thing is located."[276] It can mean "from" or "to" respectively. The spatial sense of עַל makes more sense in the context rather than the directional sense of מִן.

Lexical analysis. The terms referring to family/kinship first appear in v. 4. The term אֲבֹתֵינוּ, "our fathers" is the plural form (with suffix) of the word אָב, "father."[277] The word אָב may refer to the patriarchs: Abraham, Isaac, and Jacob or the "first or the former generations of the people, i.e., the forefathers."[278] Another term used for kinship/family appears in v. 7. The term עַם, "people, nation"[279] originally means people who are "united, connected, related."[280] It refers to "agnate relationship"[281] "both individually and collectively."[282] It can refer to "members of a family line"[283] or "fellow tribe member, relative."[284] In this psalm, this kinship/family group is hostile to the psalmist.

In v. 10, the term גֹחִי from גחה or גִּיחַ indicates God as the progenitor. The closest meaning is "give birth."[285] The passage uses this term metaphorically. The other word, מַבְטִיחִי, from בָּטַח, "to feel secure, be unconcerned"[286] discussed further below relates to God as the progenitor.

In v. 11, the next term, הָשְׁלַכְתִּי, from שָׁלַךְ, "to throw, fling, cast"[287] is a verb that indicates kinship. The metaphorical sense of שָׁלַךְ means to "express a lifelong dependence and reliance upon God."[288] For the salvific act of God, the most likely meaning is "save, deliver, provide for."[289] The preposition עַל, when used with deliverance and trust, has the sense "of trust, reliance, support, upon, on, in, to."[290]

The term רֶחֶם, "womb"[291] comes from the verb root רָחַם, "love, have compassion."[292] The noun form רַחֲמִים means "intense compassion."[293] The origin of the word means "brotherhood, brotherly feeling, of those born from the same womb."[294] In this context, the psalmist recognizes his "existential dependence on Yahweh from the womb."[295] From his mother's womb, he already received love and compassion from the Yahweh himself who adapted and took care of him.

Grammatical and syntactical analysis. In v. 4, the substantive אֲבֹתֵינוּ functions as the subject of בָּטְחוּ, "they trusted." It emphasizes the psalmist's claim of belongingness to the descendants of the fathers. The repetition of בָּטְחוּ from בָּטַח, "to trust" three times in this passage indicates the essentiality of the fathers' trust in Yahweh for their deliverance. The psalmist's allusion to Yahweh's deliverance of the fathers is an encouragement for him.[296]

The conjunction כִּי, opening v. 10, emphasizes God's act as the progenitor. God is addressed in the vocative אַתָּה. The transitive and active fientive participle גֹחִי functions as predicative that describes the subject אַתָּה. The antecedent of אַתָּה is God. The *hiphil* participle מַבְטִיחִי indicates that God continuously[297] causes the psalmist to trust in him. It functions as a predicative.

In v. 11, the perfective present continuous *hophal*[298] הָשְׁלַכְתִּי has a salvific sense in reference to deliverance. The preposition עַל shows that the salvific act is done on behalf of the psalmist. God's salvific act causes a change in the psalmist's life.[299]

Structure. The structure of v. 10 is a synonymous parallelism. The text has an interjection. The subject of the two clauses, B and B', shows Yahweh as a father and parent. The object, C and C', indicates the psalmist trusting his mother's care. The structure of v. 11 is an inverted parallelism. A and A' indicate Yahweh as progenitor and God. B' and B' point to the psalmist being taken care of even from the womb and birth.

> v. 10: A Interjection
> > B Yahweh as progenitor
> > > C Psalmist from the womb
> >
> > B' Yahweh secures
> > > C' Psalmist on mother's breast
>
> v. 11: A Yahweh as progenitor
> > B Psalmist from birth
> > B' Psalmist from the womb
> > A' Yahweh as God

Text and translation. This section presents the Hebrew text and the working translation.

Hebrew Text		Working Translation
בְּךָ בָּטְחוּ אֲבֹתֵינוּ	5a	In you our fathers trusted.
כִּי־אַתָּה גֹחִי מִבָּטֶן מַבְטִיחִי עַל־שְׁדֵי אִמִּי:	10	Surely you are the one who took me from the womb making me trust upon my mother's breast.
עָלֶיךָ הָשְׁלַכְתִּי מֵרָחֶם מִבֶּטֶן אִמִּי אֵלִי אָתָּה: [300]		Unto you, I am caused to be cast out from the womb. From the womb of my mother, you are my God.

Interpretation. The referent of אֲבֹתֵינוּ, "our fathers" may find a clue in David's thanksgiving prayer for the offerings brought by the people of Israel for the rebuilding of the temple. In his prayer, he mentions the names of Abraham, Isaac, and Jacob as "our fathers" (1 Chr 29:18). Collectively, the people of Israel refer to these personalities as "our fathers" (2 Chr 20:6–7, Mic 7:20) or "your fathers" (Deut 6:10).

The OT records how God takes care of the fathers, who most likely represent the whole people of Israel. Most prominent of God's deliverance of the fathers is Israel's deliverance from their bondage in Egypt.[301] This deliverance becomes a paradigm for later generations to call on the Lord whenever they are in trouble, distress, and oppression.[302] When they cry for God's help, God saves, delivers, and protects them (Neh 9:9–14). Chronicles record the closest example where בָּטַח and זָעַק are used. The Reubenites, the Gadites, and the half-tribe of Manasseh cry to the Lord for help (זָעַק) in the war against the Hagrites and their allies. Because they trust (בָּטַח) in him, God grants them victory over their enemies (1 Chr 5:20).

Notably, in Ps 89:26, the psalmist claims that the God of salvation, Yahweh, is "my father." Although the psalm is attributed to Ethan the Ezrahite, the context reveals the anointing of David as king. Here, David calls on Yahweh as "my father." Figuratively, God serves as David's "father" who establishes him as king.

In Ps 22, David recognizes Yahweh as his progenitor. As progenitor, Yahweh serves as protector and deliverer in a covenantal saving relationship. David may have recounted how God delivered the fathers from their bondage in Egypt. God took away their shameful state as slaves in Egypt. He rescued them from a dangerous situation to a place of peace and quiet. By his power and might, he sustained them until they could settle in the land they could call their own.

David recalls the father's deliverance as his encouragement[303] that God, as a faithful patron, will grant him the same salvation the fathers received.[304] He seems to declare that "he belongs to the offspring of those who have been heard"[305] so he should also have the opportunity to be heard. His close association with God is expressed in the vocative אַתָּה to address God, like a son addressing his father. Thus, God has "the obligations of a parent"[306] towards him.

The following statements emphasize Yahweh's act as a progenitor. First, the psalmist's metaphorical extraction from the womb of his mother signifies God's care towards him from his being a helpless babe at birth until he can be taken care of by his mother (v. 10).[307] God himself presents the psalmist to the world to be seen by others. Even when the psalmist is on his mother's breast, he still depends upon God.[308] This means that God made the psalmist secure upon the care of his mother, as Jamieson, Fausset, and Brown commented.[309] God serves as the protector and provider of everything he needs in his infancy as the father does for his newborn child. The psalmist can put his confidence and be dependent on God because of this.[310]

Second, the metaphoric casting of the psalmist indicates that Yahweh adopts the psalmist so that he can take care of him.[311] The psalmist has not identified the subject of the casting. Yet, the intention is clear. Yahweh, the adoptive father, loves and shows compassion to him as a father to his son. Mitchell J. Dahood summarizes the sense of the verse this way: "I was placed in your custody."[312] The psalmist can trust and rely upon Yahweh to sustain (Ps 55:23) him throughout his life. Also, all the honor attributed to a natural-born son becomes his, including salvation and deliverance from his enemies.

In vv. 20–22, the kinship/family social institution seems to appear again. The psalmist's declaration that Yahweh is "my help" and "my aid" (v. 19) indicates that he has a direct relationship with Yahweh. The relationship began when Yahweh adopted the psalmist (vv. 10–12). Again, the psalmist's directly addressing Yahweh as אַתָּה emphasizes so well their close affinity. He invokes Yahweh's name to keep his distance close. He petitions him to help, deliver, save, and rescue him from his enemies.

Yahweh has always faithfully fulfilled his part of the covenant. Every time Israel is in trouble, he acts according to his vow to them (Hos 8:2, 9:17).[313] The psalmist has Yahweh's covenant faithfulness always in his mind. When his enemies beset him, he does not hesitate to call Yahweh for his deliverance, salvation, and rescue. The psalmist thought that Yahweh is his divine protector, a winning warrior who never loses to the powerful and mighty enemies surrounding him.

Honor and shame implication. David alludes to Yahweh's deliverance of the fathers from their bondage in Egypt. The fathers' shameful status of their slavery, including the whole of Israel, must be rectified. They are humiliated. They alone cannot save themselves. Yahweh's intervention is necessary to deliver them from their shame. To bring about the intervention, they need to trust in Yahweh's salvific and redemptive power and bring their cry for help before God's presence. Indeed, Yahweh hears their cry and brings deliverance to Israel.

Deliverance ends all the mystery and bondage of the fathers. It gives them a new identity as an honored nation. First, it implies that bondage and slavery brings them shame and humiliation. Yahweh's act of deliverance alone can end these and he alone can give a new status of honor to them. He needs to change their shame and disgrace by taking them away from (*mlt*) a place of danger and bringing them to (*plt*) a place of safety and deliverance.

Second, for this deliverance to take effect, the afflicted must belong to the family of Israel. This means that non-Israelites have no chance of being honored. For David, he claims Yahweh as his father, who adopts and takes care of him from birth to the present time. Yahweh created him, so he deserves the honor of deliverance. It implies that a person adopted in the family of Israel has the privilege of God's protection, care, and salvation. As the progenitor, Yahweh serves as the psalmist's parent who takes good care of him and provides him with an identity.

Third, in the kinship relationship, compassion is a peripheral value that has roots in "kinship obligations." Compassion is "defined as the caring concern that ought to be felt and acted upon between real or fictive kin, specifically between brothers since the basic connotation of *rhm* was brotherhood or brotherly feeling."[314] In this psalm, Yahweh serves as David's parent, who cares and protects him from birth until his present situation. Their relationship is based on Yahweh's love and compassion upon David; thus, they formed a fictive kin relationship.[315]

Summary. This section identifies the fathers as Abraham, Isaac, Jacob, and the long line of descendants of the people of Israel. The bondage of Egypt brought the fathers' shame and humiliation. Yet the Israelites needed to trust Yahweh's deliverance and salvific power. Yahweh took them out of slavery and brought them to a place of safety and salvation. He also gave them a new status—an honorable, independent nation. What Yahweh did for the fathers the psalmist wanted to be done for him, too. The psalmist also claimed honor by declaring that Yahweh was his progenitor who adopted and took care of him from birth to his present status.

Trust. Trust is a value in the honor and shame context. It is a vital part of a society where some aspects of daily life are beyond people's control. People under this context "search for security, for someone or something in which they can trust, in which they can place their allegiance, upon which they can base their hope."[316] Pilch explains that "trust or hope is ... a value that serves as a means to attaining an honorable existence, so long as the source is trustworthy and reliable."[317] Words referring to security and trustworthiness are the nouns "hope," "trust," "confidence," and "allegiance" and the verbs "to have hope" and "to hope."[318]

Textual criticism. In v. 9, the Hebrew גֹּל is translated into Greek as ἤλπισεν. The Greek word comes from ἐλπίζω, defined as "to look forward to something, with implication of confidence about something coming to pass, hope, hope for"[319] with the sense of "rely on, trust."[320] It corresponds with גָּלַל, "commit"[321] which has a sense of trust.[322] The implication is that the Greek rendering of גָּלַל as ἐλπίζω significantly supports the understanding of trust in this psalm. The Targum translation of גָּלַל is שבחית ,ישבח, "to praise."[323] The translation seems unlikely because its meaning and sense do not correspond with the Hebrew גָּלַל nor the Greek ἐλπίζω.

Lexical analysis. Trust is an essential aspect of this psalm. The word בָּטַח, "to trust"[324] or "have confidence"[325] appears four times (vv. 5[2x], 6, 10) in Ps 22. The Hebrew sense means "to have strong confidence or reliance upon someone or something."[326] The word זָעֲקוּ from זָעַק, "cry, cry out, call"[327] stems from the petitioner's confidence in Yahweh who answers the call.[328] The Egyptian sources indicate that "the crying can be directed 'to (r) the heavens' as a cry for help."[329] The primary emphasis of זָעַק is the loud and disturbing cry "of someone in acute distress, calling for help and seeking deliverance with this emotion-laden utterance."[330]

In response to the trust and agonizing cry of the fathers, God's first act of deliverance (v. 5) for the fathers is וַתְּפַלְּטֵמוֹ from פָּלַט, "rescue"[331] or "to save."[332] The sense of פָּלַט means that one has to escape from hostile person(s),[333] oppressors, and distress, especially from the war zone.[334] The focus is not the departure from danger but on the escapee's arrival at a place of safety.[335] In that place of protection or deliverance, the escapee is secure and has come out of danger.

The next act God does (v. 6) is וְנִמְלָטוּ from מָלַט, "to rescue, to save,"[336] or "to deliver."[337] The sense of מָלַט is to "deliver one from danger and so cause one to be safe, often with a focus of physically leaving an area."[338] The synonymous פָּלַט and מָלַט differ in the direction of the motion—"motion toward a place of safety ... motion away from a place of danger"[339] respectively.

The last act of God (v. 6) for the fathers in this passage is וְלֹא־בוֹשׁוּ, "and they were not shamed." The word בּוּשׁ, "be ashamed"[340] carries the idea of humiliation, disgrace, and dishonor.[341] The particle לֹא negates בּוּשׁ. The phrase לֹא־בוֹשׁוּ means that God's deliverance of the fathers kept their honor unimpaired by abandonment (v. 2) or the attacks of the enemies (vv. 7–9, 12–22). In v. 9, the word גֹּל from גָּלַל, "roll" or "commit"[342] is a parallel of בָּטַח. The sense of the word is "to commit (trust)" that a specific person may do something.[343]

Grammatical and syntactical analysis. Three times in this psalm, the verb בָּטַח appears in the perfective fientive[344] sense (vv. 5[2x], 6). The perfective aspect of the word is continuous. All three occurrences of בָּטַחin this psalm indicate that the fathers continue to trust in Yahweh amidst their predicament. The *hiphil* causative מַבְטִיחִי (v. 10) suggests that Yahweh causes the psalmist to trust or to hope upon him as the person who adopts him as his son.

Verses 5–6 are one line with a quatrain. The antecedent of the suffix of the preposition of circumstances בְּךָ is אֵל בְּךָ (v. 2) or אֱלֹהַי (v. 3), the same referent of אַתָּה (v. 4). The subject of the fientive verb is אֲבֹתֵינוּ. The perfective fientive בָּטְחוּ is preterite.[345] The first of the two verbal clauses in the second colon repeats the fientive verb בָּטְחוּ of the previous colon. The repetition indicates emphasis. The conjunctive-sequential *waw* in the second verbal clause of the second colon indicates a sequential action. The *piel* resultative וַתְּפַלְּטֵמוֹ expresses the sequential action.[346]

The antecedent of the prepositional phrase אֵלֶיךָ is the same as בְּךָ. The verb זָעֲקוּis in fientive preterite sense. The *waw* attached to the *niphal* fientive נִמְלָטוּ functions as a conjunctive-sequential. The subject of the passive[347] fientive בְּנִמְלָטוּ is Yahweh.

The first part of the fourth colon parallels the first colon. The negation לֹא, "not" negates the fientive stative[348] בּוֹשׁ. In v. 9a, the fientive imperative גֹּל functions as a command, a directive[349] addressed to an inferior. The preposition אֶל concerns the "perceptual and verbal acts and dispositions of one person to(wards) another person, place, etc."[350] יְהוָה is the object of the preposition.

The subject אַתָּה fills the ellipsis in the dependent clause in v. 10b. The participle מַבְטִיחִי functions as a causative attributive adjective.[351] The phrase עַל־שְׁדֵי אִמִּי is a prepositional objective accusative. The preposition עַל indicates a direction of attention.

Structure. The structure of v. 5 shows a staircase parallelism. The center of the chiasm is trust. A indicates the fathers' trust in God. B emphasizes A. C is the climax indicative of the result of A and B; that is, God delivers the fathers. The structure of v. 6 is a synthetic parallelism. A and A' are the direct address. B' and B' indicate the fathers' cry and trust. C and C' are the result of their call for help. The fathers were rescued and not shamed.

> v. 5: A Fathers trusted in God
>   B Fathers trusted
>   C God delivers the fathers
> v. 6: A Direct address
>   B Fathers cried
>   C Fathers rescued
>   A' Direct address
>   B' Fathers trusted
>   C' Fathers not shamed

Text and translation. This section presents the Hebrew text and the working translation.

Hebrew Text		Working Translation
בְּךָ בָּטְחוּ אֲבֹתֵינוּ בָּטְחוּ וַתְּפַלְּטֵמוֹ׃	5	In you our fathers trusted. They trusted so that they were indeed delivered.

JOSE MANUEL S. ESPERO

אֵלֶיךָ זָעֲקוּ וְנִמְלָטוּ בְּךָ בָטְחוּ וְלֹא־בוֹשׁוּ:	6	Unto you they cried so that they were rescued. In you they trusted so that they were not shamed.
גֹּל אֶל־יְהוָה	9a	Commit unto Yahweh.
מַבְטִיחִי עַל־שְׁדֵי אִמִּי:	10b	*You* make me trust upon my mother's breast.

Interpretation. David, at this time, is in a state of trouble, abandoned by God, and oppressed by his enemies. To gain trust and confidence in God, he alludes to God's deliverance of the fathers. He points out that the fathers' trust in God was so important so that they were delivered from their predicament. The predicament could refer to the bondage in Egypt (i.e., Exod 2:23, 25; 5; 13:3) or the different periods in the long course of Israel's history when they were oppressed by their enemies (Judg 10:7, 8). The most likely reference to the deliverance could be the former.

The Israelites suffered oppression and ruthless slavery in the hands of the Egyptians (Exod 1:12–13). Their male children were also ordered to be killed by Pharaoh (vv. 16, 22). The bondage curtailed Israel's freedom beyond their control. Israel needed security, safety, and deliverance from their enslavement. In God alone could Israel put their trust and allegiance. To him, they cried out for help and rescue (2:23). "And God heard their groaning" (v. 24, ESV) in their time of shame and humiliation. Indeed, God delivered (מָלַט) Israel out of danger by removing them out of Egypt. He rescued (פָלַט) them by bringing them into the wilderness and cared for them there (Deut 32:10–14). He took them out of distress (20:2) and placed them in a position to become honored people.[352]

The Israelites' deliverance from bondage in Egypt is David's hope to gain his security and honor again. In alluding to the deliverance of the fathers, he asserts that God is trustworthy and reliable. He cannot be wrong to put his trust and hope in God for the removal of his shame and restoration of his honor.

The OT records Hezekiah's and Jerusalem's deliverance from Sennacherib, the Assyrian king. Hezekiah was known to trust (בָּטַח)

Yahweh, the God of Israel (2 Kgs 18:5). The account about him indicates that he was an honorable king because he trusted Yahweh. He instituted reforms to Yahweh's worship, including the keeping of the commandments. With his trust and goodly deeds, Yahweh's presence was always with him so that Yahweh granted him success (v. 7). One of the successes Hezekiah had, because he trusted in Yahweh, was the repulsion of Sennacherib. When the Assyrians attacked Judah, both Hezekiah (king of Judah) and Isaiah (the prophet) cried to the Lord for deliverance from the Assyrians. Yahweh killed many of the great Assyrian warriors so that Judah was saved. Sennacherib, king of Assyria, went home ashamed (2 Chr 32:17, 20–22). Hezekiah was honored or exalted by all nations "from that time onward" (v. 23).

Psalms calls for the people of Israel to trust in Yahweh for help, deliverance, and salvation.[353] For the people of Israel who do not trust in God, they receive his wrath (78:19–22). During Israel's monarchial period, the people of Israel failed to trust God so that they were oppressed and subdued by their enemies.[354] Shame came to those who trusted in kings and had confidence in themselves (Job 6:20, Isa 36:6).

David declares, in the song he has written, his deliverance from his enemies. He recognizes the Lord as his deliverer, savior, the one who gave him victory and exaltation. He declares that the Lord himself brought him out of strife, from legal battle, and made him ruler over all other nations (2 Sam 22:1–3, 44; Ps 18:44, 49). Some psalmists petition the Lord to deliver them from evil, enemies and persons of violence, deceitful and unjust persons, and the wicked (17:13; 22:5, 9; 31:2; 37:40; 43:10; 71:2, 4). The Lord promises to deliver and protect them (91:14).

The book of Isaiah gives an example of Yahweh saving and helping the people of Israel, resulting to them not being shamed (Isa 45:17, 49:23, 50:7). The psalms of David state that God does not put the blameless to shame. Instead, they will have abundance in times of famine (Pss 37:18–19, 119:80). The eyes fixed on God's commandments are not put to shame (119:6, 116). These events indicate that when a group or an individual believer puts their trust in Yahweh, shame will never come to them. Instead, Yahweh himself provides them honor.

Honor and shame implication. In vv. 5–6, David recognizes that the fathers experienced distress and bondage. Misery and slavery are shameful states. The fathers needed to trust in someone more powerful than them who can alleviate their shame and restore their honor. God is the only one who is "reliable and trustworthy."[355] He indeed brought the fathers out of their shameful situation, from oppression and bondage in Egypt. By God's act of deliverance, Israel was accorded the honor as the apple of God's eye (Deut 32:10). The attribution of their honor reverses their status from shame to honor. The experience of the fathers gave David a sense of security on the trustworthiness of God.

The enemies insulted the psalmist by undermining God's trustworthiness. Yahweh's supposed untrustworthiness would result in David's total devastation and shame. Yahweh's failure to defend David would cause disappointment and rejection in the process. Yet, David asserts that his trust does not come to waste. From David's birth to the present, Yahweh's protective care, provision of identity for David, and love and compassion prevail. Yahweh still delights in him (v. 9). Yahweh's benevolent acts towards David make Yahweh trustworthy. In another psalm, David petitions Yahweh: "Keep me as the apple of your eye; hide me in the shadow of your wings" (Ps 17:8, ESV).

The confidence must be placed in Yahweh alone.[356] As in the Greek sense, the feeling of complete security ought to be in God alone. Those who trust in "Yahweh can know for sure that it [community of Yahweh] can rely on him."[357] They can feel safe and secure in him.[358] Also, they "are refreshed, protected, surrounded by good things, and will not fall."[359]

Summary. Trust is a value where a person or community maintain honor. In a situation beyond control, a person or community calls for someone trustworthy and reliable in whom they can hope for security. God is the person one can rely on. The fathers acted rightly to put their trust in God. They became David's inspiration to claim complete security from God also. The psalmist's enemies who coaxed him to commit to God expected the opposite result. Devotion to God brings honor, but rejection by God leads to shame. His trust does not fail because he finds security in God through his mother's care.

Feast/meal. A feast/meal is a means of communication people use all over the world to convey an essential non-verbal "social message"[360] to each other. In the OT and the NT, it is an important means of "sealing friendships, celebrating victories, and for other joyous occasions (Dan 5:1, Lk 15:22–24)."[361] The kind of food and drink, mode of preparation, and the seating arrangement transmit a message from the host to those invited. An elaborate meal called a banquet or a feast,[362] as opposed to a common meal, is a "formal communication, usually with messages of great significance."[363] It is a means of the restoration of the honor of someone neglected, outcast, or disconnected from the family or society. This section looks into the entities involved in the meals and the effect upon those involved.

Textual criticism. In the LXX and the Syr. translations, the word לֵבָב has the third person singular suffix. The MT rendering לְבַבְכֶם is the most probable since the psalmist addresses the participants of the worship in the second person (i.e., "You who fear the LORD," "All you offspring of Jacob," v. 24).

The word וַיִּשְׁתַּחֲוּוּ (v. 30) is a case of textual error. Verse 28 has the correct spelling וְיִשְׁתַּחֲווּ. The emendation of the Hebrew manuscript, the LXX, and the Hebrew text of Kennicott is the most likely spelling. The revision of the *shewa* to *patach* under the *waw* of וְיִשְׁתַּחֲווּ corrects the spelling and follows the frequent occurrence of the שחה *hithpael*, [364] וַיִּשְׁתַּחֲוּוּ.

Also, the proposed word יְשֵׁנֵי for דִּשְׁנֵי seems to parallel כָּל־יוֹרְדֵי עָפָר, "those who go down to the dust" and "those who could not keep himself alive." However, the revision may not be necessary. The MT takes precedence over the suggested emendation.

Lexical analysis. This section deals with the terms that refer to meals, those involved, and the activities accompanying the meals. The two occurrences (vv. 27, 30) of the Hebrew word for a meal have the same conjugation, יֹאכְלוּ from אָכַל. The word's primary meaning is "to eat."[365] The word יִשְׂבָּעוּ, "be sated, satisfied, surfeited with food" or "to have enough"[366] is the outcome of the meals.

Those involved in the meals are the עֲנָוִים, דֹּרְשָׁיו, כָּל־דִּשְׁנֵי־אֶרֶץ, כָּל־יוֹרְדֵי עָפָר, and נַפְשׁוֹ לֹא חִיָּה. The first group is the עֲנָוִים, the poor, afflicted, humble, meek.[367] They may refer to the "lowly, pious, and modest mind, which prefers to bear injuries rather than return them."[368] They have "been a victim of some pain, injury, or harm, either physically or mentally."[369]

The other group is דֹּרְשָׁיו, "the ones who seek" Yahweh. The stem דָּרַשׁ, "resort to, seek"[370] may figuratively mean "to earnestly try to encounter the presence of a deity; often involving requests or petitions to the deity."[371] The other group is the כָּל־דִּשְׁנֵי־אֶרֶץ, "all the fat of the earth." The word דֶּשֶׁן, "fat"[372] may refer to "people who have possessions and wealth considered as a group."[373]

The next group is כָּל־יוֹרְדֵי עָפָר, "all who goes down to the dust." The word יוֹרְדֵי comes from יָרַד, meaning "to come or go down, descend."[374] In this verse, the word עָפָר may mean "human transience and nothingness before Yahweh"[375] or the dead itself. The phrase may indicate a person who is already at the brink of death but not yet dead. The description of the next group is חִיָּה לֹא וְנַפְשׁוֹ, "his life he cannot indeed keep." In this passage, נֶפֶשׁ refers to "life (state) … the condition of living or the state of being alive; especially healthiness, happiness, exuberance, energy, vitality, and the like."[376] This group is the people who cannot keep their state of living.

The feast/meal is also a festival of praise and worship. People involved in the festive meal honor Yahweh for their deliverance with the following acts: יְהַלְלוּ, יִשְׁתַּחֲווּ, and יִכְרְעוּ. The word הָלַל, "praise" means to "extol the greatness or excellence of a person, object, or event."[377] It is accompanied by the glorifying and standing in awe before Yahweh. Part of praise is indicated in the term יִשְׁתַּחֲווּ from שָׁחָה, "bow down, prostrate oneself … before God, in worship."[378]

The posture suggests making "a low stance as a sign of honor, worship, and homage of deity, with an associative meaning of allegiance to that deity."[379] DeSilva adds, "Bowing down low, even stretching out upon the ground, was a prominent gesture by which one party showed honor to another, recognizing and acting out the proportionately greater honor of the one to whom one bowed."[380] The next act is יִכְרְעוּ, "they bow down" from כָּרַע, "to bow down"[381] or bending one's knee, "either [with] the back bent down or straight."[382] This posture of kneeling is associated with "giving respect or worship."[383] It is the opposite of kneeling as being subdued or defeated by an enemy.[384]

Grammatical and syntactical analysis. This verse (v. 27) belongs to the praise of the psalmist. The subjects of the previous verses who praise Yahweh shifts from "I" (the psalmist, v. 23) to "you" (those who fear the Lord, the offspring of Jacob/Israel, v. 24), then "I" (v. 26). Verse 27 has another shift of the subject to the third person plural—the afflicted and those who seek him. These subjects may be parallel.

Verse 27 has two lines. The two fientive progressive non-perfective verbs יֹאכְלוּ and יִשְׂבָּעוּ are consequences of the previous act—Yahweh's succoring "the affliction of the afflicted" (v. 25). The earlier verb is persistent (present): "the afflicted will continue eating." The latter verb is "a stative (non-changing) present situation"[385]: "and they will always be satisfied." The factitive non-perfective *piel* יְהַלְלוּ, "they praise" "is the result of a sensory causation."[386] The direct object of the objective event[387] is יְהוָה. The fientive jussive יְחִי functions as a benediction— "may he lives." The subject of the verb is לְבַבְכֶם, "your heart." The benediction is given a duration, לָעַד, "until forever."

Verse 30 seems to be a parallel of v. 27 with modification of the subjects. The fientive non-perfective אָכְלוּ (v. 30) parallels the fientive non-perfective יֹאכְלוּ (v. 27). The subject refers to the people of wealth coming from the different parts of the world. The *hithpael* non-perfective וְיִשְׁתַּחֲווּ is "iterative or durative."[388] The "habitual non-perfective" denotes a "habitual activity with no specific tense value."[389] The translation of וְיִשְׁתַּחֲווּ is "They themselves repeatedly worship." The fientive non-perfective יִכְרְעוּ parallels the verb יִשְׁתַּחֲווּ.

Structure. Verses 27 and 30 seem to form a synonymous parallelism. The A's refer to the subjects of vv. 27, 30. The B's represent the acts of the participants of the feast/meal. The acts of eating and the resulting satisfaction refer to the benefits they receive from Yahweh. The praise, worship, and kneeling are reciprocal acts to honor the benefactor identified in C as Yahweh. C' shows the place where the worshipful acts are done. D pronounces the benediction for the A's. The benediction is resultative of Yahweh's beneficent actions toward the A's. The structure is indicated below.

A The afflicted
　B Eat and satisfied (v. 27a)
A' The ones who seek him
　B' Praise
　　C Yahweh (v. 27b)

D Benediction (v. 27c)
A''' All the fat of the earth
  B''' Eat and worship (v. 30a)
A'''' All going down to dust
  B'''' Kneel
    C'' Before him (v. 30b)
A''''' He who cannot keep himself alive (v. 30c)

Text and translation. This section presents the Hebrew text and the working translation.

Hebrew Text		Working Translation
יֹאכְל֨וּ עֲנָוִ֨ים ׀ וְיִשְׂבָּ֗עוּ יְהַֽלְל֣וּ יְ֭הוָה דֹּרְשָׁ֑יו יְחִ֖י לְבַבְכֶ֣ם לָעַֽד׃	27	The afflicted eat and they are satisfied. Those who seek him praise Yahweh. May your hearts live forever!
אָכְל֬וּ וַיִּֽשְׁתַּחֲו֨וּ ׀ כָּֽל־דִּשְׁנֵי־אֶ֗רֶץ לְפָנָ֥יו יִ֭כְרְעוּ כָּל־יוֹרְדֵ֣י עָפָ֑ר וְ֝נַפְשׁ֗וֹ לֹ֣א חִיָּֽה	30	All the rich of the earth eat and they (themselves) repeatedly worship him. All those going to dust bow down before him. Even he [who] does not have his life [praise him].

Interpretation. Verses 27 and 30 show the means of meals which indicates the integration of the psalmist and the afflicted into the worshipful community. The attendees to the festive meals are the distressed, well-to-do, those going to dust, and the barely alive. There seems to be a significant gap in the social status of the attendees. However, the festive meal levels the ground. The distressed receive their honor back by merely attending the festive meal. The well-to-do maintain their honor.

The afflicted belongs to the class of the lowly who are products of oppression.[390] They are miserable (Ps 9:12), poor (Ps 9:18; Prov 14:21), oppressed (Ps 9:9, Amos 2:7), downtrodden, and needy (Ps 74:20). They may be blind, broken-hearted, captives, or bound (Isa 61:1). In Ps 22, they are the afflicted, those going down to the dust, and those who cannot keep themselves alive (vv. 27, 30). Because of their status, they are shameful and have no honor. They are also targets of violence. They may turn out shamed (Ps 74:20–21).

Nevertheless, Yahweh protects them from exploitation (Ps 14:4). They call on Yahweh to defend their cause and not send them to oppression (vv. 19, 22). They challenge Yahweh "as [the] saving judge, now at last to exercise his twofold office, namely effecting justice in the cosmos and in his people, against the oppressors and for the oppressed—out of mercy for the victims of injustice to judge or effect rescue."[391] In 2 Macc, those in bondage, despised, hated, and oppressed have the same plight of being shamed by their enemies. They call on God to torment those who oppress them (1:27–28). In Job's suffering, he equates his affliction with shame.[392] He describes himself as full of shame and satiated with his affliction (Job 10:15). His misery leaves him without self-esteem.[393]

The phrase "all the fat of the earth" is a figurative expression of those well-to-do or the rich. They obtain great possessions and wealth.[394] They are privileged to have the abundance and the richness of the land. They live a satisfying life, not needing anything. Proverbs 3:16 indicates that riches and honor come hand-in-hand.[395] A rich man also receives the honor.[396]

However, God warns the people of Israel to "neither show partiality to the poor nor honor the rich" (Exod 23:3, Lev 19:15) for Yahweh is the source and giver of both riches and honor[397] and he will defend the cause of the oppressed, the poor, and the needy (Ps 74:20). Also, there is danger in having much riches and honor, relying too much on self, and making an alliance with those who hate God. Those who hate God earn the ire of Yahweh (2 Chr 18:1, 19:2).

On the meal occasion of Ps 22, both the afflicted and the rich are present (vv. 27, 30). Yet, the assembly is not limited to them. The group includes the "fearers of the LORD" (vv. 23, 25), "descendants of Jacob/Israel" (v. 23), "seekers of the LORD," and "the afflicted" (v. 26). Indirectly, people from different areas of the earth including the families of nations, those who worship Yahweh, shall be part of the festive meal. Mays indicates that they have a theological spiritual identity. "They are brothers (v. 22) in a religious sense."[398]

The sight at the gathering for the meal seems to be awe-inspiring because of the all-inclusive circumstances. The gathering produces no discrimination of ethnicity and social status. It breaks the barrier of social strata between the poor and the rich drawn together in unity.[399] It attributes honor to both the distressed and the well-to-do. The distressed and the well-to-do achieve the same level of satisfaction from the provision and the occasion.

The occasion in Ps 22 is a stark contrast to the Mediterranean meal customs, especially of the 2nd century BC. In the Mediterranean, only the elite come together for the meal. However, in the meal, the seating arrangement indicates the status of the attendees. Commonality does not exist in this gathering. Slaves served in the gathering and women were excluded. The society's poor and ordinary never adopted the custom.[400]

One significant scenario in David's life involving abundant eating and drinking was his coronation as king of Israel. David had been successful in his military campaigns from the time he became Saul's soldier until he became king. He rose from being a lowly person to being the most honored individual in the kingdom. Yet the story is not all about David. His rise to power was orchestrated by God himself who provided him the honor. Ralph W. Klein succinctly observes that "David became king because God chose him to be king."[401]

The celebration of eating and drinking was appropriate for the occasion. The people of Israel came from different parts of the land and gathered together with the intent to crown him as king.[402] David's brothers prepared a great meal for such an occasion. This festive meal is another sharp contrast to David's exclusion in Samuel's sacrificial ritual (זֶבַח), which comprises of "slaughtering, a libation, and meal or a festive meal at which meat was consumed"[403] during his anointment as king of Israel (1 Sam 16:1–13). Even their neighbors came and brought meals for this celebration. The celebration of eating and drinking was of no ordinary magnitude, for it lasted three days (1 Chr 12:38–40).

Probably, the distressed, debtors, and disgruntled (those of lowly status) came and joined the eating of food and the drinking with those who are of a better state. The gathering broke the wall that divided the weak (the poor and afflicted) and the strong (the rich and well-to-do).

The feast formalized the people of Israel's alliance, including the nations beyond Hebron, and the kingship of David.[404]

The OT records the invitation of certain kings to persons to eat at the king's table as a sign of the restoration of honor. One OT narrative goes back to David's invitation of Mephibosheth, the son of his intimate friend Jonathan, to eat at the king's table. He did it to honor his commitment to Jonathan by showing kindness to his descendants displaced from the throne. Before the presence of David, who was already the king of Israel at that time, Mephibosheth "paid homage" (2 Sam 9:6). He attributes shame upon himself by considering himself as an outcast, unworthy to be part of the king's party (v. 8). His shame stemmed from the loss of his right to Israel's throne as the king's descendant when his grandfather king and father died in the war. He suffered a crippling accident while escaping from the onslaught of the war (2 Sam 4:4, 9:3). Right after the war, someone not on his patristic lineage sat on the throne (5:1–5).

The verb used to describe Mephibosheth's homage is the same verb used in Ps 22:30 to describe the act of worship before Yahweh. In Mephibosheth's case, it was an act of respect and honor to the monarch on the throne. Essentially, his honor returned when he ate at the king's table as one of the king's sons (v. 10). Also, all the land that belongs to Saul were returned to him (v. 7). David's "magnanimous decree … changed Mephibosheth's fortunes forever."[405]

Jehoiachin, an exiled king of Judah to Babylon, had his honor restored by Evil-Merodach, king of Babylon. He was freed from prison and was given "a place of honor"[406] before the other exiled kings in Babylon. Hobbs holds that "'the seat of seats' presupposes a hierarchy of royal prisoners in the Babylonian jails. The chair was a symbol of important social status."[407] The removal of Jehoiachin's prison clothes, an indication of defeat and shame, and his eating at the king's table regularly (2 Kgs 25:27–30) meant the removal of shame and the restoration of honor.[408] The stories of Mephibosheth and Jehoiachin are two incidents that show the importance of gathering together for a meal. They were removed from their shameful status and honored to be part of the royal entourage again.

The festive meal in vv. 27–29 includes praise, worship, and kneeling. Verse 29 adds further details of those who do these worshipful acts. Those who seek God and who go down to the dust are probably in distress and trouble, so they seek Yahweh for respite. The figurative expression "those who go down to the dust" indicates that this group of people is on the brink of extinction, yet they are still alive. As with the עָנִי, "afflicted," "poor," "humble"[409] (v. 25), the psalmist can relate with their sufferings and afflictions.[410]

Also, he considers himself as if dead at the height of his enemies' attacks (v. 17). He was once miserable, distressed, and about to die. Yahweh turns his face towards him in his affliction and listens to his cries (v. 22). Yahweh's turning and hearing of the psalmist's prayer is a total reversal of the psalmist's previous situation. Previously, the psalmist was forsaken and turned away. His prayers were not heard and answered (vv. 2–3). Yet, Yahweh has seen his affliction and responded to his prayers.[411] In the same sense, he also sees and answers the prayers of the afflicted.

The meal provided for the afflicted means that Yahweh had already delivered them and had brought them out of shame and attributed them the honor. For this reason, the afflicted responded with praise, worship, and obeisance before him. They did these to pay homage to Yahweh, honoring and fearing him as a deliverer. "He [psalmist] now sits with his fellow human beings and participates in a feast which symbolizes fellowship with God,"[412] as Craigie states succinctly.

An expression in Isaiah mimics eating and praising. The people of Yahweh, Jerusalem's inhabitants, experienced affliction when their provisions and resources were taken away by their enemies and they were left forsaken and abandoned (49:14). Their reputation was restored when Yahweh put an end to their affliction by restoring their city and giving them their own food (Isa 62:12).[413] The place of eating, honoring, and drinking is the sanctuary (Isa 62:8–9). Yahweh's ending the people's affliction also brought salvation, reward, recompense, and redemption. Yahweh also changes the status of his people to "a sought out one, a city not forsaken" (vv. 11–12). Yahweh's acts on behalf of his people mean a "restored relationship."[414]

In the same context, Isaiah shows Yahweh's ascription of honor to his people. The people were afflicted and taken into captivity. Amid their suffering, Yahweh let his people eat, drink, rejoice, and be satisfied. He had delivered them from their bondage in Babylon (Isa 65:13–15). Psalm 23:5 may be a fitting response to this act of Yahweh: "You have prepared a table before me in the presence of my enemies." This is probably the same kind of feasting Yahweh prepares for his people in Ps 22:27, 30.[415]

Amid their feasting, praise, and worship, the psalmist pronounced a benediction for both the afflicted and the well-to-do. A benediction is a "pronouncement of God's favor upon an assembled congregation."[416] In the OT, usually, a priest pronounces the blessing, especially during the morning and evening sacrifices (Lev 9:22, 1 Chr 23:13). In some instances, "the king, as the viceroy of the Most High, might give the blessing"[417] (2 Sam 6:18, 1 Kgs 8:55, 1 Chr 16:2). Levites also pronounce blessings to the people (2 Chr 30:27).

The superior one usually utters the benediction to an inferior. If the psalmist indeed pronounced the blessing, he may be of superior status. Probably, the psalmist declared this blessing at the time when he became the leader of all the distressed who came to him (1 Sam 22:2). The blessing requested Yahweh to satiate the needs and the prosperity of both the distressed and the well-to-do. The request included the blessing of protection, deliverance, salvation, and rescue that Yahweh provided. The pronouncement of the blessing was without exclusivity. It suggested that both the distressed and the well-to-do should receive the blessing. Both received the honor attributed to them.

Honor and shame implication. In vv. 27 and 30, three groups belong to the lower class of society. These are the afflicted, those going to the dust, and those who cannot keep their lives. They are oppressed and exploited by the strong and the powerful. Their retaliation is futile due to their meager resources and physical capabilities. Their enemies reduce them to shame. In the honor and shame context, they are the economically poor and the politically powerless.

One other group mentioned in v. 30 is the well-to-do, prosperous, rich, and wealthy. They possess the fat of the land and satiated with its abundance. In the honor and shame context, they are economically prosperous and politically influential. Also, because of their wealth and prosperity, they gain honor.

Yahweh's meal brought the afflicted, the shamed, and the well-to-do together. It was a leveling ground because it attributed honor to both the afflicted and well-to-do. The afflicted were delivered from their affliction while the well-to-do preserved their prosperity. Both stood honored as a consequence. In response, they honored Yahweh with their acts of praise, worship, and prostration. They honor Yahweh as the deliverer, savior, and rescuer.

Summary. This section deals with feast or meal, a means of communication. Yahweh set the meal for the afflicted, the shamed, who were satisfied with the meals. The prosperous of the earth, the honored, partook of the same meal. The feast attracted the afflicted and the affluent together, thus placing them on the same honorific status. The meal indicated Yahweh's deliverance of the afflicted from their affliction and the preservation of the well-to-do. Here, honor was attributed to both the afflicted and the well-to-do. The acts of worship of both the afflicted and the well-to-do honored Yahweh.

The New Testament Use of Psalm 22

Psalm 22 is quoted or alluded to by different authors of the NT. The quotations are about Jesus's passion and his proclamation of those sanctified as his brothers. This section briefly discusses these select quotations from the context of the values and means mentioned.[418] Abandonment/forsakenness, taunt, nakedness, and kinship/family appear in the passion experience of Jesus.

In the Gospel accounts, before and during his crucifixion, Jesus experiences taunting from his crucifiers: the soldiers, the passersby, the chief priests, scribes, and elders.[419] The subject of their mockery is Jesus's kingship, power to save others, trust in God (cf. Ps 22:7), God's ability to deliver and affection towards Jesus (cf. v. 7), and Jesus's being the son of God.[420] The purpose of the taunters' mockery is to shame Jesus negatively. It is a challenge to Jesus's innocence.

To defend his honor, Jesus has to respond to it. Yet, he does not, as Isaiah states: "He was oppressed, and he was afflicted, yet he opened not his mouth; like a lamb that is led to the slaughter, and like a sheep that before its shearers is silent, so he opened not his mouth" (53:7, ESV). He does not need to since the people have declared him innocent of all the mockers' accusations.[421] Thus, Jesus's honor is restored.

The Gospels also record the dividing of Jesus's garments, alluding to Ps 22:19.[422] In this passion experience of Jesus, nakedness seems to appear. The division or distribution of the garments is customary in that the executioners are entitled to the victim's garments. According to W. D. Davies and Dale C. Allison Jr., there are two things to note here: (a) the victim experiencing the shame of nakedness because the crucified were crucified naked and (b) the fulfillment of Ps 22:19.[423] Jesus experiences the most shameful and "gruesome forms of torture and death humans have ever invented."[424]

Further, in his cry on the cross, Jesus quotes Psa 22:2.[425] His cry on the cross indicates the value of kinship and the means of abandonment. The vocative Ἠλὶ ἠλὶ, "My God, my God" (Matt 27:46) or Ἐλωῒ ἐλωῒ, "My God, my God" (Mark 13:54) seems to indicate the close and intimate kinship relationship between Jesus and God.[426] This kinship relationship is between a father and son (cf. Ps 22:10–11), as revealed in the context through the centurion's words, "Truly this man was the son of God" (Matt 27:54, Mark 15:39). Luke also catches this kinship relationship when he records Jesus's last words, before giving up his life, calling God as father (23:46).

Yet, amid his agony, Jesus feels that God the Father has abandoned him.[427] The Greek word ἐγκαταλείπω means that the connection between Jesus and the Father is separated,[428] and Jesus is left uncared.[429] At this time, Jesus's primary need is for God, the Father, to deliver him from his suffering (Luke 22:42). The Greek σῴζω, "save, deliver"[430] means "to deliver when there is a particularly perilous situation, a mortal danger."[431] This deliverance seems to reflect what the psalmist also needed from God when he faced suffering from his enemies' hands (cf. Ps 22:2).[432]

The Gospel writers mark that the Father did not deliver Jesus from death during his crucifixion. Yet, Jesus's shameful death on the cross turns into an honorable triumph.[433] First, the people confirm the innocence of Jesus, thus shaming his accusers. Second, his persecutors declared his kingship over Israel, an honorific title (Matt 27:37; Mark 15:26; Luke 23:38; John 19:3, 19).[434] Third, the centurion acknowledged that indeed Jesus is the son of God, another honorific title. It also indicates that the kinship between Jesus and God was not severed. Fourth, the mockery was disputed through the resurrection of Jesus. God also did not abandon him, even at his death. God the Father did not leave Jesus in the grave, for he resurrected him (Matt 28:5–6, Mark 16:6, Acts 2:30–33, 1 Cor 15:4). Jesus's shame of death turned into honor because of his resurrection. Also, Jesus was exalted to the right hand of (Acts 2:33), bestowed with the name which is "above every name so that at the name of Jesus every knee should bow, in heaven and on earth and under the earth, and every tongue confess that Jesus Christ is Lord, to the glory of God the Father" (Phil 2:9–10, ESV).

Hebrews 2:10–12 talks about the close unity of Jesus with the believers.[435] In this passage, the value of kinship is evident. Jesus, the creator, controller of all things, and the founder of salvation (v. 10) came to earth and made himself a human being to die for everyone (Heb 2:9). He was not ashamed to call humans his brethren (v. 11). The word ashamed means to "lose face" especially of someone "treated without respect for his position or status."[436] Paul Ellingworth and Eugene Albert Nida fittingly state that "although Jesus is supreme, he nevertheless has so much in common with men that he can call them his brothers without any risk of losing his status."[437]

Verse 12 emphasizes Jesus's commonality with humanity by quoting Ps 22:23: the opening statement of the praise part of the psalm indicates the psalmist's triumph over his enemies' attacks. This is a fitting statement of Jesus, who identified himself with his brethren and experienced the "suffering of death" (v. 9), yet was victorious. Jesus exclaims, "I will tell of your name to my brothers; in the midst of the congregation I will sing your praise" (v. 12). Donald Guthrie intimates that Hebrews quotes the psalm because it "sees the suffering [of Jesus] in the light of [his] ultimate glory."[438] Also, Jesus's glory is shared with the community. Two things are evident in this passage: (a) it indicates that the honor of an individual is connected with the community and (b) the purpose of Jesus identifying himself with humanity provides them salvation.

In summary, the NT use of Ps 22 reflect some of the values and means found in the psalm. In his passion experience, Jesus experiences the shame of abandonment, taunting, and nakedness. Yet, his shameful crucifixion and death turns into honor because he is acknowledged as God's son, pronounced as the king of Israel and innocent of any wrong doing. He is not abandoned to eternal death but is resurrected and exalted at the right hand of God. With his victory over death, he calls the sanctified people as his own brothers, so that he will be glorified and his people honored.

Summary

This present chapter presented the following themes: God as savior and king, deliverance, and trust. It holds that Ps 22 is a lament psalm with a section of praise in it. The structure shows the division between the lament and the praise, emphasizing deliverance in the context of honor and shame. The analysis of the honor and shame passages in Ps 22 reveals that the psalmist is shamed. It also shows that his deliverance is necessary for the restoration of his honor.

The following statements show the psalmist's shame experience. (a) The abandonment resulted in the fractured patronage relationship between the psalmist and Yahweh, causing shame to the psalmist. (b) The fractured relationship exposed the psalmist to attacks of the enemies which reduced him to utter shame. (c) He faced taunts from the people and his family, which indicated his separation from his familial affiliation and dishonorable state.

The following reasons indicate the reasons for the psalmist's desires for his honor. (a) Yahweh, as a patron, plays a vital role in removing the psalmist's shame and restoring his honor because he can rescue, save, and restore the psalmist's health. (b) Yahweh delivered the fathers from their shame and humiliation, so the psalmist seems to desire such deliverance from his shameful state as well, for he declares that Yahweh is his progenitor. (c) The fathers trusted in Yahweh, so they were rescued, delivered, and not put to shame. Yahweh made the psalmist trust in him, providing him security. At long last, the psalmist appears to have received deliverance from Yahweh. The feast indicates such deliverance.

In this chapter, the NT use of Ps 22 is also presented. The NT reveals that Ps 22 was quoted in relation to the passion of Jesus Christ. The means of abandonment, taunt, and nakedness and the value of kinship are evident in the context of the passages where the psalm is quoted. These values and means are also related to the deliverance of Jesus from shame. The next chapter elaborates on the deliverance terms the psalmist used to express his quest for deliverance. The frequency of the terms shows the dire need of the psalmist for deliverance. The next chapter also presents deliverance as the means to the reversal of the psalmist's status, from shame to honor.

---

[1] As indicated in the study of the structure, vv. 2 and 12 serve as an inclusio of the first part of the lament section. The word *rḥq*, "to be far" serves as the marker of the inclusio. In v. 12, the word *qrb* appears to complete the figure of speech indicating the total distance the Lord has from the psalmist. To complement this figure of speech in v. 2, the LXX adds the phrase πρόσχες μοι. Thus, the terms far and near now appear in vv. 2 and 12 completing the inclusio of the first part of the lament.

[2] The imperative indicates a positive "request, petition, supplication, or prayer." Wesley J. Perschbacher, *New Testament Greek Syntax: An Illustrated Manual* (Chicago: Moody Press, 1995), 347. The request is addressed to a superior, in this case God. The imperative is "used in the aorist tense" that belongs to the constative category. Daniel B. Wallace explains that a constative indicates that "this is a solemn or categorical command. The stress is *not* 'begin an action,' nor 'continue to act.' Rather, the stress is on the *solemnity* and *urgency* of the action." Daniel B. Wallace, *The Basics of New Testament Syntax: An Intermediate Greek Grammar* (Grand Rapids: Zondervan, 2000), 211. The emphasis is in the original.

[3] The word שָׁאַג or שְׁאָגָה means "groaning." *DBLH*, s.v. "שְׁאָגָה." The BDAG defines the word as "in imagery of one making a false step so as to lose footing: a violation of moral standards, offense, wrongdoing, sin." BDAG, s.v. "Παράπτωμα, Ατος Τό." A shorter meaning is "to go astray," "transgression, trespass," "false step, slip, … blunder, … defeat, error in amount of payments." W. Michaelis, "Píptō, Pt Ma, Pt Sis, Ekpíptō, Katapíptō, Parapíptō, Paráptōma, Peripíptō," *TDNTA* 846; *LALGNT*, s.v. "Παράπτωμα"; *LSJ*, s.v. "Παράπτωμα."

[4] Jer 9:13, 17:13.

[5] Carl Schultz, "עֲזַב," *TWOT* 2:658. See also BDB, s.v. "עֲזַב." The root of עֲזַב appears in Psalms twenty-three times (Pss 9:11; 10:14; 16:10; 22:2; 27:9–10; 37:8, 25, 28, 33; 38:11, 22; 40:13; 49:11; 71:9, 11, 18; 89:31; 94:14; 119:8, 53, 87).

6 The Aramaic translation of עָזַב is *šbq*, "leave, leave behind." The Akkadian *ezēbu* may refer to an "abandoned child," "malformed newborn," "divorce," which indicate a condition of shame. Gerstenberger, *TDOT* 10:584. The Ethiopic meaning is "widowed, unmarried." *HALOT*, s.v. "עָזַב." A. Schoors, referring to the widowhood of Israel because Yahweh abandoned her, holds that widowhood is a shame. A. Schoors, *I Am God Your Saviour: A Form-Critical Study of the Main Genres in Is. 40–55* (Leiden: Brill, 1973), 82.

7 *LALHB*, s.v. "עָזַב."

8 *DCH* 6, s.v. "עָזַב"; Gerstenberger, *TDOT* 10:586; *HALOT*, s.v. "עָזַב."

9 *HALOT*, s.v. "יְשׁוּעָה." The other meaning is "acts of salvation." *LALHB*, s.v. "יְשׁוּעָה."

10 *BDB*, s.v. "יְשׁוּעָה."

11 *NSDHGW*, s.v. "יְשׁוּעָה."

12 The KJV translates יְשׁוּעָה in different ways: "salvation (65x), help (4x), deliverance (3x), health (3x), save (1x), saving (1x), welfare (1x)." "יְשׁוּעָה," blueletterbible, https://www.blueletterbible.org/kjv/gen/1/1/s_1001. The NASB has a different rendering of the distribution of *yĕšûʿâ*. See *NASH AGD*, s.v. "יְשׁוּעָה."

13 *HALOT*, s.v. "שְׁאָגָה." See also *DBLH*, s.v. "שְׁאָגָה."

14 Gary G. Cohen, "שָׁאַג," *TWOT* 2:890. The word also refers to the roaring "specifically of the young lion already capable of bringing down prey ... as well as of the mature animal." M. Graupner, "שְׁאָגָה; שָׁאַג," *TDOT* 14:232–33. The Ugaritic refers it "to the bellowing of a bull" or in Arabic it refers to the "roaring of various animals." Graupner, *TDOT* 14:233.

15 These are: (a) "cry of war of the 'nation far away'"; (b) the roaring of the hostile powers, adversaries, or demonic beings encircling the petitioner; (c) the deadly and destructive behavior of "certain groups in the society"; (d) the expression of the "intensity of the lament ... and expression of suffering"; and (e) the roaring of Yahweh. Graupner, *TDOT* 14:234.

16 The other meanings of this word are "to give evidence, testify; to respond to what was said, follow willingly." *LALHB*, s.v. "עָנָה." See also the homonyms indicating the different meanings of the ʿnh. C. J. Labuschagne explains that the verb "does not primarily mean 'to answer' but 'to react.'" C. J. Labuschagne, "עָנָה," *TLOT* 1:926. Also, the sense of עָנָה means "favorable answer." *GHCLOT*, s.v. "עָנָה." When Pharaoh dreamt and his dream caused him distress, Joseph came to his presence and told him that "God will give Pharaoh a favorable answer" (Gen 41:16). Indeed, God revealed to Pharaoh what he was about to do in the land of Egypt (v. 25). Through Joseph, Pharaoh was spared from the onslaught of the seven-year drought that came to Egypt (41:56–57).

17 Labuschagne, *TLOT* 1:928. For the other senses of the word *ʿānâ*, see *LALHB*, s.v. "עָנָה."

18 *BDB*, s.v. "דּוּמִיָּה"; *HALOT*, s.v. "דּוּמִיָּה."

[19] The word has another meaning, "awaits." *DBLH*, s.v. "דּוּמִיָּה." Isaiah Hoogendyk also adds the meaning "the absence of sound." *LALHB*, s.v. "דּוּמִיָּה."

[20] *GHCLOT*, s.v. "דּוּמִיָּה." Another sense is "the state of being silent (as when no one is speaking)." *LALHB*, s.v. "דּוּמִיָּה." In this present passage, this is not most likely indicated by the act of crying by the psalmist. The other sense of the word is "awaits" which details "the expectation of something that is rightfully, properly due." *GHCLOT*, s.v. "דּוּמִיָּה."

[21] *LALHB*, s.v. "דּוּמִיָּה."

[22] Robert D. Culver, "דּוּמִיָּה," *TWOT* 1:186.

[23] The sense of the preposition מִן is dynamic. The ablative designates a "movement away from a specified beginning point." BDB, s.v. "מִן." The basic meaning of the preposition *min* is "out of, from, on account of, off, on the side of, since, above, than, so that not; out of" (BDB, s.v. "מִן"); "part of, made of, by means, since, because of, than, more than" (*DBLH*, s.v. "מִן"); "away from, because, without, beside, over, above" (*LALHB*, s.v. "מִן") indicating the idea of separation. For the different senses of the uses of the preposition מִן, see Bruce K. Waltke and M. O'Connor, *An Introduction to Biblical Hebrew Syntax* (Winona Lake, IN: Eisenbrauns, 1990), 212–14.

[24] Weiser holds that the psalmist imagines that God has forsaken him. The fact is that there is no reason for God's abandonment of the psalmist here in this psalm. Artur Weiser, *The Psalms: A Commentary*, trans. Herbert Hartwell, 5th and rev. ed., OTL (Philadelphia: Westminster, 1962), 220. Derek Kidner describes the psalmist's cry as a cry of disorientation because God had withdrawn his protective care while the enemies closed in. Derek Kidner, *Psalms 1–72: An Introduction and Commentary*, TOTC 15 (Downers Grove, IL: InterVarsity Press, 1973), 123.

[25] Ernst R. Wendland summarized the "four types of God's apparent 'negligence' that the Psalmists lament" as presented by Ross. Ernst R. Wendland, *Studies in the Psalms: Literary-Structural Analysis with Application to Translation* (Dallas: SIL International, 2017), 138. The types are "God hides himself, God has forgotten, God has forsaken, God is hostile." Wendland, *Studies in the Psalms*, 139. See A. P. Ross, "The 'Thou' Sections of Laments: The Bold and Earnest Prayers of the Psalmists," in *The Psalms: Language for All Seasons of the Soul*, ed. Andrew J. Schmutzer and David M. Howard Jr. (Chicago: Moody Press, 2013), 136–41.

[26] Eugene H. Merrill, *Deuteronomy*, NAC 4 (Nashville: Broadman & Holman, 1994), 397.

[27] Robert G. Bratcher and Howard A. Hatton, *A Handbook on Deuteronomy*, UBS Handbook Series (New York: United Bible Societies, 2000), 513.

[28] Ibid., 521.

[29] The disasters and sufferings that came upon Israel were "famines, droughts, epidemics, and hostile enemies." Ibid.

[30] Gerstenberger, *TDOT* 10:519.

[31] Salvation may be received from different sources: God, human beings, and things. *HALOT*, s.v. "יְשׁוּעָה."

[32] The term תְּיַשְּׂטְמֵנִי comes from שָׂטַם, "to hate, bear a grudge against, to harass." *CWSDOT*, s.v. "שָׂטַם."

[33] Job describes God as a "ferocious beast ([v.] 9f.), a traitor ([v.] 11), a wrestler ([vv.] 12a, b), an archer ([vv.] 12c, 13a), a swordsman ([vv.] 13b, 14)." Francis I. Andersen, *Job: An Introduction and Commentary*, TOTC 14 (Downers Grove, IL: InterVarsity Press, 1976), 195.

[34] See also Samuel Rolles Driver and George Buchanan Gray, *A Critical and Exegetical Commentary on the Book of Job*, 3rd ed., ICC (Edinburgh: T&T Clark, 1921), 145.

[35] Andersen, *Job*, 197. Emphasis in the original.

[36] Robert L. Alden, *Job*, NAC 11 (Nashville: Broadman & Holman, 1993), 187.

[37] William David Reyburn, *A Handbook on the Book of Job*, UBS Handbook Series (New York: United Bible Societies, 1992), 777.

[38] BDB, s.v. "יְשׁוּעָה."

[39] *DBLH*, s.v. "יְשׁוּעָה."

[40] *DBLH*, s.v. "יְשׁוּעָה."

[41] This sense of salvation appears at least fifty-one times out of seventy-eight times in the OT. Another example of this is indicated in David's psalm about God's deliverance of him from the hand of Saul (2 Sam 22:51).

[42] *DBLH*, s.v. "יְשׁוּעָה."

[43] *DBLH*, s.v. "שָׂגַב."

[44] BDB, s.v. "יְשׁוּעָה."

[45] BDB, s.v. "נְדִיבָה." Nobility means "the quality of being noble in character, mind, birth, or rank." *Lexico Dictionaries: English*, s.v. "nobility." The words related to this—virtue, goodness, honor, honesty, decency, integrity, magnanimity, generosity, selflessness or bravery—may describe who Job is. The other meaning of *nĕḏîḇâ* may be "dignity." *HALOT*, s.v. "נְדִיבָה." Dignity means "the state or quality of being worthy of honor or respect." *Lexico Dictionaries: English*, s.v. "dignity."

[46] This state of salvation appears approximately twenty-six times (i.e., in the book of Psalms, it appeared at least eighteen times; in the book of Isaiah, it appears five times; in the book of Job, it appears once) out of the seventy-eight times where this word appears in the OT.

[47] Nupanga Weanzana et al., "Psalms," in *Africa Bible Commentary: A One-Volume Commentary Written by Seventy African Scholars*, ed. Tokunboh Adeyemo, 2nd ed. (Grand Rapids: Zondervan, 2010), 634.

[48] F. J. Stendebach, "עָנָה," *TDOT* 11:223.

[49] J. J. Pilch and Bruce J. Malina, eds., *Biblical Social Values and Their Meaning: A Handbook* (Peabody, MA: Hendrickson, 1993), xxiv.

[50] Bruce J. Malina, "Grace/Favor," in *Biblical Social Values and Their Meaning: A Handbook*, ed. J. J. Pilch and Bruce J. Malina (Peabody, MA: Hendrickson, 1993), 85.

[51] Timothy C. Tennent, *Theology in the Context of World Christianity: How the Global Church Is Influencing the Way We Think About and Discuss Theology* (Grand Rapids: Zondervan, 2007), 86.

[52] Robert L. Reymond, *A New Systematic Theology of the Christian Faith*, 2nd ed. (Nashville: Nelson, 2010), 236. Christopher West describes the nakedness without shame as "the gift," the nakedness between man and woman called as "one flesh." Christopher West, *Theology of the Body Explained: A Commentary on John Paul II's "Gospel of the Body"* (Herefordshire, UK: Gracewing, 2003), 19. In the beginning, both Adam and Eve were naked before the presence of God yet felt no shame. It was only after the fall that they recognized they were both naked. The recognition of their nakedness and covering themselves up indicated their feeling of shame. Peter J. Leithart, *A Great Mystery: Fourteen Wedding Sermons* (Moscow, ID: Canon, 2006), 34.

[53] Kenneth A. Mathews, *Genesis 1–11:26*, NAC 1A (Nashville: Broadman & Holman, 1996), 225.

[54] L. E. P. Erith, *Genesis*, ed. Charles Gore, Henry Leighton Goudge, and Alfred Guillame, A New Commentary on Holy Scripture: Including the Apocrypha 1 (New York: MacMillan, 1928), 43.

[55] Ḥayim Navon, *Genesis and Jewish Thought*, trans. David Straus (New York: Ktav, 2008), 137.

[56] Horst Robert Balz, "Γυμνότης, Ητος, ἡ," *EDNT* 265. Cf. Gen 3:7.

[57] Harvey Newcomb, *The Young Lady's Guide to the Harmonious Development of Christian Character*, 3rd, rev. and enlarged ed. (Boston: James B. Dow, 1841), 232.

[58] John Skinner, *A Critical and Exegetical Commentary on Genesis*, ICC (New York: Scribner's Sons, 1910), 76.

[59] William David Reyburn and Euan McGregor Fry, *A Handbook on Genesis*, UBS Handbook Series (New York: United Bible Societies, 1998), 76.

[60] Dan Lé, *The Naked Christ: An Atonement Model for a Body-Obsessed Culture*, Distinguished Dissertations in Christian Theology 7 (Eugene, OR: Pickwick, 2012), 124.

[61] A. Robert Hirschfeld, *Without Shame or Fear: From Adam to Christ* (New York: Church Publishing, 2017), 26. Rabbi Boruch David explains that "after Adam and Eve sinned, they understood that they had taken G[o]d's protection for granted, and they concluded that they no longer deserved it. Frightened of their vulnerability, they attempted to deal with it on their own. G[o]d explained the consequences and changes that would occur and then made them garments of leather." Rabbi Boruch David, *Adam and Eve: The Rest of the Story Secrets*

from the Ancient Wisdom of the Jews (Bloomington, IN: Xlibris, 2016), Conversation No. 2, "On Wearing Clothing and Uniqueness," para. 2.

[62] Lé, *The Naked Christ*, 119.

[63] Ibid., 122.

[64] Reyburn and Fry, *A Handbook on Genesis*, 98.

[65] Mathews, *Genesis 1–11:26*, 255.

[66] Arnold Andersen, Leigh Cohn, and Tom Holbrook, *Making Weight: Men's Conflicts with Food, Weight, Shape and Appearance* (Carlsbad, CA: Gurze Books, 2010), ch. 3, "The Clothes Make the Man," para. 3.

[67] Leithart, *A Great Mystery*, 34.

[68] Sheila Bridge, *How to Feel Good Naked: Learning to Love the Body You've Got* (Oxford: Monarch Books, 2012), 75.

[69] Jerome H. Neyrey, "Clothing," in *Handbook of Biblical Social Values*, ed. J. J. Pilch and Bruce J. Malina, updated ed. (Peabody, MA: Hendrickson, 2000), 23.

[70] Lé, *The Naked Christ*, 118. Lé discusses in his book the antithesis of nakedness and clothing. He states that it elicits discussion on the concept of nakedness in relation to the original sin. He points out "the metaphorical role of nakedness in relation to the 'brokenness' or 'lack of wholeness' in the concepts of sin and shame." See Ibid., 119.

[71] Ibid., 118.

[72] Bridge, *How to Feel Good*, 73.

[73] *LSJ*, s.v. "Θηράω."

[74] Dahood, *Psalms 1:1–50*, 140.

[75] This paper directs the readers to the work of Carl Friedrich Keil and Franz Delitzsch for the detailed explanation of these variants. Carl Friedrich Keil and Franz Delitzsch, *The Psalter*, trans. James Martin, K&D 5 (Peabody, MA: Hendrickson, 1996), 199.

[76] G. Johannes Botterweck, "כֶּלֶב," *TDOT* 7:147.

[77] Ibid., 149.

[78] Ibid., 156.

[79] The following are articles that dealt with solving the textual variant of the word כָּאֲרִי/כָּאֲרוּ. Samuel Daiches, "The Meaning of כָּאֲרִי in Psalm 22, v. 17," *JRAS* 1.2 (1933): 401–3; Gregory Vall, "Psalm 22:17B: 'The Old Guess,'" *JBL* 116.1 (1997): 45–56, https://doi.org/10.2307/3266745; John Kaltner, "Psalm 22:17b: Second Guessing 'The Old Guess,'" *JBL* 117.3 (1998): 503–6, https://doi.org/10.2307/3266445; Brent A. Strawn, "Psalm 22:17b: More Guessing," *JBL* 119.3 (2000): 439–51, https://doi.org/10.2307/3268408; Kristin M. Swenson, "Psalm 22:17: Circling around the Problem Again," *JBL* 123.4 (2004): 637–48, https://doi.org/10.2307/3268463; James R. Linville, "Psalm 22:17b: A New Guess," *JBL* 124.4 (2005): 733–44, https://doi.org/10.2307/30041067; Shon Hopkin, "The Psalm 22:16 Controversy: New Evidence from the Dead Sea Scrolls," *Brigham Young University Studies* 44.3 (2005): 161–72; Conrad R.

Gren, "Forcing the Ambiguities of Psalm 22:16 and the Messiah's Mission," *JETS* 48.2 (2005): 283–99.

[80] Conrad R. Gren presents a detailed study on the different translations of Ps 22:17. Gren, "Forcing the Ambiguities," 288–95.

[81] *DCH* 2, s.v. "בֶּגֶד"; BDB, s.v. "בֶּגֶד."

[82] BDB, s.v. "לְבוּשׁ"; *HALOT*, s.v. "לבושׁ."

[83] BDB, s.v. "בֶּגֶד."

[84] *DBLH*, s.v. "בֶּגֶד."

[85] Seth Erlandsson, "בֶּגֶד," *TDOT* 1:470.

[86] *DBLH*, s.v. "לְבוּשׁ." Emphasis in the original.

[87] *DCH* 4, s.v. "לְבוּשׁ"; BDB, s.v. "לְבוּשׁ."

[88] *DBLH*, s.v. "לְבוּשׁ."

[89] M. Tsevat, "מַחֲלֹקֶת; חָלַק; חֵלֶק; חֶלְקָה; חֲלָקָה," *TDOT* 4:448.

[90] *GHCLOT*, s.v. "נָפַל"; BDB, s.v. "נָפַל."

[91] Tsevat, *TDOT* 4:449.

[92] The objects distributed are things (plunder), clothing, or land. H. H. Schmid, "חָלַק," *TLOT* 1:431–32.

[93] *GHCLOT*, s.v. "נָפַל."

[94] BDB, s.v. "גּוֹרָל"; *HALOT*, s.v. "גּוֹרָל"; *DCH* 2, s.v. "גּוֹרָל."

[95] כִּי is used as a "relative causal particle: because, since, while." *GHCLOT*, s.v. "כִּי."

[96] Waltke and O'Connor, *Biblical Hebrew Syntax*, 487.

[97] The verbal clauses of the second line are an irreal resultative non-perfective clause, a causative non-perfective clause, a fientive incipient progressive non-perfective clause, a resultative non-perfective clause, and another causative non-perfective clause.

[98] The verb also changes to causative active from the fientive perfective appearing in the previous colon. The irreal resultative non-perfective verb "describes an irreal version of the action of the Qal" indicating a metaphorical action. Waltke and O'Connor, *Biblical Hebrew Syntax*, 407. The psalmist now "grasps the full measure of his suffering." Helmer Ringgren, "סָפַר," *TDOT* 10:311.

[99] Waltke and O'Connor, *Biblical Hebrew Syntax*, 503.

[100] Briggs and Briggs, *The Book of Psalms*, 197.

[101] Goldingay, *Psalms*, 110; Mays, *Psalms*, 110.

[102] Bratcher and Reyburn, *Book of Psalms*, 219.

[103] Goldingay, *Psalms*, 332.

[104] John H. Walton, Victor H. Matthews, and Mark W. Chavalas, *The IVP Bible Background Commentary: Old Testament* (Downers Grove, IL: InterVarsity Press, 2000), 533. On the ANE background of scattering the bones of enemies killed in battle, see also Walton, Matthews, and Chavalas, *The IVP Bible*, 524.

[105] Heinz-Josef Fabry, "לֵב," *TDOT* 7:412.

[106] Craigie, *Psalms 1–50*, 200.

107 Bratcher and Reyburn, *Book of Psalms*, 219.

108 Kenneth L. Barker and Waylon Bailey, *Micah, Nahum, Habakkuk, Zephaniah*, ed. E. Ray Clendenen, NAC 20 (Nashville: Broadman & Holman, 1999), 210.

109 T. Laetsch, *The Minor Prophets* (St. Louis: Concordia, 1956), 305.

110 *GHCLOT*, s.v. "חָרַשׁ."

111 Helmer Ringgren, "כֹּחַ," *TDOT* 7:124.

112 Ibid.

113 Reyburn, *Book of Job*, 525.

114 Allen P. Ross, *Psalms*, ed. John F. Walvoord and Roy B. Zuck, vol. 1 of *The Bible Knowledge Commentary: An Exposition of the Scriptures* (Wheaton, IL: Victor Books, 1985), 890.

115 R. E. O. White, "Psalms," in *Evangelical Commentary on the Bible*, vol. 3 of *Baker Reference Library* (Grand Rapids: Baker Books, 1995), 396.

116 The term תִּשְׁפְּתֵנִי second person singular is probably שְׁפָתֵנִי third person plural. The third is probably basing on the sequence of the passage (vv. 15–16). The Latin translation is *deduxerunt*, "to be reduced." This seems to get the sense of the situation of the psalmist that he was reduced to death.

117 1 Sam 2:8; 1 Kgs 16:2; Job 42:6; Pss 7:6; 44:26; 113:7; 119:25; Isa 29:4, 4; 47:1; 52:2; Lam 3:29; Mic 1:10. See also *DCH* 6, s.v. "עָפָר."

118 Job 7:21; 17:16; 20:11; 21:26; 24:12; Pss 22:16, 30; 30:10; Isa 26:19; Dan 12:2; 1QH 14_{34}, 19_{12}, 20_{26}. See also *LALHB*, s.v. "סָבַב."

119 L. Wächter, "עָפָר," *TDOT* 11:264.

120 *GTWGTHB* 2, s.v. "מָוֶת."

121 *GHCLOT*, s.v. "פַּר."

122 Bratcher and Reyburn, *Book of Psalms*, 219.

123 F. W. Dobbs-Allsopp, *Lamentations*, IBC (Louisville: Westminster John Knox, 2002), 70.

124 Donald Fowler, "Lion," *EDB*, 811.

125 Bradley S. Butler, "Dog," *Holman Illustrated Bible Dictionary* 438.

126 Michelle Ellis Taylor, "Dog," *EDB*, 352.

127 See also Helmer Ringgren, "נָבַט," *TDOT* 9:127.

128 John Peter Lange et al., *A Commentary on the Holy Scriptures: Psalms* (Bellingham, WA: Logos, 2008), 173.

129 Some examples show how clothing reveals the status of an individual: torn clothes for the leprous (Lev 13:45), and purple garments worn by the kings of Median (Judg 8:26), and some others (1 Sam 28:8, 2 Sam 1:2, 14:2).

130 Kenneth A. Mathews, *Genesis 11:27–50:26*, NAC 1B (Nashville: Broadman & Holman, 2005), 718.

131 Ibid.

132 George W. Coats, *Genesis, with an Introduction to Narrative Literature*, FOTL 1 (Grand Rapids: Eerdmans, 1983), 274. See also Lina Toth, *Transforming the*

Struggles of Tamars: Single Women and Baptistic Communities (Eugene, OR: Wipf & Stock, 2014), 1.

[133] Gordon J. Wenham, *Genesis 16–50*, ed. John D. W. Watts, WBC 2 (Waco, TX: Word, 1994), 367.

[134] Walter Brueggemann, *Genesis*, IBC (Atlanta: John Knox, 1982), 307. Gordon J. Wenham emphasizes that prostitution is of such disreputable status as indicated by Judah's "furtive way in which he sends his friend to make the payment, rather than go himself." Wenham, *Genesis 16–50*, 367.

[135] Mathews states that "the text's description of her dress incognito ... exhibited the depths of her [Tamar's] humiliation. She set aside her widowhood for the demeaning status of a prostitute." Mathews, *Genesis 11:27–50:26*, 718.

[136] Lé, *The Naked Christ*, 131.

[137] John E. Goldingay, *Israel's Gospel*, Old Testament Theology 1 (Downers Grove, IL: InterVarsity Press, 2003), 109.

[138] Alden, *Job*, 231.

[139] Bin Kang, *Honor and Shame in 1 Samuel 1–7* (Carlisle, Cumbria: Langham, 2022), 2.9 The Disgrace of Nakedness. Lé, *The Naked Christ*, 132.

[140] Lamar Eugene Cooper Sr., *Ezekiel*, NAC 17 (Nashville: Broadman & Holman, 1994), 169.

[141] Ibid.

[142] G. A. Cooke, *A Critical and Exegetical Commentary on the Book of Ezekiel*, ICC (Edinburgh: T&T Clark, 1936), 162.

[143] Ronald M. Hals, *Ezekiel*, FOTL 19 (Grand Rapids: Eerdmans, 1989), 100. See Ezek 16:9–14.

[144] Mosheh Greenberg, *Ezekiel 1–20: A New Translation with Introduction and Commentary*, AB 22 (New Haven: Yale University Press, 1983), 277.

[145] Cooper Sr., *Ezekiel*, 171.

[146] Leslie C. Allen, *Ezekiel 1–19*, WBC 28 (Dallas: Word, 1994), 242.

[147] Cooper Sr., *Ezekiel*, 174.

[148] Greenberg, *Ezekiel*, 242.

[149] Robert B. Chrisholm, "The Major Prophets," in *Holman Concise Bible Commentary: Simple, Straightforward Commentary on Every Book of the Bible*, ed. David S. Dockery, Holman Reference (Nashville: Broadman & Holman, 1998), 298.

[150] Lé, *The Naked Christ*, 132.

[151] Ibid.

[152] Ibid.

[153] Allen, *Ezekiel 1–19*, 242.

[154] Cooper Sr., *Ezekiel*, 174.

[155] Brandon Fredenburg, *Ezekiel*, The College Press NIV Commentary (Joplin, MO: College Press, 2002), 241.

[156] John F. Walvoord and Roy B. Zuck, eds., *The Bible Knowledge Commentary: An Exposition of the Scriptures* (Wheaton, IL: Victor Books, 1985), 1:1279.

[157] For the role of David as the Philistines' mercenary, see Walton, Matthews, and Chavalas, *The IVP Bible*, 316–17.

[158] Marvin A. Sweeney, *Isaiah 1–39, with an Introduction to Prophetic Literature*, FOTL 16 (Grand Rapids: Eerdmans, 1996), 540.

[159] *SDABD*, s.v. "taunt."

[160] Burke O. Long, *2 Kings*, FOTL 10 (Grand Rapids: Eerdmans, 1991), 316.

[161] Michael H. Floyd, *Minor Prophets: Part 2*, FOTL 22 (Grand Rapids: Eerdmans, 2000), 649.

[162] Lyn M. Bechtel, "The Perception of Shame within the Divine-Human Relationship," in *Uncovering Ancient Stones: Essays in Memory of H. Neil Richardson*, ed. Lewis M. Hopfe (Winona Lake, IN: Eisenbrauns, 1994), 80.

[163] Leland Ryken, "Taunt," *Dictionary of Biblical Imagery* 841.

[164] Ibid.

[165] BDB, s.v. "תּוֹלֵעָה"; *HALOT*, s.v. "תּוֹלֵעָה."

[166] Diether Kellerman and Helmer Ringgren, "תלע; תלעתלע; תּוֹלֵעָה; תּוֹלַעַת," *TDOT* 13:589.

[167] תּוֹלֵעָה is not strictly limited to worms but also "caterpillars, maggots, and the larvae of beetles." Ibid. These destroy vineyards and even the castor bean plant Jonah took shelter under (Jon 4:7). The maggots destroyed the left-over manna the Israelites took for themselves (Exod 16:20, 24). Ibid.

[168] Thomas E. McComiskey, "אִישׁ," *TWOT* 1:39. As a man of worth, he must possess masculine "properties such as strength, influence, courage." J. Kühlewein, "אִישׁ," *TLOT* 1:100. The use of this in Ps 22's context may be synonymous to the word גֶּבֶר, *geber*, meaning "a valiant man." John McClintock and James Strong, "גֶּבֶר," *Cyclopædia of Biblical, Theological, and Ecclesiastical Literature* 3:760.

[169] *HALOT*, s.v. "חֶרְפָּה."

[170] BDB, s.v. "חֶרְפָּה."

[171] *GHCLOT*, s.v. "חֶרְפָּה."

[172] *HALOT*, s.v. "חֶרְפָּה."

[173] E. Kutsch, "חָרַף," *TDOT* 5:211.

[174] There are different variations of situations in the OT where it is considered as a reproach: runaway slave, celibacy, widowhood, childlessness, and suffering and humiliation. Ibid., 213–14.

[175] BDB, s.v. "בָּזָה."

[176] BDB, s.v. "בָּזָה."

[177] *LALHB*, s.v. "בָּזָה."

[178] M. Görg, "בּוּז; בּוּז; בָּזָה," *TDOT* 2:60.

[179] Ibid., 2:61.

[180] Ibid.

181 *DBLH*, s.v. "רָאָה."

182 *LALHB*, s.v. "רָאָה."

183 BDB, s.v. "לָעֵג"; *GHCLOT*, s.v. "לָעֵג"; *DCH* 4, s.v. "לָעֵג."

184 *LALHB*, s.v. "לָעֵג."

185 *CWSDOT*, s.v. "לָעֵג."

186 C. Barth, "לָעֵג; לַעַג; לָעֵג," *TDOT* 8:13.

187 Ibid.

188 The topic of trust deals with the meaning of פָּלַט.

189 BDB, s.v. "נָצַל."

190 *GHCLOT*, s.v. "נָפַל."

191 U. Bergmann, "נָצַל," *TLOT* 2:760.

192 Ibid., 761.

193 BDB, s.v. "חָפֵץ." The Arabic of חָפֵץ attests to the idea of protection and preservation. In the North and Semitic languages, the element of protection also predominates. G. Johannes Botterweck, "חָפֵץ," *TDOT* 5:93; G. Gerleman, "חָפֵץ," *TLOT* 2:466.

194 *LALHB*, s.v. "חָפֵץ."

195 The participle denotes linear aspect: "The [participle] or *nomen agentis* … presents the person or subj[ect] in the continuous exercise or exhibition of the action or condition denoted by the verb." Waltke and O'Connor, *Biblical Hebrew Syntax*, 613.

196 Ibid., 441. See also Bruce K. Waltke, James M. Houston, and Erika Moore, *The Psalms as Christian Lament: A Historical Commentary* (Grand Rapids: Eerdmans, 2014), 363.

197 Alden, *Job*, 256.

198 Driver and Gray, *Book of Job*, 72.

199 Reyburn, *Book of Job*, 158.

200 Kidner, *Psalms 1–72*, 82.

201 Pilch, *A Cultural Handbook*, 159.

202 J. M. Ford, "Defeat," in *Biblical Social Values and Their Meaning: A Handbook*, ed. J. J. Pilch and Bruce J. Malina (Peabody, MA: Hendrickson, 1993), 42.

203 Ibid., 42–43.

204 *LGT*, s.v. "patronage."

205 Philip R. Davies, *Scribes and Schools: The Canonization of the Hebrew Scriptures* (Louisville: Westminster John Knox, 1998), 60.

206 The preposition *en* modifies *hagiois* and functions as a preposition of location. The prepositional phrase *en hagiois* functions as a substantive of location. *Hagios* refers to "things, places, and persons connected with the (Jewish) cult and the OT-Jewish tradition." Horst Robert Balz, "Άγιος," *EDNT* 17. The prepositional phrase may be translated as "in a holy place."

207 A participial phrase "indicates that the phrase, … described is marked by a participle." Roger L. Omanson and John Ellington, *A Handbook on the First*

Book of Samuel, UBS Handbook Series (New York: United Bible Societies, 2001), 621.

[208] The vocative אֵלִי appears in the OT twelve times: Exod 15:2; Pss 18:3; 22:2, 11; 63:2; 68:25; 89:27; 102:25; 118:28; 140:7; Isa 44:17. The vocative אֵלִי appears three times in this psalm (vv. 2, 11)

[209] BDB, s.v. "אֵל"; *DBLH*, s.v. "אֵל." The word אֵל appears in the OT about 230 times.

[210] In the East Semitic use, אֵל is named as 'Il. The name "was the proper name of a deity." Mark S. Smith, "El," *EDB* 384. In the Canaanite myth, he is called the eternal king. Also, he is known to be a "lusty old man" who is fittingly "the primordial procreator and patriarch." Frank M. Cross, "אֵל," *TDOT* 1:243, 247.

[211] BDB, s.v. "אֵל."

[212] The name יְהוָה appears in this psalm six times (vv. 9, 20, 24, 27, 28). "Yahweh is the proper name of the God of Israel" given to Moses. Mark Nicholas, *The Rules: Ten to Live By* (Nashville: Transit, 2003), 33. See also *LALHB*, s.v. "יהוה." Outside of Israel, the reference to Yahweh as the cult god does not exist. It means that the name is exclusive to the God of Israel. K. van der Toorn suggests that since the name Yahweh does not exist in Syria and Palestine, as well as in the West Semitic world, he "does not belong to the traditional West Semitic deities." K. van der Toorn, "Yahweh," *DDD* 911. Only in the Victory Stela of Mesha did it exist, not as his own personal god but rather as the official God of the Israelites whom he had defeated. The practice of putting up a stela after a victory in the war campaign is common in the Mediterranean context. Anybody defeated in a battle loses his honor. This indicates that the battle between Israel and Mesha, king of Moab, Israel loses its honor and is placed in a state of shame because of the defeat and Mesha receives the due honor because of his victory over Israel. This victory stela is a declaration of such honor for which Mesha is attributed with. Toorn, "Yahweh," 911. The counting of the occurrence of the personal name of God, "The Tetragrammaton YHWH, the LORD" differs (6823, 5,321, 6,700). J. B. Payne, "יהוה," *TWOT* 1:210. The name Yahweh is called a Tetragrammaton because it is always written with four letters *yod, he, waw, he.* Henry O. Thompson, "Yahweh (Deity)," *AYBD* 1011.

[213] The occurrences of אֱלֹהַי in the OT refer to Yahweh as Israel's God (i.e., Num 22:18, Deut 4:5, Josh 14:8, Ps 7:3, Isa 49:4), except for two where idols are referred to as personal gods (Gen 31:30, Judg 18:24).

[214] BDB, s.v. "אֱלֹהִים." אֵל may also mean "gods, judges, angels." *CWSDOT*, s.v. "אֱלֹהִים." This term appears 119 times in the OT.

[215] Swanson comments that the term God is "a title of the true God, with a focus on the might and power of God (Josh 22:22)." *DBLH*, s.v. "אֵל." See also BDB, s.v. "אֵל."

[216] BDB, s.v. "קָדוֹשׁ." קָדוֹשׁ means "holy, commanding respect, awesome, singled out, consecrated for," "sacred." *LALHB*, s.v. "קָדוֹשׁ." See also *HALOT*, s.v. "קָדוֹשׁ."

[217] BDB, s.v. "קָדוֹשׁ." See Craig Keen, "A 'Quick' Definition of Holiness," in *The Holiness Manifesto*, ed. Kevin W. Mannoia and Don Thorsen (Grand Rapids: Eerdmans, 2008), 237.

[218] BDB, s.v. "קָדוֹשׁ."

[219] BDB, s.v. "יָשַׁב." Other meanings of this word is "inhabit, be settled, be inhabited, ... establish a dwelling place, settle, marry, sit, seat, crouch, meet, restore." *DBLH*, s.v. "יָשַׁב."

[220] *DCH* 4, s.v. "יָשַׁב." The ESV, NASB, NIV, and NKJV use *enthroned*, the most probable translation of the term.

[221] BDB, s.v. "תְּהִלָּה." See also *LALHB*, s.v. "תְּהִלָּה"; *HALOT*, s.v. "תְּהִלָּה."

[222] The word תְּהִלָּה offers different senses. (a) In relation to worship, it is an offering of words of homage as an act of worship. (b) In an honorific status, it is the state or quality of being widely honored or acclaimed. (c) As an object, it is an object that inspires praise. (d) As an act, it can refer to the glorious deed, an act of wonder and glory that is deserving of praise. *LALHB*, s.v. "תְּהִלָּה."

[223] Exod 15:11, Pss 50:3, 71:22, 145:17, Isa 57:15, Jer 17:14.

[224] Hans-Jürgen Zobel, "יִשְׂרָאֵל," *TDOT* 6:399. Hans-Jürgen Zobel suggests that the root of the name יִשְׂרָאֵל is *śrh*, "persevere, persist" or *rîb,* "contend." Ibid., 6:400. However, he prefers the root *rbb*, "be exalted, reign" as it is the most likely root. The suggested meaning would be "El reigns, El is supreme." Ibid.

[225] Ibid., 6:401.

[226] E. Ruprecht, "פָּצַח," *TLOT* 2:583.

[227] Heinrich Ewald, *Syntax of the Hebrew Language of the Old Testament* (Edinburgh: T&T Clark, 1891), 162. See also Frederic Clarke Putnam, *Hebrew Bible Insert: A Student's Guide to the Syntax of Biblical Hebrew* (Quakertown, PA: Stylus, 2002), 10.

[228] אֵל is a noun masculine construct with a pronominal suffix first person singular. The noun in the nominative functions as the grammatical case of direct address otherwise called as a vocative. The suffix functions as a pronominal possession. Waltke and O'Connor, *Biblical Hebrew Syntax*, 129; *PDSBH*, s.v. "vocative."

[229] Waltke and O'Connor, *Biblical Hebrew Syntax*, 147.

[230] BDB, s.v. "אַתָּה"; *CDWGTHB* 2, s.v. "אַתָּה"; *DCH* 1, s.v. "אַתָּה."

[231] Waltke and O'Connor, *Biblical Hebrew Syntax*, 292.

[232] Joshua R. Westbury et al., eds., "The Lexham Figurative Language of the New Testament Dataset," in *Lexham Figurative Language of the Bible Glossary* (Bellingham, WA: Lexham, 2016), "Orientational Metaphor," para. 1.

[233] Waltke and O'Connor, *Biblical Hebrew Syntax*, 143.

[234] Synthetic parallelism is "a growing or expanding parallelism." Leland Ryken, *Sweeter than Honey, Richer than Gold: A Guided Study of Biblical Poetry*

(Bellingham, WA: Lexham, 2015), 72. See also Philip P. Jenson, *New Bible Commentary: Twenty-First Century Edition*, ed. D. A. Carson et al., 4ᵗʰ ed. (Leicester: Inter-Varsity Press, 1994), 453–54; Tremper Longman III, *How to Read the Psalms* (Leicester: Inter-Varsity Press, 1988), 100; *PDSBH*, s.v. "synthetic parallelism"; Kim Williams Bodenhamer, "Poetry, Biblical," *Lexham Bible Dictionary*, "Synthetic," para. 1. For the meaning of complementary parallelism, see Jenson, *New Bible Commentary*, 454.

235 A. J. Köstenberger, "Nations," *NDBT* 676.

236 Wendland, *Studies in the Psalms*, 138; Samuel L. Terrien, *The Psalms: Strophic Structure and Theological Commentary* (Grand Rapids: Eerdmans, 2003), 230.

237 The obligation of the psalmist towards God is clearly fulfilled in the praise section of the psalm.

238 Bratcher and Reyburn, *Book of Psalms*, 212.

239 Jayson Georges, *Ministering in Patronage Cultures: Biblical Models and Missional Implications* (Downers Grove, IL: InterVarsity Press, 2019), 148.

240 Ernst R. Wendland, *Contextual Frames of Reference in Translation: A Coursebook for Bible Translators and Teachers* (London: Routledge, 2014), 63.

241 Ibid.

242 deSilva, *Honor, Patronage, Kinship*, 96.

243 See Georges, *Ministering in Patronage Cultures*, 9; deSilva, *Honor, Patronage, Kinship*, 97; David F. Watson, *Honor Among Christians: The Cultural Key to the Messianic Secret* (Philadelphia: Fortress, 2010), 43; Seneca, *Ben*, n.d., 1.2.4.

244 deSilva, *Honor, Patronage, Kinship*, 97.

245 Alan B. Wheatley, *Patronage in Early Christianity: Its Use and Transformation from Jesus to Paul of Samosata* (Eugene, OR: Wipf & Stock, 2011), 3. See also S. N. Eisenstadt and Luis Roniger, *Patrons, Clients and Friends: Interpersonal Relations and the Structure of Trust in Society*, Themes in the Social Sciences (Cambridge: Cambridge University Press, 1984), 43–49.

246 Charles H. Kraft, *Power Encounter in Spiritual Warfare* (Eugene, OR: Wipf & Stock, 2017), 12.

247 Moreno Dal Bello, *For God so Loved...Who?* (Morrisville, NC: Lulu Press, 2017), 76.

248 Kent Gramm, *The Prayer of Jesus: A Reading of the Lord's Prayer* (Eugene, OR: Wipf & Stock, 2015), 40.

249 Jacob Neusner, *A Theological Commentary to the Midrash: Pesiqta DeRab Kahana* (Lanham, MD: University Press of America, 2001), 181.

250 Mark D. Roberts, *Ezra/Nehemiah/Esther*, The Preacher's Commentary 11 (Nashville: Nelson, 2004), "The People Celebrate the Passover," para. 3.

251 Peter J. Bellini, *Truth Therapy: Renewing Your Mind with the Word of God* (Eugene, OR: Wipf & Stock, 2014), 135.

252 Jerry Bridges, *The Pursuit of Holiness: Run in Such a Way as to Get the Prize 1 Corinthians 9:24* (Carol Stream, IL: Tyndale House, 2014), 13.

[253] Francis Frangipane, *Holiness, Truth, and the Presence of God: For Those Who Are Unsatisfied with Their Spiritual Life and Willing to Do Something About It* (Lake Mary, FL: Charisma Media, 2011), 48.

[254] Pss 10:16, 22:28, 24:7, 29:10, 84:3, 146:10.

[255] Niels Peter Lemche, *Ancient Israel: A New History of Israel*, 2nd ed. (London: Bloomsbury, 2015), 242.

[256] Meredith G. Kline, *Treaty of the Great King: The Covenant Structure of Deuteronomy: Studies and Commentary* (Eugene, OR: Wipf & Stock, 2012), 16.

[257] Curtis Giese and Paul Puffe, *Called To Be God's People, Abridged Edition: An Introduction to the Old Testament* (Eugene, OR: Wipf & Stock, 2015), 32.

[258] Stephen L. Cook, *The Social Roots of Biblical Yahwism* (Atlanta: SBL Press, 2004), 38.

[259] Bill T. Arnold, *Introduction to the Old Testament* (New York: Cambridge University Press, 2014), 180.

[260] David A. deSilva, "Grace," *EDB* 525.

[261] Toorn, "Yahweh," 915.

[262] See also Payne, *TWOT* 1:211.

[263] Walter A. Elwell and Barry J. Beitzel, "Names, Significance Of," *BEB* 2:1523–24.

[264] Stephen R. Miller, *Daniel*, ed. E. Ray Clendenen, NAC 18 (Nashville: Broadman & Holman, 1994), 244.

[265] Ibid.

[266] P. R. Williamson, "Covenant," *NDBT* 424.

[267] Peter Toon, "Remember, Remembrance," *Baker's Evangelical Dictionary of Biblical Theology* 668.

[268] Arthur G. Patzia and Anthony J. Petrotta, "Holy War," *Pocket Dictionary of Biblical Studies* 59–60.

[269] Thompson, *AYBD* 1012.

[270] M. Smith, "El," 385. M. Smith mentions, "Like El, Yahweh is a father (Deut 32:6; Isa 63:16; 64:8; Jer 3:14, 19; 31:9; Mal 1:6, 2:10; cf. Exod 4:22; Hos 11:1), with a compassionate disposition ("merciful and gracious god"; Exod 34:6, Neh 9:17, Pss 86:15, 103:8, 145:8, Joel 2:13, Jonah 4:2). Like El, Yahweh is the progenitor of humanity (cf. Deut 32:6–7). Both El and Yahweh appear to humans in dream-visions and function as their divine patron. Like El, Yahweh is a healing god (Gen 20:17; Num 12:13; 2 Kgs 20:5, 8; Ps. 107:20)." Ibid.

[271] Pilch and Malina, *Biblical Social Values*, xv.

[272] Ibid.

[273] Ibid., xviii.

[274] Jerome H. Neyrey, "Dyadism," in *Biblical Social Values and Their Meaning: A Handbook*, ed. J. J. Pilch and Bruce J. Malina (Peabody, MA: Hendrickson, 1993), 51.

275 Waltke and O'Connor, *Biblical Hebrew Syntax*, 216. אֲבֹתֵינוּ appears fifty-four times in the OT.

276 Ibid., 212.

277 BDB, s.v. "אָב." The pronominal suffix is genitival.

278 Helmer Ringgren, "אָב," *TDOT* 1:7. Examples of the OT occurrences for the *patriarchs* are Deut 1:8, 6:10, 9:5, 29:12(13), 30:20; 1 Chr 29:18. Some examples of passages that refer to *forefathers* are Gen 15:15; 46:34; 1 Kgs 19:4; 21:3, 4; 2 Kgs 19:12; 20:17.

279 *DCH* 6, s.v. "עַם."

280 BDB, s.v. "עַם."

281 W. Von Soden and E. Lipiński, "עַם," *TDOT* 11:164.

282 Ibid., 168.

283 *LALHB*, s.v. "עַם." Members of family line denotes "an eponymous ancestor, a great-grandfather, … a paternal uncle, or … a father-in-law." Von Soden and Lipiński, *TDOT* 11:169-70. The collective relationship may mean "people as a whole, a multitude, or a religious assembly." Ibid.,170.

284 A. R. Hulst states that the original meaning of this "paternal uncle" and later it developed to "tribe." A. R. Hulst, "עַם," *TLOT* 2:896. "*'am* emphasizes the relationship of the members." Ibid.

285 *DBLH*, s.v. "גחה." Other translations are "one who draws me forth" (BDB, s.v. "גיח"); "one who extracts me" (*DCH* 2, s.v. "גחה"); or "pull out" (*HALOT*, s.v. "גחה").

286 Alfred Jepsen, "בָּטח," *TDOT* 2:89.

287 BDB, s.v. "שָׁלַךְ."

288 W. Theil, "שָׁלַךְ," *TDOT* 15:95.

289 Ibid., 89.

290 *DCH* 6, s.v. "עַם."

291 BDB, s.v. "רְחָם"; *HALOT*, s.v. "רְחָם." "*Rehem/raham* is to be distinguished from *beten* 'belly.' *Beten* and *rehem/raham* are used as parallels only when speaking of conception and birth." Leonard J. Coppes, "רְחָם," *TWOT* 2:842.

292 T. Kronholm, "רְחָם," *TDOT* 13:454.

293 BDB, s.v. "רְחָם."

294 Ibid.

295 Kronholm, *TDOT* 13:457.

296 Ross, *Psalms*, 810.

297 Waltke and O'Connor, *Biblical Hebrew Syntax*, 433.

298 The *hophal* "represents the subject as being caused to be acted upon or to suffer the effects of having been acted upon (usually by an unnamed agent)." Ibid., 447.

299 M. Oeming, "שׁד," *TDOT* 14:411.

300 Num 20:15; Deut 26:7; 1 Kgs 8:53; Neh 9:9; Josh 24:17; Ps 78:3–4.

301 Judg 6:13, 1 Kgs 8:57–58, Neh 9:32, Ps 44:2.

302 Ross, *Psalms*, 810.

303 James Montgomery Boice, *Psalms* (Grand Rapids: Baker Books, 2005), 194.

304 John Calvin, *Psalms*, Calvin's Commentaries (Albany, OR: Ages Software, 1998), Psalms 22:4.

305 Erhard Gerstenberger, *Psalms, Part 1, with an Introduction to Cultic Poetry*, FOTL 14 (Grand Rapids: Eerdmans, 1988), 111.

306 Bratcher and Reyburn, *Book of Psalms*, 217. The act is just like how a midwife catches a baby when the mother gives birth and takes care of him/her until he/she is ready to be moved to the mother's care.

307 Craigie, *Psalms 1–50*, 119.

308 Jamieson, *Genesis-Esther*, 1:353.

309 Erhard Gerstenberger, "בָּטַח," *TLOT* 1:228.

310 Bratcher and Reyburn, *Book of Psalms*, 218.

311 Dahood, *Psalms 1:1–50*, 139.

312 Margaret S. Odell, "Hosea," *EDB*, 609.

313 J. J. Pilch, "Compassion," in *Biblical Social Values and Their Meaning: A Handbook*, ed. J. J. Pilch and Bruce J. Malina (Peabody, MA: Hendrickson, 1993), 28.

314 Ibid., 29. Fictive kin relation is a "relation between individuals unrelated by either birth or marriage who have an emotionally significant relationship similar to those of a family relation." Charlotte Linde, *Working the Past: Narrative and Institutional Memory* (Oxford: Oxford University Press, 2008), 29. See also Pearl A. Dykstra, "Kin Relationship," *Encyclopedia of Human Relationships* 952; Maria Schmeekle, "Extended Families," *Encyclopedia of Human Relationships* 574. One of the widespread forms of fictive kinship is adoption. Cristian Alvarado Leyton, "Fictive Kinship," *Encyclopedia of Human Relationships* 682. In Ps 22, the psalmist is adopted by Yahweh who acted as his loving and compassionate adoptive father.

315 J. J. Pilch, "Trust," in *Handbook of Biblical Social Values*, ed. J. J. Pilch and Bruce J. Malina, Update ed. (Peabody, MA: Hendrickson, 2000), 178.

316 Ibid.

317 Ibid., 178–79.

318 BDAG, s.v. "Ἐλπίζω."

319 BDAG, s.v. "Ἐλπίζω." The other meaning of *elpizō* is "to look forward to something in view of the measures one takes to ensure fulfillment, expect." BDAG, s.v. "Ἐλπίζω." The short meanings are "hope for, look for, hope to, hope, expect that." BDAG, s.v. "Ἐλπίζω."

320 *DBLH*, s.v. "גָּלַל."

321 To commit means "to dedicate or trust entirely to a specific person or activity or cause." *LALHB*, s.v. "גָּלַל."

322 *Targum Lexicon*, s.v. "גָּלַל." The meaning of *šbḥ* is "to praise, to be of the opinion, to polish, to commend, to be glorified, to be commended, to be praiseworthy." *Targum Lexicon*, s.v. "גָּלַל."

323 BDB, s.v. "בָּטַח"; *HALOT*, s.v. "בָּטַח." The LXX translates this word to ηλπισεν, *ēlpisen*, "to hope." The Greek sense indicates "complete security in God alone" and total reliance upon him. Jepsen, *TDOT* 2:89.

324 *DCH* 2, s.v. "בָּטַח." בָּטַח may also mean "to believe." Chris Kugler, "Faith," *Lexham Theological Wordbook* Logos book, "Faith," para. 1; *DBLH*, s.v. "בָּטַח."

325 *LALHB*, s.v. "בָּטַח."

326 BDB, s.v. "זָעַק"; *HALOT*, s.v. "זָעַק."

327 The parallel nouns עָנָו, עָנִי, "poor, afflicted, humble, meek" (Ps 22:25, 27) and their verbal counterparts עָנָה, "afflicted" (Exod 1:11–12) and זָעַק, "to cry" (Exod 2:23; Ps 22:6) link the Exodus experience of the Israelites with the Davidic experience. See BDB, s.vv. "עָנִי," "עָנָה," "זָעַק."

328 G. Hasel, "זָעַק," *TDOT* 4:112.

329 Ibid., 115.

330 *DBLH*, s.v. "פָּלַט."

331 Ruprecht, *TLOT* 2:986.

332 *DCH* 6, s.v. "פָּלַט."

333 Ruprecht, *TLOT* 2:988. The idea here is that a person "slips out." *GTWGTHB* 2, s.v. "פָּלַט." It indicates an escape from either a hostile person, from the guards or a dangerous place towards a place of safety or deliverance.

334 *DCH* 6, s.v. "פָּלַט."

335 BDB, s.v. "מָלַט"; *HALOT*, s.v. "מָלַט."

336 Ruprecht, *TLOT* 2:986; BDB, s.v. "מָלַט."

337 *LALHB*, s.v. "מָלַט." Someone needs to be saved from the place of "ruin, destruction, or harm." *LALHB*, s.v. "מָלַט." He needs to be rescued "from harm or evil" or, in some cases, "from prison." *DBLH*, s.v. "מָלַט."

338 *DCH* 6, s.v. "פָּלַט."

339 BDB, s.v. "בוש."

340 *DCH* 2, s.v. "בוש."

341 BDB, s.v. "גָּלַל." The other meaning of *gālal* is "roll down, roll on, roll off, roll up, be rolled, wallow, remove." *DBLH*, s.v. "גָּלַל."

342 The following are the Bible senses that Hoogendyk suggests on the word *gālal*: "to roll (turn over)"; "to commit (trust)"; "to remove ⇔ roll away" "to be rolled up"; "to pass through ⇔ roll on"; "to roll"; "to roll down"; and "to wallow." *LALHB*, s.v. "גָּלַל."

343 "A *fientive verb* is one that designates a dynamic situation." Waltke and O'Connor, *Biblical Hebrew Syntax*, 363.

344 Ibid., 486, 693. Preterite is a "simple past tense form that is not marked for aspect." Christo H. J. van der Merwe, Jackie A. Naudé, and Jan H. Kroeze, *A Biblical Hebrew Reference Grammar* (Sheffield: Sheffield Academic, 1999), 363.

345 The *piel* functions as a resultative (terminal *Aktionsart*). Waltke and O'Connor, *Biblical Hebrew Syntax*, 406.

[346] "The subject is in the state of being acted upon or of suffering the effects of an action by an implicit or explicit agent." Ibid., 382.

[347] A stative verb denotes "a mental or psychological state and take an object." Ibid., 491.

[348] There are different types of directives: command, permission, request, and invitation. The context suggests that the directive is a command by a hostile party towards the psalmist whom they consider as inferior. van der Merwe, Naudé, and Kroeze, *Biblical Hebrew Reference*, 150.

[349] *DCH* 1, s.v. "אַל."

[350] Waltke and O'Connor, *Biblical Hebrew Syntax*, 619.

[351] Deut 7:6–8, 14:2, 26:17–19; Pss 105:8–15, 135:4; Isa 43:1–3.

[352] Pss 22:5–6, 33:20–22, 62:8–9, 91:2–4, 115:9–11, 119:41–42.

[353] 2 Chr 32:10, Jer 13:25, Ezek 16:15, Zep 3:2.

[354] Pilch, "Trust," 179.

[355] Gerstenberger, *TLOT* 1:229.

[356] Jepsen, *TDOT* 2:92.

[357] Gerstenberger, *TLOT* 1:228.

[358] Jepsen, *TDOT* 2:92.

[359] Malina, "Feast," 76.

[360] W. Thomas Sawyer, "Banquet," *Holman Illustrated Bible Dictionary*, 170.

[361] Ibid.

[362] Malina, "Feast," 76.

[363] Mark D. Futato, *Beginning Biblical Hebrew* (Winona Lake, IN: Eisenbrauns, 2003), 244.

[364] *DCH* 1, s.v. "אָכַל"; BDB, s.v. "אָכַל"; *LALHB*, s.v. "אָכַל"; *HALOT*, s.v. "אָכַל." The context means "to eat a meal."

[365] G. Gerleman, "שָׂבַע," *TLOT* 3:1268.

[366] See also BDB, s.v. "עָנָו"; *HALOT*, s.v. "עָנָו"; *DBLH*, s.v. "עָנָו."

[367] *GHCLOT*, s.v. "עָפָר."

[368] *LALHB*, s.v. "עָפָר." Those who cause harm are "the wealthy or powerful." *DCH* 6, s.v. "עָנָו."

[369] BDB, s.v. "דָּרַשׁ."

[370] *LALHB*, s.v. "דָּרַשׁ."

[371] BDB, s.v. "דָּשֵׁן."

[372] *LALHB*, s.v. "דָּשֵׁן." דָּשֵׁן could refer to all humankind living on the earth who are wealthy or affluent.

[373] BDB, s.v. "יָרַד."

[374] G. Wanke, "עָפָר," *TLOT* 2:940. See also *GHCLOT*, s.v. "עָפָר"; BDB, s.v. "עָפָר"; *HALOT*, s.v. "עָפָר."

[375] *LALHB*, s.v. "נֶפֶשׁ."

[376] *DBLH*, s.v. "הָלַל."

[377] BDB, s.v. "שָׁאֲגָה."

378 *DBLH*, s.v. "חָוָה."

379 David A. deSilva, "Honor and Shame," *Dictionary of the Old Testament: Pentateuch; A Compendium of Contemporary Biblical Scholarship* 432.

380 BDB, s.v. "קָרָא."

381 *DBLH*, s.v. "קָרָא."

382 Ibid.

383 Ibid.

384 Waltke and O'Connor, *Biblical Hebrew Syntax*, 505. The "stative non-perfective represents the internal temporal structure of a stative (non-changing) present situation," Ibid.

385 Ibid., 401. This "factitive piel is the result of sensory causation … a 'real' result available to the physical senses, or of psychological or linguistic causation, a mental change or a speech act that reflects a mental change." Ibid.

386 The objective event is "an event that can be seen or felt apart from the participants." Ibid.

387 Ibid., 427.

388 Ibid.

389 J. David Pleins, "Poor, Poverty: Old Testament," *AYBD* 5:413.

390 Frank-Lothar Hossfeld, Erich Zenger, and Linda M. Maloney, *Psalms 2: A Commentary on Psalms 51–100*, ed. Klaus Baltzer, Hermeneia: A Critical and Historical Commentary on the Bible (Philadelphia: Fortress, 2005), 250.

391 Reyburn states that שְׂבַע קָלוֹן, to be "filled with disgrace" means to be "'covered with shame,' 'dishonored,' 'humiliated.'" Reyburn, *Book of Job*, 209.

392 John E. Hartley, *The Book of Job*, NICOT (Grand Rapids: Eerdmans, 1988), 189.

393 *CDWGTHB* 2, s.v. "דָּשֵׁן."

394 Leo G. Perdue states that "long life (Prov. 3:2; 22:4), riches (Prov. 14:24), and honor (Prov. 8:18) are among the greatest values in wisdom literature (1 Kgs 3:1–15)." Leo G. Perdue, *Proverbs*, IBC (Louisville: Westminster John Knox, 2000), 101.

395 I.e., David, Solomon, Jehoshaphat, and Hezekiah (1 Kgs 3:13; 2 Chr 17:5, 29:28, 32:27).

396 1 Kgs 3:13; 1 Chr 29:11, 12; Prov 8:18; Eccl 6:2.

397 Mays, *Psalms*, 111.

398 "Our fathers trusted" [Ps 22:4], *SDABC*, ed. Francis D. Nichol, rev. ed. (Washington, DC: Review & Herald, 1976), 3:684.

399 Dennis Edwin Smith, *From Symposium to Eucharist: The Banquet in the Early Christian World* (Minneapolis: Augsburg Fortress, 2002), 11; Bincy Mathew, *The Johannine Footwashing as the Sign of Perfect Love: An Exegetical Study of John 13:1–20* (Tübingen: Mohr Siebeck, 2018), 113.

400 Ralph W. Klein, *1 Samuel*, ed. John D. W. Watts, WBC 10 (Waco, TX: Word, 1983), 159.

[401] Steven Shawn Tuell, *First and Second Chronicles*, IBC (Louisville: Westminster John Knox, 2001), 59.

[402] U. Bergmann, "זָבַח," *TDOT* 4:8.

[403] Walvoord and Zuck, *Bible Knowledge Commentary*, 1:605. See also Walton, Matthews, and Chavalas, *The IVP Bible*, 1 Chronicles 12:40; John Mark Hicks, *1 and 2 Chronicles*, The College Press NIV Commentary (Joplin, MO: College Press, 2001), 138.

[404] Robert D. Bergen, *1, 2 Samuel*, NAC 7 (Nashville: Broadman & Holman, 1996), 355.

[405] Paul R. House, *1, 2 Kings*, NAC 8 (Nashville: Broadman & Holman, 1995), 400.

[406] T. Raymond Hobbs, *2 Kings*, ed. John D. W. Watts, WBC 13 (Waco, TX: Word, 1985), 367.

[407] Jesse C. Long Jr. states, "As Yahweh prospered Joseph and raised him from prison to a position of honor in Egypt, he has released Jehoiachin from prison in Babylon and given him a position above the kings who were with him in exile." Jesse C. Long Jr., *1 and 2 Kings*, ed. Terry Briley and Paul Kissling, The College Press NIV Commentary (Joplin, MO: College Press, 2002), 538.

[408] BDB, s.v. "עָנִי." See also *HALOT*, s.v. "עָנִי"; *GHCLOT*, s.v. "עָנִי."

[409] Mays, *Psalms*, 111.

[410] Craigie, *Psalms 1–50*, 201.

[411] Ibid.

[412] John D. W. Watts, *Isaiah 34–66*, ed. John D. W. Watts, rev. ed., WBC 25 (Nashville: Nelson, 1999), 888.

[413] John N. Oswalt, *The Book of Isaiah: Chapters 40–66*, NICOT (Grand Rapids: Eerdmans, 1998), 589.

[414] For the unity of Pss 22–24, see Davidson, "Psalm 22, 23," 25.

[415] Thomas E. McComiskey, "Benediction," *BEB* 1:280.

[416] John McClintock, "Benedictions," *Cyclopædia of Biblical, Theological, and Ecclesiastical Literature, Supplement—A–Z* 11:427.

[417] An exhaustive discussion of Jesus's passion in relation to the values studied in this paper is not the aim of this paper. The exhaustive study of Jesus's passion in correlation with the values considered in this paper is given as part of the recommendation for further study.

[418] Matt 27:39, 41, 46; Mark 15:20, 29, 31; Luke 23:35–38.

[419] See Matt 27:37, 42–44, 49; cf. Mark 15:18, 30; Luke 22:63, 66, 70; 23:35–37.

[420] Matt 27:19, 54; Luke 23:4, 15, 41, 47; John 19:4; cf. Isa 53:8–9.

[421] See Matt 27:35; Mark 15:24; Luke 23:32; John 19:20.

[422] W. D. Davies and Dale C. Allison Jr., *A Critical and Exegetical Commentary on the Gospel According to Saint Matthew*, ICC 3 (New York: T&T Clark, 2004), 613. See also Leon Morris, *The Gospel according to Matthew*, ed. D. A. Carson, PNTC (Grand Rapids: Eerdmans, 1992), 715. Craig L. Blomberg is doubtful whether Jesus was totally left naked or some clothing was left to cover

his private parts. Craig L. Blomberg, *Matthew*, ed. David S. Dockery, NAC 22 (Nashville: Broadman & Holman, 1992), 416.

[423] Blomberg, *Matthew*, 416.

[424] There is a slight difference in the versions and translations between Matthew and Mark. Matthew records, "Ἠλὶ ἠλὶ λεμὰ σαβαχθάνι; τοῦτ' ἔστιν· Θεέ μου θεέ μου, ἱνατί με ἐγκατέλιπες;" "*Eli, Eli, lema sabachthani?*' that is, 'My God, my God, why have you forsaken me?'" Mark accounts "Ἐλωῒ ἐλωῒ λεμὰ σαβαχθάνι; ὅ ἐστιν μεθερμηνευόμενον Ὁ θεός μου ὁ θεός μου, εἰς τί ἐγκατέλιπές με;" "*Eloi, Eloi, lema sabachthani?*' which means, 'My God, my God, why have you forsaken me?'" For the discussion on the difference between the two accounts, see Willoughby C. Allen, *Matthew*, 3rd ed., ICC (Edinburgh: T&T Clark, 1907), 294; Morris, *Matthew*, 740; Blomberg, *Matthew*, 419; R. T. France, *Matthew: An Introduction and Commentary*, TNTC 1 (Downers Grove, IL: InterVarsity Press, 1985), 403; D. A. Carson, *The Expositor's Bible Commentary: Matthew, Mark, Luke*, ed. Frank E. Gaebelein (Grand Rapids: Zondervan, 1984), 8:578; Robert G. Bratcher and Eugene Albert Nida, *A Handbook on the Gospel of Mark*, UBS Handbook Series (New York: United Bible Societies, 1993), 491; Ezra Palmer Gould, *Mark*, ICC (Edinburgh: T&T Clark, 1922), 294; James R. Edwards, *The Gospel according to Mark*, ed. D. A. Carson, PNTC (Grand Rapids: Eerdmans, 2002), 476; James A. Brooks, *Mark*, NAC 23 (Nashville: Broadman & Holman, 1991), 260; R. Alan Cole, *Mark: An Introduction and Commentary*, TNTC 2 (Downers Grove, IL: InterVarsity Press, 1989), 325; Walter W. Wessel, *The Expositor's Bible Commentary: Matthew, Mark, Luke*, ed. Frank E. Gaebelein (Grand Rapids: Zondervan, 1984), 8:782.

[425] The people understand the term Ἠλὶ as Elijah. Both passages indicate that Jesus is referring to God (Matt 27:47; Mark 15:34).

[426] According to Blomberg, "Christian theology developed the belief that at this moment Christ bore the sins of all humanity, spiritually separating him from his Heavenly Father." Blomberg, *Matthew*, 419. The text is understood as Jesus's recitation of the psalm to give him comfort at the hour of his need while hanging on the cross. Morris, *Matthew*, 720. There are different interpretations on the status of Jesus in relation to his sinlessness and the sinfulness of humanity. Some believe that Jesus is a pious man crying the words of the psalm while dying on the cross. See Carson, Wessel, and Leifeld, *The Expositor's Bible Commentary. Vol. 8*, 8:578. Stuart K. Weber indicates that Jesus was "completely alone, bearing the guilt of all sinners." Stuart K. Weber, *Matthew*, HNTC 1 (Nashville: Broadman & Holman, 2000), 465.

[427] *BDAG*, s.v. "Ἐγκαταλείπω."

[428] *L&N*, s.v. "Ἐγκαταλείπω."

[429] *BDAG*, s.v. "Σῴζω."

[430] Ceslas Spicq, "Σῴζω," *TLNT* 3:982.

[431] In Jesus's passion, the mockers seem to emphasize this need in two instances. The first instance was when the passersby, the chief priest, and the scribes mocked Jesus right before he cried, "My God, my God." The mockers stated "Save yourself, and come down from the cross!" "He saved others; he cannot save himself" (Mark 15:30–31; cf. Matt 27:40). The second time was when the onlookers mocked Jesus before he yielded up his life. The onlookers said among themselves, "Wait, let us see whether Elijah will come to save him" (Matt 27:49; cf. Mark 15:33).

[432] See Santos on Mark's Gospel about how the shameful death of Jesus is turned into honor. Santos, *Turning Our Shame*, 221–25.

[433] Santos indicates that Mark had unwittingly recorded the persecutor's recognition of Jesus as the king of Israel. Ibid., 225.

[434] Paul Ellingworth and Eugene Albert Nida, *A Handbook on the Letter to the Hebrews*, UBS Handbook Series (New York: United Bible Societies, 1994), 37.

[435] Ibid., 42.

[436] Ibid.

[437] Donald Guthrie, *Hebrews: An Introduction and Commentary*, TNTC 15 (Downers Grove, IL: InterVarsity Press, 1983), 94.

CHAPTER 4

DELIVERANCE AS A RESTORATION OF HONOR

Deliverance plays an essential role in Ps 22. Ten synonymous terms on deliverance occur in the psalm, relevant to the psalmist's restoration of honor. One word appears which refers to the outcome of the deliverance. The frequency of the occurrences of the deliverance terms means that David, the psalmist of Ps 22, is in dire straits and indeed he is in a status of shame. The psalmist yearns for deliverance to reverse his situation, from shame to honor. The present section deals with the psalmist's use of these deliverance terms to communicate his supplications to Yahweh to restore his honor.

The Psalmist's Need of Salvation

The word salvation, יְשׁוּעָה, (v. 2) is the first of the series of synonymous words the psalmist uses to refer to his need for deliverance and restoration of his honor. It appears right at the beginning of the complaints of the psalmist. Its occurrence at the beginning of the complaint indicates the urgency of the psalmist's deliverance. The psalmist's call for salvation comes at a critical time when salvation is far from him. The structure of the passage shows the placement of this word.

> A The psalmist's address to God (v. 2a)
> > B Question 1: Why did God forsake the psalmist (v. 2b)
> > B' Question 2: Why is his salvation far (v. 2c)
> > B'' Question 3: Why is there no mitigation of his groanings (v. 2d)

The psalmist's complaints begin with a direct address, "My God" (v. 2a), which indicates his closeness with God[1] and dependence on him.[2] Two sentences follow the direct address in three questions,[3] which contradict the psalmist's intimacy with God. The questions express the psalmist's rejection and sense of desperation,[4] the far distance of his salvation, and the non-mitigation of his groanings. They seem to indicate the enormity of the psalmist's situation.

The onset of the psalm immediately displays the psalmist's questions about his rejection by God. Augustin holds that the psalmist's sins cause his rejection.[5] His thoughts are based on Ps 119:155 and, probably, from scriptural records where God rejected Israel's people because of their sins: breaking God's commandments and statutes.[6] Although shaming is a social control to make an individual conform to society's norms and the family in the honor and shame context, Ps 22 shows no indication that the psalmist did ever deviate from the standards.

Keil and Delitzsch make it clear that the abandonment was not because of God's wrath against sin.[7] Even Walter A. Elwell holds that the psalmist is faithful to God.[8] Waltke, James M. Houston, and Erika Moore, who seem to contradict Augustin, claim that "none accused the psalmist"[9] of breaking the covenant, but God himself did break the covenant. Tremper Longman III correctly holds that the psalmist has not specified the details of his troubles to tame the discussion. According to Waltke, Houston, and Moore, which Matthew Henry and Thomas Scott seem to view similarly,[10] the intention is to have a prayer model for the believers when they experience similar dire predicament.[11] Yet, Jamieson, Fausset, and Brown succinctly state that the psalmist is an innocent sufferer.[12] If the psalmist is sinless, God seems to have no basis for rejecting the psalmist.

Whatever the circumstances behind the rejection, God's refusal to acknowledge his relationship[13] with the psalmist is tantamount to a shameful situation. It thereby breaks the kinship[14] between them. It costs the psalmist his ascribed honor, thus bringing him shame and causing him despair.

The psalmist continues to find a solution in God to restore him from his rejection. Already in dire circumstance, salvation becomes critical to and the ultimate need of the psalmist. God seems to be the only source of this salvation from shame and rejection. The psalmist needs God to restore his relationship with him. However, as indicated in the second complaint, this needed salvation looks far-fetched (v. 2c). C. Briggs and E. Briggs describe the distance of the psalmist's salvation as "an awful gap and appalling distance between the agony and the salvation."[15] The gap between his suffering and deliverance seems to complicate and aggravate the psalmist's shame and rejection. At this point, God himself appears to be disinterested in his responsibility as a patron of the psalmist.

The psalmist's abandonment affects the provisions attached to the patron-client relationship. First, his salvation (v. 2b), the spring of his honor and dignity, is beyond reach. God, his patron, whose physical presence should be around him during his distress which is now aggravated by the attacks of his enemies that resulted in his emotional agony and physical sickness,[16] seems out of his situation to deliver him. There are two aspects of salvation that the psalmist appears to lose here. (a) Physically, the psalmist lost his state and freedom from danger, harm or unpleasantness, and distress.[17] God's salvation that should shield and protect him from the enemies' attacks no longer exists (Isa 26:1). (b) He lost his prosperity.[18] Prosperity means friendship with God, being with family, the ability to do humanitarian work, and respect. The inaccessibility of his salvation brings distress and shame. The loss makes the enemies taunt and ridicule him (vv. 7–9). Ultimately, the psalmist experiences humiliation and disgrace before his enemies.

Second, God intensifies the distance between him and the psalmist. With this, the psalmist questions God the third time on God's non-mitigation of his intense lamentation. God fails to hear his cry of loudest agony, שַׁאֲגָתִי (v. 2d), an expression of the intensity and the power of the pain and suffering he endures.[19] In his helplessness, God's silence seems louder than his salvation. The psalmist needs an answer to his complaints and he needs to find rest.

The Psalmist's Need of an Answer and Rest

The psalmist uses two terms here that are related to deliverance: עָנָה, "answer, respond"[20] and דּוּמִיָּה, "silence, still waiting, repose"[21] (v. 3). As mentioned, the former term does not refer to a verbal dialogue but a beneficial act towards someone. In this psalm, the psalmist expects God to respond to him helpfully, especially in restoring the broken relationship between God and him. The latter term indicates that a person expects divine aid from God who provides relief from trouble on the basis of being in a right relationship with him. The parallel structure below seems to suggest that the favorable response the psalmist expects from God is to aid him from his trouble, rejection, and abandonment; to restore him into a right relationship with God; and to end his abandonment and forsakenness.

    A Direct address
      B Psalmist cries by day
        C God does not answer
      B' Psalmist cries by night
        C' He does not find rest for himself

The psalmist continuous his complaints to God. The word קָרָא indicates the use of the voice to attract attention. "This action serves to establish communication over some distance. The act of calling can preserve this distance or abolish it."[22] The psalmist intends to catch God's attention to end his forsakenness or abandonment by God. The act of deliverance he expects from God is an act beneficial to him,[23] that is to be restored to his welfare and his kinship with God.

The psalmist's cry for help is prolonged as God continues to be silent. Kidner mentions that this cry is "not a lapse of faith, nor a broken relationship, but a cry of disorientation as God's familiar, protective presence is withdrawn … and the enemy closes in."[24] He is correct about the psalmist's faith, God's distancing, and the enemies closing in. However, he fails to understand the matter of the psalmist's relationship with God. Keil and Delitzsch correctly state that there is a "great gulf between the two."[25] The broken relationship causes the gulf. God does not answer the cry of the individual or group because of rebellion, wickedness, and their neglect of God.[26] In David's case, he does not belong to those against God.

However, God has not acted beneficially towards David's predicament. Also, he offers no relief for the broken relationship. The psalmist's salvation seems to be far away still. His communication with

God is not established. The hyperbole[27] יוֹמָם/לַיְלָה, "day/night" indicates that the psalmist has been crying a great deal towards God, meaning his agony continues "without interruption."[28] God's act of deliverance from the psalmist is still evidently far amidst his cry. God has not fulfilled his obligation as a faithful patron of the psalmist. His presence as a deliverer of the psalmist's distress is far. He leaves him without salvation. He abandons him to sink into a status of shame. David asks God superlatively why these are so (v. 2).

The psalm of David in 2 Sam 22 seems related to Ps 22. Specifically, in v. 4, David accentuates the reversal of his status, for Yahweh has delivered him from his enemies and from Saul (v. 1). He declares, "I cry [אֶקְרָא] to Yahweh, the one who is praiseworthy, because I was saved [אִוָּשֵׁעַ] from my enemies" (ESV). Two terms David uses in this verse parallel with words he uses in Ps 22:2–3: קָרָא and יְשׁוּעָה. Significantly, in both instances, the first person is used to express that Yahweh is very personal to David. Also, in both cases, Yahweh's intervention in David's life spells the difference between life and death.[29] The difference, however, is that 2 Sam 22:4 "sums up the purpose of the entire psalm [2 Sam 22],"[30] but Ps 22:2–3 still looks forward to the summing up of the purpose of his cry for deliverance. The psalmist alludes to the deliverance of the fathers to emphasize his need of salvation.

The Fathers Were Delivered, Rescued, and Not Shamed

In vv. 5–6, three words that are synonymous to deliverance appear: פָּלַט, מָלַט, and לֹא־בוֹשׁ. The essence of פָּלַט means that someone rescued, freed, and removed another from "harm or evil, … a certain place, environment, or mental or emotional state."[31] The translation of the noun form of the verb is "deliverer"[32] and the result of the action is "deliverance."[33] The word מָלַט is synonymous with פָּלַט. The form of מָלַט in this passage refers to "to cause to escape, to deliver from danger."[34]

Interestingly, C. Briggs and E. Briggs favor the passive meaning "be delivered."[35] The verb בוּשׁ, "shame" is the opposite of the two previous words. The word shame in Hebrew, which is different from the English meaning, means "'to come to shame' and stresses the sense of public disgrace, a physical state."[36] The negation לֹא, a prohibition of permanent effect, negates the word בּוֹשׁ to make it parallel with the two previous terms.

The passage (vv. 5–6) contrasts the previous section (vv. 2–3) of abandonment and rejection and continues the praise in v. 3.[37] It also reverses the psalmist's earlier direct address to God, speaking about his complaints. The subject of the passage, the fathers (אֲבֹתֵינוּ) is "the common subject of the four lines."[38]

The structure of the passage, as presented above, indicates that the three words parallel each other. The staircase parallelism suggests that the climax of deliverance and rescue is the negation of the shame of Israel's people. Also, it means that the ultimate aim of Israel's redemption is to bring them into honor.

The psalmist changes his tone in this passage, from one with complaints to one with great hope. Erhard Gerstenberger agrees that the passage (vv. 4–6) "represent[s] a strong AFFIRMATION OF CONFIDENCE in the same God just accused of infidelity."[39] He further says that it "counterbalances … the desperate and accusatory complaint of vv. 2–3."[40] The psalmist points out that the fathers trusted because he offers deliverance, escape, and freedom from shame. The psalmist's paradigm for his deliverance is the thought that God can be trusted to deliver because he delivered the fathers and did not permit them to be shamed. C. Briggs and E. Briggs correctly put that the fathers' deliverance is the climax of the psalm.[41] The psalmist believes that the experience of the fathers is the "truth about God"[42] for him. He expresses hope that the covenant God who has not "deserted his faithful people"[43] would not let him slip away into shame. Here, the psalmist shows hope of deliverance based on the fathers' previous experiences of deliverance.

In v. 9, the object of deliverance shifts from the fathers to the psalmist. The enemies scorned the psalmist, reminding him that God had deserted him. However, Craigie states that though their words were spoken in mockery, an essence of truth seems to be in it,[44] the affirmation that Yahweh delivers. The psalmist has one thing that he is sure of, "God has been faithful in the past."[45]

The fathers most probably refer to the people of Israel's bondage in Egypt whom Yahweh, the God of Israel, freed from the bondage in

Egypt and delivered to a place of safety in the wilderness until they could reach the land of Canaan, the promised land. Goldingay indicates that though the terms used in the Exodus may differ from the words the psalmist used, the psalmist seemingly alludes to Israelites' bondage.694 Besides, the deliverance God did to Israel was not limited only to the exodus experience of the Israelites but until they had settled in the promised land.

The book of Daniel made significant use of מָלַט (Dan 12:1). The context of the passage—God's people persecuted—seems to have similarities with Israel's people during their bondage in Egypt. In Daniel and Exodus, they had Michael and Yahweh, respectively, who delivered them from their trouble and brought them to safety. Stephen R. Miller indicates that in Daniel's context, many of the faithful become martyr. However, those who trust in the Lord will "ultimately 'be delivered' from the oppression of the Antichrist."[46] The Lord will appear "to rescue the faithful."[47]

Zdravko Stefanovic succinctly states that "even though Michael is the great Prince, he does not prevent the faithful 'from enduring the suffering; rather, he delivers them in the midst of it."[48] The case of God's people in Daniel seems to be true to the psalmist as well. In the case of Ps 22, as Ross indicates, when David recalls Israel's experience of continued prayer so that God delivered them from their distress, he was "encouraged to keep on praying."[49] Indeed, the psalmist believes that since God rescued, delivered, and did not put the fathers to shame, surely God would also deliver him.[50]

Like the previous verse, vv. 5–6 seem related to 2 Sam 22:2 on the term פָּלַט. Although the subject of deliverance in vv. 5–6 is the fathers, the psalmist tries to claim that Yahweh may also be his personal deliverer just like the fathers. In 2 Samuel, David claims that Yahweh is his deliverer. The apparent similarity between the passages is that both express the psalmist's trust in Yahweh, who delivers those who call on him in times of calamity and trouble.[51]

Yahweh Rescues the Psalmist

The terms נָצַל, פָּלַט, and חָפֵץ appear in Ps 22:9. The three verbs are all associated with deliverance. The verb פָּלַט is discussed previously. The term נָצַל predominantly occurs in the "various aspects and moods of the Hiphil ... and that generally with the sense of deliverance or rescue."[52] The sense of the term indicates removal from harm or trouble. U. Bergmann suggests that when the object benefits from the removal, it "produces the meaning 'to rescue.'"[53] In v. 9, the subject of the verb is Yahweh and the object is the psalmist. It appears in the causative and permissive[54] sense, translated as "let him rescue him." The persons giving permission are those who mock the psalmist.

The relationship of the word חָפֵץ with deliverance may be derived from the south Semitic and northwest Semitic languages; it means "protection" and "care for."[55] Another sense of this word indicates that a superior is willing to do something towards the inferior.[56] Yahweh is superior but the psalmist is inferior. In this psalm, Yahweh delights פָּלַט, "to deliver" and נָצַל, "rescue" the psalmist.

The passage (v. 9) is the psalmist's direct quotation of the mockers' taunts against him.[57] It is part of the passage where the psalmist narrates, in the first person, his shameful state: his sense of worthlessness and "un-humanness" and the taunt speeches and actions of the mockers directed at him (vv. 7–8). The direct quotation is a challenge thrown by the mockers to shame the psalmist effectively. The direct quote is one way because the psalmist makes no riposte.

From an expression of hope, the psalmist again sinks into despair in the second round of complaint.[58] In vv. 4–6, the psalmist focuses on the fathers' deliverance and their freedom from shame. The fathers' salvation provides him the hope of the same. However, in vv. 7–9, the psalmist complains of his desperate situation because of his fellow human beings' mockery. As indicated above, the fathers' trust in God produced deliverance. However, the psalmist's confidence in God yields no result.

Instead, the psalmist becomes an object of mockery.[59] In his sense of shame, he lost his manhood, became an object of reproach of humankind in general, and despised by the people surrounding him. All who saw him showed no compassion upon him, acted maliciously towards him, and derided him with their acts.[60] Gerstenberger indicates that "such experiences are typical of the sufferer."[61]

The psalmist then directly quotes the mockers. Gerstenberger rightly holds that the "quotation of the enemy certainly is a climax of lament."[62] In mockery, the enemies deride the psalmist to "roll-on Yahweh" (v. 9). To roll-on means to trust or to rely on Yahweh.[63] The abuse should prompt the psalmist not to trust in Yahweh anymore. Yet, the insult is not directed to the psalmist alone but to Yahweh as well. It reduced Yahweh to being untrustworthy. C. Briggs and E. Briggs state that the "derision of suffering Israel is here, as ever, accompanied with the derision of Yahweh their God by the hostile nations."[64] As mentioned previously, however, the essence of the insult is that Yahweh cannot be trusted.

The taunt continues with the challenge of Yahweh to deliver and rescue the psalmist. The nature of deliverance indicates the psalmist's liberation and removal from personal trouble. The psalmist indicates that he is worthless; rejected by humankind; and taunted by the enemies by mockery, insult, and ridicule. The enemies emphasize that Yahweh will not deliver the psalmist from his troubles. They also cast doubt in the affections of Yahweh upon the psalmist. This affection involves caring for and providing protection to the psalmist. They scoff on the psalmist's deliverance from personal and relational shame. With his predicament, the psalmist calls for deliverance.

The Psalmist Calls for Deliverance

In the section call for deliverance (vv. 20–22), five synonymous words related to deliverance appear: אֱיָלוּת, עָזַר, נָצַל, יֵשַׁע, and עָנָה. The aggression of the enemies prompted the psalmist to call for deliverance (vv. 13–19). The psalmist directs his call to Yahweh, who is described by the psalmist with different deliverance terms.

The term אֱיָלוּת, a *hapax legomenon*,[65] is a noun used as a direct address in place of the name Yahweh. It means "strength or help"[66] and also implies protection.[67] It is closely related to the word אַיָּלָה, "hind." Dahood suggests that this reading may be the correct one.[68] However,

Swanson holds that the context suggests the correct meaning of the word. He also states that אֱיָלוּת is used as a title of Yahweh that focuses on "his potency to help and give aid."[69] This paper follows that the psalmist uses the word to indicate Yahweh's title, "my strength," implying Yahweh as his protector, aid, and the "ideal of strength."[70]

The terms עוֹזֵר is also associated with deliverance. The verb עָזַר "conveys the notion of protection."[71] It especially indicates military assistance.[72] Its Ugaritic derivative *dr* means "to rescue/save."[73] The term appears again in its derivative noun עֶזְרָה, "help, assist" (v. 20). The appearance of לְעֶזְרָתִי frequently refers to "help in battle."[74] Dahood correctly translates לְעֶזְרָתִי as "to my war."[75] The terms עוֹזֵר and לְעֶזְרָתִי seem to form an inclusio of the psalmist's trouble through their common root עָזַר. They indicate the importance of Yahweh's military aid. The structure below illustrates the inclusio:

A Call for help [עוֹזֵר] (v. 12)
   B Enemies' aggression (vv. 13–19)
A Call for help [לְעֶזְרָתִי] (v. 20)

In v. 21, the verb נָצַל appears again here for the second time but in the imperative, הַצִּילָה. From the speaker's perspective, the command indicates the urgency of the needed action.[76] The *hiphil* form carries the modal form of compulsion.[77] The verb seems to describe Yahweh as someone who would physically snatch the psalmist out of the grasp of the enemies: the sword (v. 21) and the dogs (vv. 17, 21).

The term הוֹשִׁיעֵנִי comes from the word יָשַׁע, "to help,"[78] "to deliver, to save."[79] It appears in the imperative, functioning like the imperative הַצִּילָה. The imperative means that the deliverance is urgent and the subject is compelled to act immediately. One of the derivatives of יָשַׁע is יְשׁוּעָה. יְשׁוּעָה appears in the complaints of the psalmist against the distance of his salvation. In this psalm, the deliverance noted is not only snatching or liberating someone in trouble. The other related meanings of יְשׁוּעָה are still true to the context. This paper may use the meanings interchangeably.

Another term related to deliverance is עָנָה, "to reply, answer,"[80] a word that appeared previously. Its previous occurrence shows that

Yahweh did not answer the cries of the psalmist (v. 3). This time, in v. 22, the psalmist positively trusts that God had already answered his call for deliverance. He indicates that Yahweh hears his cry and acts on behalf of him for his deliverance from shame. The perfect עֲנִיתָנִי is the concluding statement of the deliverance of the psalmist. Dahood is correct that the Hebrew perfect conjugation is a precative perfective[81] or perfective of prayer, as indicated in the context. The inverted parallel structure of v. 22 supports the perfective of prayer. The translation of עֲנִיתָנִי as "respond to me," which parallels the volitional term הוֹשִׁיעֵנִי, "make me victorious," is probable. The series of imperatives, something that "seek to induce Yahweh to save the afflicted,"[82] reinforces the precative perfect.

The structure of Ps 22, as stated above, demonstrates that vv. 2–3 and vv. 20–22 form an inclusio of the lament. The terms enclosing the lament are רָחוֹק (vv. 2, 20), יָשַׁע (vv. 2, 22), and עָנָה (vv. 2, 22). The first part of the inclusio laments the lack of deliverance that brought the psalmist down to shame. The second part reverses the situation of the psalmist. The center of the inclusio details the psalmist's claim to honor and the shame that he experienced in the hands of the enemies. This part of the inclusio proclaims the psalmist's deliverance and the restoration of his honor.

The psalmist endures the shame of abandonment (vv. 2–3), the taunts of the enemies (vv. 4–6), and his despoiled state of defeat in the hands of his enemies (vv. 13–19). Amidst his trouble, he calls Yahweh for help. He displays his full trust in Yahweh "who, in His strength and faithfulness, is contrasted with the urgent dangers describe."[83] He pleads that Yahweh's divine distance, which has been his complaint (v. 2), be removed from his troubled situation.[84] He has previously complained about the drying up of his strength (v. 16) because of the attacks of the enemies. The power or weapons of the enemies described in metaphorical terms are חֶרֶב, "sword"; יָד, "hand, paw" (v. 21); פֶּה, "mouth, jaw"; and קֶרֶן, "horn" (v. 22).[85] The metaphorical terms connote the use of military oppression to attack the psalmist. Against such the psalmist has no protection. Only Yahweh, acknowledged as the ideal of strength, can protect and aid him against the power of his enemies.

Addressing Yahweh as his protector and aid, he prays Yahweh to hasten to come to his help, עֶזְרָ (v. 20), to come quickly to his aid amid the enemies' attack (vv. 13–19). The psalmist uses the term עֶזְרָ correctly because of its connotation of "military assistance." The OT is replete with experiences of people who had God as their heavenly assistance amidst their struggles. David received assistance from God under Saul when he received the additional recruits from Benjamin and Judah (2 Chr 12:18). "Asa is divinely assisted against Egypt (2 Chr 14:10); Uzziah, against Philistia and other nations (2 Chr 26:7, 13); and Amaziah, against Edom (2 Chr 25:8)."[86] In this psalm, the psalmist does not expect that Yahweh will send military assistance to help him. Rather, he expects Yahweh himself to come and be his helper in the military conquest.

The psalmist continues to show confidence and complete trust in God who can deliver him from the shame of worthlessness, being an outcast, and being an object of ridicule and insult. The call for deliverance (vv. 20–22), where the term נֶצֶל appears, is the third confirmation of the psalmist's trust in God. The previous affirmations of trust in God refer to God's holiness and his acts of deliverance of the fathers (vv. 4–6) and acknowledging that God is the psalmist's progenitor and protector (vv. 10–11). The call to deliver from the sword and the dog's paws (v. 21) rebuffs the enemies' insult in v. 9. It indicates the psalmist's total trust in God despite the enemies taunting (vv. 7–9) and oppression (vv. 13–19) to put him to shame. The psalmist trusts that God delivers the only life he has from violent death and cruel enemies.[87]

In addition to the prayer of deliverance, the psalmist prays for victory over the "lion's mouth and the oxen's horn" (v. 22). The parallel animal metaphors refer to the psalmist's enemies.[88] The concluding part of the prayer indicates that the psalmist highly expects that God would respond to his prayer of deliverance. The expected response would be beneficial to the psalmist.

If there is any indication that God indeed answers the psalmist's prayer, the praise section tells it all (vv. 22–32). God's favorable response to the psalmist's prayer has changed everything. Mays has a fitting statement for the change of the psalmist's status: "Instead of forsakenness, an answer has come to his cry (v. 24). Instead of the scorn of his fellows and the threat of evildoers, he is surrounded now by a company of brothers in praise and faith. Instead of laments at the encroachment of death, he can offer his brothers a wish for enduring life (v. 26)."[89]

Deliverance as a Restoration of Honor in the Psalms

The previous section shows the psalmist's prayers for deliverance from shame and his expectations in Yahweh as his Deliverer to restore his honor. Some Davidic and non-Davidic psalms have similarities with David's deliverance experiences and the restoration of honor, as described in Ps 22. This section presents a brief survey of the psalms which contain these parallel occurrences.

Psalm 62 parallels Ps 22 in terms of confidence in God as the source of salvation amidst the enemies' aggression to shame David. Here, David's statement as God is יְשׁוּעָתִי, "my salvation," (vv. 2, 7) indicates a complete trust or full confidence in God and a total resignation that God alone can save him, as some scholars agree.[90] Psalm 62 parallels Ps 22 in the psalmist's experience of shame from the enemies, although in different circumstances. Here, his shame occurs when his enemies attempt to destroy his dignity by falsehood and curses (v. 5).

Yet, in both psalms, the enemies use the mouth to hurl their attacks. Speaking of the restoration of David's honor in Ps 62, Keil and Delitzsch state that David renounces the vengeance to restore his honor and puts his confidence in God.[91] By his mouth, God will do it for him (v. 11). In Ps 22, the guests in the feast/meal proclaim that God delivered the psalmist, including the afflicted, from the mouth of his enemies.

Psalms 88 and 22 have similarities in terms of God as being the source of salvation, their predicament, and the source of honor. (1) The psalmists use the term יְשׁוּעָתִי, "my salvation" (22:2, 88:2) to refer to their need for salvation amidst their distress. Indeed, Yahweh is the source of their salvation. (2) The psalmists resolutely cry out to God for deliverance.[92] In Ps 88, the psalmist uses different terms to emphasize his distress and need of God's help to deliver him in his situation (vv. 2, 3, 10, 14).[93] The verb קָרָא, "to cry out for help" appears in Pss 88 and 22.

(3) God's abandonment and rejection of the psalmists are evident.[94] Also, the abandonment is questioned, which appears to have no answer at all (22:3, 88:15).[95] As indicated previously, God's abandonment is tantamount to a broken kinship relationship, causing shame. (4) God brought the psalmists to the brink of death (88:16, 22:16). In Ps 88, the psalmist's suffering is caused by God's wrath towards the psalmist. In Ps 22, the psalmist's physical and emotional distress causes his moving towards the brink of death.

(5) The deliverance of the psalmist is not expressed explicitly in Ps 88. However, in Ps 89, a continuation of Ps 88,[96] Ethan claims for the restoration of honor by alluding to the covenant relationship God has established with David (89:20–22, 49), which appears to be similar to God's established relationship with David's in Ps 22:5–6. The declaration of Ethan's praise can be surmised as his deliverance (89:53). (6) The apex of both psalms is Yahweh's rulership over all nations and created things (22:28, 89:10–15). Yahweh's rulership indicates his exalted status over everything. It makes the psalmist's deliverance from shame imminent. Also, those who worship Yahweh are exulted.

Psalm 25 portrays the struggle between honor and shame and the importance of deliverance to keep the psalmist from shame. The reason for David's petition to Yahweh is to spare him from shame. A consequent reversal of status will develop if Yahweh fails to deliver (נָצַל) him. David's shame will cause his enemies' exultation (vv. 1–2). However, his petition for protection and deliverance from the hatred of his enemies would preserve his honor (vv. 19–21). The psalm ends with the petition for a communal deliverance (v. 22). In this psalm, deliverance, with integrity and uprightness (יֹשֶׁר), is crucial to the preservation of honor.

Summary

This chapter covers the different terms that are related to deliverance. The words are יְשׁוּעָה, "salvation" or יָשַׁע, "to save, be victorious"; עָנָה, "to act favorably, respond"; דּוּמִיָּה, "rest"; פָּלַט, "to rescue, deliver"; מָלַט, "to slip away, escape"; לֹא־בְוֹשׁוּ "they were not shamed"; נָצַל, "to snatch away, deliver"; עָזַר, "to help" or עֶזְרָה, "helper, support, assistance"; and אֱיָלוּת, "strength, protector." In the psalmist's experience, deliverance seems so far from him. Yet, he continues to trust and call Yahweh to deliver, rescue, save, protect, and give him victory. His prayers are no longer ignored nor met with silence.

Yahweh indeed favorably answers the psalmist's prayers. Some other psalms indicate that deliverance, although in different terms, initiated by Yahweh is crucial to the psalmist's restoration of honor. The next chapter presents how God works his deliverance through his being a patron, holiness, abandonment and restoration, taunts, nakedness, and feast/meal as seen in Ps 22 and other parts of the OT.

---

[1] Goldingay, *Psalms*, 325.

[2] Bratcher and Reyburn, *Book of Psalms*, 214; Gerstenberger, *Psalms, Part 1*, 109.

[3] John E. Goldingay holds that the psalmist's complaint has threefold question, as opposed to Bratcher and Reyburn's idea of a twofold question. Goldingay, *Psalms*, 324. See also Bratcher and Reyburn, *Book of Psalms*, 214.

[4] John Calvin, *John Calvin's Commentaries on the Psalms 1–35* (Altenmünster, Germany: Jazzybee Verlag, 2012), 275.

[5] Augustine of Hippo, *Expositions on the Book of Psalms*, ed. Philip Schaff, trans. A. Cleveland Coxe, vol. 8 of *A Select Library of the Nicene and Post-Nicene Fathers of the Christian Church* (New York: Christian Literature, 1888), 58.

[6] See Jer 12:7, Ezek 9:9.

[7] Keil and Delitzsch, *The Psalter*, 195.

[8] Walter A. Elwell, *Evangelical Commentary on the Bible*, Baker Reference Library 3 (Grand Rapids: Baker Books, 1989), 377.

[9] Waltke, Houston, and Moore, *Psalms as Christian Lament*, 399.

[10] Henry and Scott hold that the psalmist's situation "may be applied to any child of God, pressed down, overwhelmed with grief and terror." Matthew Henry and Thomas Scott, *Matthew Henry's Concise Commentary* (Oak Harbor, WA: Logos, 1997), ch. 22, vs. 1–10.

[11] Tremper Longman III, *Psalms: An Introduction and Commentary*, ed. David G. Firth, TOTC 15–16 (London: Inter-Varsity Press, 2014), 129.

[12] Jamieson, *Genesis-Esther*, 1:353.

[13] The sense of the term עזב means refusal to accept or acknowledge something. In Ps 22:2, the thing that is not acknowledged is the kinship of God with the psalmist. *LALHB*, s.v. "עזב."

[14] The honor of the person, called ascribed honor, comes from "family, name, house, the honor of the world into which a man is born." Richard E. DeMaris and Carolyn S. Leeb, "Judges–(Dis)Honor and Ritual Enactment," in *Ancient*

Israel: The Old Testament in Its Social Context, ed. Philip F. Esler (Minneapolis: Augsburg Fortress, 2006), 182.

15 Briggs and Briggs, *The Book of Psalms*, 192.

16 Hartley, *TWOT* 1:414.

17 *LALHB*, s.v. "יְשׁוּעָה"; *DBLH*, s.v. "יְשׁוּעָה."

18 BDB, s.v. "יְשׁוּעָה."

19 Graupner, *TDOT* 14:233.

20 BDB, s.v. "עָנָה."

21 BDB, s.v. "דּוּמִיָּה."

22 Frank-Lothar Hossfeld and E. M. Kindl, "קָרָא," *TDOT* 13:110–11.

23 See p. 102.

24 Kidner, *Psalms 1–72*, 123.

25 Keil and Delitzsch, *The Psalter*, 195.

26 Job 35:12–13; Prov 1:24–25; Isa 59:2; Jer 14:10; Mal 1:7–9.

27 E. W. Bullinger, in explaining what hyperbole means, states, "The figure is so called because the expression adds to the sense so much that it exaggerates it, and enlarges or diminishes it more than is really meant in fact. Or, when more is said than is meant to be literally understood, in order to heighten the sense. It is the superlative degree applied to verbs and sentences and expressions or descriptions, rather than to mere adjectives." E. W. Bullinger, *Figures of Speech Used in the Bible: Explained and Illustrated* (New York: E. & J. B. Young, 1898), 422.

28 Briggs and Briggs, *The Book of Psalms*, 192.

29 Bergen, *1, 2 Samuel*, 452.

30 Roger L. Omanson and John Ellington, *A Handbook on the Second Book of Samuel*, UBS Handbook Series (New York: United Bible Societies, 2001), 1114.

31 *LALHB*, s.v. "פָּלַט."

32 *LALHB*, s.v. "פָּלַט."

33 *LALHB*, s.v. "פָּלַט."

34 *GHCLOT*, s.v. "מָלַט."

35 Briggs and Briggs, *The Book of Psalms*, 202.

36 John N. Oswalt, "בּוֹשׁ," *TWOT* 1:222.

37 Goldingay, *Psalms*, 327.

38 Briggs and Briggs, *The Book of Psalms*, 193.

39 Gerstenberger, *Psalms, Part 1*, 110. Emphasis in the original.

40 Ibid.

41 Briggs and Briggs, *The Book of Psalms*, 194.

42 Mays, *Psalms*, 109.

43 Craigie, *Psalms 1–50*, 198.

44 Ibid., 199.

45 S. Edward Tesh and Walter D. Zorn, *Psalms*, The College Press NIV Commentary (Joplin, MO: College Press, 1999), 205.

[46] Goldingay, *Psalms*, 328.

[47] S. Miller, *Daniel*, 315.

[48] Ibid.

[49] Zdravko Stefanovic, *Daniel: Wisdom to the Wise; Commentary on the Book of Daniel* (Nampa, ID: Pacific Press, 2007), 435.

[50] Ross, *Psalms*, 811.

[51] "Our fathers trusted" [Ps 22:4], *SDABC* 3:683.

[52] Henry Preserved Smith, *A Critical and Exegetical Commentary on the Books of Samuel*, ICC (New York: Scribner's Sons, 1899), 378.

[53] Milton C. Fisher, "נָצַל," *TWOT* 2:594. The concept of this word is closely related to three verbs: *gāʾal*, *ḥālaṣ*, and *pādâ*; two closely related words: *mālaṭ* and *pālaṭ*; and with the sense of rescue: *yāša*, *šûb*, *ḥāyâ*, and *yātar*. Ibid.

[54] Bergmann, *TLOT* 2:760. Bergmann states that the *hiphil* of נָצַל indicates "removal or liberation from all types of restrictions." Ibid.

[55] Bill T. Arnold and John H. Choi, *A Guide to Biblical Hebrew Syntax* (New York: Cambridge University Press, 2003), 61–62.

[56] Botterweck, *TDOT* 5:93.

[57] *LALHB*, s.v. "חָפֵץ."

[58] Bratcher and Reyburn, *Book of Psalms*, 216.

[59] Gerstenberger, *Psalms, Part 1*, 111.

[60] J. A. Motyer, "The Psalms," in *New Bible Commentary: Twenty-First Century Edition*, ed. D. A. Carson (Leicester: Inter-Varsity Press, 1994), 499.

[61] Briggs and Briggs, *The Book of Psalms*, 194.

[62] Gerstenberger, *Psalms, Part 1*, 112.

[63] Ibid., 111.

[64] Bratcher and Reyburn, *Book of Psalms*, 216.

[65] Briggs and Briggs, *The Book of Psalms*, 195.

[66] Dahood, *Psalms 1:1–50*, 140.

[67] *CWSDOT*, s.v. "אֱיָלוּת."

[68] *CDWGTHB*, s.v. "אֱיָלוּת."

[69] Dahood, *Psalms 1:1–50*, 140. See also Briggs and Briggs, *The Book of Psalms*, 197.

[70] *DBLH*, s.v. "אֱיָלוּת."

[71] Keil and Delitzsch, *The Psalter*, 202.

[72] E. Lipiński, "עָזַר," *TDOT* 11:14.

[73] Carl Schultz, "עָזַר," *TWOT* 2:660.

[74] Ibid.

[75] Lipiński, *TDOT* 11:14.

[76] Dahood, *Psalms 1:1–50*, 140.

[77] Arnold and Choi, *Biblical Hebrew Syntax*, 64.

[78] Ibid., 51.

[79] F. Stolz, "יָשַׁע," *TLOT* 2:584.

[80] BDB, s.v. "יָשַׁע."

[81] *LALHB*, s.v. "עָנָה."

[82] Dahood, *Psalms 1:1–50*, 142. The precative perfective refers to "situations the speaker prays for and expects to be realized." Waltke and O'Connor, *Biblical Hebrew Syntax*, 594–95.

[83] Gerstenberger, *Psalms, Part 1*, 111.

[84] Jamieson, *Genesis-Esther*, 1:354.

[85] Craigie, *Psalms 1–50*, 200.

[86] See Keil and Delitzsch, *The Psalter*, 202.

[87] Schultz, *TWOT* 2:660.

[88] Bratcher and Reyburn, *Book of Psalms*, 223.

[89] Ibid.

[90] Mays, *Psalms*, 111.

[91] Bratcher and Hatton, *A Handbook on Deuteronomy*, 541; Longman III, *Psalms*, 244; Mark D. Futato and George M. Schwab, *The Book of Psalms, the Book of Proverbs*, ed. Philip W. Comfort, vol. 7 of *Cornerstone Biblical Commentary* (Carol Stream, IL: Tyndale House, 2009), 211; John Wesley, *Explanatory Notes upon the Old Testament* (London: William Pine, 1765), 2:1717; Keil and Delitzsch, *The Psalter*, 418.

[92] F. Delitzsch, *Psalms* (Grand Rapids: Eerdmans, 1980), 418.

[93] David uses the merismus "day and night" referring to his resolute cries for help to God.

[94] The terms used are צָעַק, "to cry out, in distress, in need"; רִנָּה, "ringing cry, lament," "cry for help"; שָׁוַע, "cry out for help." See BDB, s.vv. ""צָעַק,""רִנָּה," "שָׁוַע""קָרָא,"; *LALHB*, s.vv. "שָׁוַע""רִנָּה,"; *DBLH*, s.v. "קָרָא."

[95] For comments on Ps 88:15, see Bratcher and Reyburn, *Book of Psalms*, 769.

[96] In Ps 88:15, the term for abandonment is זָנַח. BDB, s.v. "זָנַח"; *LALHB*, s.v. "זָנַח."

[97] The superscriptions of both Pss 88 and 89 indicate Ethan the Ezrahite as the author of these psalms. It is most likely that these psalms are connected with each other. Themes that connect these two psalms are God's abandonment of the psalmist (88:14–15, 89:46–48), cry for help (88:15, 89:27), and Yahweh as God of salvation (88:2, 89:26) and God of steadfast love (88:11, 89:14).

CHAPTER 5

THE THEOLOGY OF HONOR AND SHAME IN PSALM 22

Presenting the theology of Ps 22 makes for a daunting task. It requires decent information to be significant, so much so that a whole study may be needed. This paper gives just a glimpse of the theology of Ps 22 as paralleled with the Scriptures as a whole. The theology looks at how God or Yahweh delivers the psalmist and his people through his being a patron and holiness and through abandonment and restoration, taunts, nakedness, and feast/meal as found in the study of Ps 22.

Yahweh Is Patron

The study of patronage in Ps 22 shows that God/Yahweh is the psalmist's patron. As Israel's chief deity, God/Yahweh acts as Israel's deliverer. He also serves as David's personal God who delivers him from distress. His attributes as the creator and warrior king make him an able patron.

First, when David calls God as the creator, David acknowledges that the world belongs to him and everything in it,[1] which are at his immediate disposal for the benefit of humanity. Nothing is withheld by God/Yahweh for humanity's honor and provision. His riches and majesty are inexhaustible. God/Yahweh provided for the fathers and David. He also provides for everyone who is in need.

As a warrior king, he provides help, deliverance, salvation, and rescue (vv. 4–5). Also, he reigns supreme over all other inutile gods considered by earthly kings and rulers as their patron gods. He is the patron par excellence of David and God's people (v. 28).

David also refers to Yahweh as the patron God of the people of Israel (vv. 4–5). The patronage relationship is based on the covenant God made with Israel. The covenant relationship spans the fathers, from Abraham's time up to the exodus. He did wondrous acts for the fathers: Abraham, from Ur to Canaan (Gen 11:27–12:8); Isaac (26:1–6); and Jacob (25:10–15). He remained a faithful patron from the peak of Israel's obedience up to their lowest ebb of rebellion. If he remained a faithful patron to the fathers and David, he would do the same with the people of God who trust in him.

God's trustworthiness as a patron is noteworthy. Israel experiences God's trustworthiness in the following ways. First, he hears the cry of his clients and he delivers them from their distress. At the time of their stay in Egypt, Israel experienced oppression under the yoke of the Egyptian pharaoh. They worked involuntarily like slaves "under harsh, oppressive conditions"[2] (See Exod 1:14). Because of their cruel situation, they cried for help under the pharaoh's hostile domain (Exod 2:23). Their cries reached God and God delivered them from their bondage in Egypt (Exod 2:23–25; cf. Ps 22:6, 25). Truly, God is a faithful patron who hears his poor people's cries for help and delivers them.

Second, God protects and provides. The psalmist's cry unto God for salvation means that God is the source of his protection, provision, and well-being. When he alludes to Israel's deliverance and rescue, he brings the thought that God had protected Israel in their wilderness wanderings from the hostility of the desert and the onslaught of enemies. He provided their needs during their exodus until he could bring them to safety and peace in the promised land of Canaan. In Canaan, he let them enjoy his protection amidst famine and pestilence, distress, and troubles (Deut 28; Josh 1:5, 11:12).

Yahweh Is Holy

Holiness is a peculiar characteristic of God as a patron. In Ps 22, it carries the idea of God's separation from humanity and the gods of the unbelievers. God's holiness shows his separateness in contrast to the helpless, desperate, and shameful state of humanity. The psalmist can just express his fearful respect and utter dependence on God's power to deliver him from his shameful state. Also, God's separateness is not defined by his abandonment of the psalmist (v. 2). Rather, it is by his faithful rescue and deliverance of the fathers of Israel. God's holiness draws the psalmist of Ps 22 to trust in him for he is faithful to fulfill his obligations as a patron. God's holy presence alone can deliver the psalmist from his predicament and from the grasp of his enemies.

God's holiness separates him from the gods. He saves human beings without appeasement, while the gods require humanity to work in exchange for their favorable acts. His acts are always meant for humanity's good, especially for the people of Israel. In contrast, the appeasement of the gods is not meant for the goodwill of humanity. As God saved the people of Israel before, he will do so again. God saved the fathers of Israel and will continue to do so on behalf of his people Israel.

Yahweh Abandons/Forsakes and Restores

The means of abandonment/forsakenness in Ps 22 is associated with the value of patronage. God/Yahweh serves as the psalmist's patron God, the patron God of Israel as well. However, the psalmist indicates that God has abandoned and forsaken him (v. 2).

In the OT, the reason God forsakes humanity is sin and infidelity towards him. Despite God's provision, sustenance, protection, and help, humanity still sin and forsake Yahweh.[3] God's chastisement upon the people would include attacks by the surrounding nations, exploitation of harvest including the population, and eventual exile and dispersion (Lev 26:40–42). God himself bring them affliction, which may include oppression and humiliation. He left them wretched, emaciated, destitute and broken, and deprived of property (1 Sam 12:8).

Confession of sins and genuine repentance averts God's chastisement. It results in a right relationship with God and the end of abandonment. As a faithful patron, God reconciles his people back to him. He also delivers his people from oppression and provides them with peace and prosperity. Yet, horrible things happen when people continue to forsake Yahweh.

The psalmist of Ps 22 has been abandoned. Sin as the basis of abandonment is not present. Not one reason is provided in this psalm for his abandonment. For this reason, the psalmist is in wonder and bewilderment. Thus, he cried, "My God, my God, why have you forsaken me?" (Ps 22:2, ESV).

Jesus used the same words as he hung in agony at the cross: "My God, my God, why have you forsaken me?" (Matt 27:46, Mark 15:34, ESV). His expression did not result from any sin that he did. Rather, it is an honest cry of deep suffering and anguish of being separated from God.[4] Jesus cries because of the sin of humanity. On the cross, he became sin for humanity (2 Cor 5:21). Humanity deserves God's abandonment because of sin. However, Jesus took his place on the cross where he was treated like a sinner. He "endured the wrath of man, so that man could escape the wrath of God."[5] He paid the penalty on the cross so God would not forsake him again.[6] Douglas Connelly states that when Jesus asked this rhetorical question, he forced humanity "to think about the real purpose of His suffering. He was dying in our [humanity's] place. He was bearing the penalty we [humanity] deserved."[7] Jesus's suffering paved the way for humanity to be reconciled back to God and be delivered from sin.

Yahweh Responds to Taunts

In the honor and shame culture, speech is a way of maintaining and defending honor. It is either to build the honor of a family/individual or tear people down to shame. Individuals or family members have to defend their honor through counter speeches or just to accept the challenge. They behave honorably when they ably uphold the honor of the household.

In Ps 22, the psalmist's enemies make a series of taunt speeches and acts to shame him. They slander, insult, and act mockingly against him (vv. 7–8). They mockingly challenge the capability of Yahweh to save (v. 9). The psalmist is expected to do a riposte to defend his honor and Yahweh. Contrary to expectation, he does not refute nor make a riposte against the enemies. Instead, he strengthens his relationship with Yahweh (vv. 11–12). Yahweh ultimately saves the psalmist from the onslaught of the enemies (v. 21).

The Scriptures record the insult or taunt of the enemy towards the people of Israel. In these passages, the people of Israel call on Yahweh to turn the insults and taunts back to their enemies (Ps 69:20, Neh 4:4, Lam 3:61–66). They appeal to Yahweh to defend his cause because the taunt speeches are not directed towards them only but towards God as well (Pss 22:9, 74:22, 79:12; Jer 15:15). Yahweh mentions that he hears the taunts and the reviling of their enemies (Zeph 2:8). He promises the righteous and the law-keepers to fear nothing because the enemies shall perish but his salvation for them shall remain (Isa 51:7). He assures the people of Israel that they will no longer hear the reproaches of the nations, neither shall they bear the reproaches of their people nor cause them to fall (Ezek 36:15). These things shall not happen to them again.[8]

The Scriptures warn against taunting the weak and defenseless for it does not please God. The weak deserve respect and honor as well. The widows and the orphans, who are weak and vulnerable, have God's special protection. The prophets plead earnestly on their behalf (Exod 22:22–23, Isa 10:1–2). Today, God's protection hovers over the widows and orphans. The people have to heed God's warning.

Yahweh Covers Nakedness

In Ps 22, the psalmist indicates that he had been subdued by his enemies. His subjection reduced him to a shameful situation (v. 19). In his humiliating situation, the enemies look upon him in disdain as if he is the most horrific being. To utterly humiliate him, his captors remove his clothing and garments, rendering him naked.

Nakedness is a removal of the garment of a person, whether voluntary or forced. In the honor and shame context and Mediterranean culture, nakedness means humiliation and shame. In the war context, it is a humiliation which indicates the shame of defeat and enslavement. It also means emptiness, vulnerability, and shame. It is almost always a symbol of shame, reserved for the destitute, the conquered, or the deranged. Conversely, clothing signifies status and honor. The tearing or removal of clothing towards nakedness means change of status, from honor to shame and humiliation.

In the beginning, nakedness was not associated with shame. Adam and Eve were both naked but were not ashamed of each other (Gen 2:25). They felt no shame in the beginning because both were right with each other and with God. They were both oblivious to evil and in a state of sinless innocence.

Adam and Eve came to know that they were naked only when sin came (Gen 3:7). The opening of their eyes saw a change of their status. They saw themselves both naked, a new sense of shame. Their newfound nakedness made them realize that something was wrong with what they had done. This nakedness leads them to a realization of a broken relationship with God and with each other. Because of this nakedness, they became unworthy to face God.

Adam and Eve tried inadequately to cover their shame because they still suffered the consequence of their act. Curses and expulsion from the garden of Eden were the direct result of this. Only God could fill their inadequacy. He made a salvific act by making "garments of skin and clothed them" (v. 21). The clothing changed their status of being cursed for it hid their nakedness and covered their shame.

References to nakedness in the OT also mention defenselessness and helplessness. It also "convey[s] the brokenness of sin in a relational aspect."[9] This relationship refers to one's relationship with God and with one another. Second, it also "implies, punishment, shame and vulnerability."[10]

For David in Ps 22, he has experienced nakedness from the hands of his enemies. He was subdued, conquered, and humiliated. The assurance of covering his nakedness was by God's deliverance of him from the grasps of his enemies. David's prayer in Ps 22 was an entreaty with the assurance that God already answered his prayers. David's deliverance was surely accomplished as evidenced in his praises to God and participation in the feast/meal. The next section discusses more on the theology of the feast/meal.

Yahweh Hosts the Feast/Meal

In Ps 22, the feast/meal is central to the praise section of this psalm (vv. 27, 30). In this feast/meal, Yahweh is the foremost subject of honor because he does not despise, abhor, nor hide his face from the afflicted in their despicable situation. He also hears their cry for help (v. 25). Although the statement is in the third person, David may be speaking of himself here. This declaration of David reverses his complaints of abandonment (v. 2). This situation also means that his shame is reversed. At the same time, he is honored since his shame of abandonment is gone by virtue of God's act of listening to his cry for help.

The theme of meal/feast remarkably appears in the Scriptures. As in the Egyptian, Palestinian, and Mediterranean contexts, a meal/feast is an indication of the strengthening of social relations. Also, it is a means of the restoration of honor for the invitees or imputation of shame to the excluded. It may also give honor to the host. In different occasions in the OT, a meal/feast accompanies reconciliation and conferral of honor.

The completion of the psalmist's restoration comes at the feast/meal. He, the afflicted, is satiated in the feast/meal. Satiation may mean the restoration of the material benefits and physical well-being he lost in the hands of the enemies. Theologically, it may mean enjoyment of the salvation Yahweh grants to him and the bestowal of the benefits of Yahweh's salvation.

Some examples of feast/meal that carry benefits are shown below. Abraham, while dwelling by the oaks of Mamre (Gen 18:1), offers a traditional near eastern hospitality to three men passing through where he is. His request for favor, חֵן (vv. 3–5b), from the strangers is "a fine example of the profuse, deferential, self-depreciatory courtesy characteristic of Eastern manners."[11] Abraham, the host, properly treats the guests thus according them honor. The guests politely accept his hospitality (v. 5b) to honor him in return.

The narrative eventually names one of the guests as Yahweh (v. 10). Yahweh's purpose of visiting Abraham is to interrupt his shame of childlessness as well as of Sarah, his wife. He bestows and restores their honor by proclaiming that Sarah will bear a child the same time the following year (v. 14). According to Yahweh's proclamation, Sarah conceives and bears Isaac (21:1–5). Sarah's "joy and wonder at what God has done for her"[12] is an expression of the end of her "hopeless despair"[13] and her praise of God (Gen 21:6–7). Sarah's expression seems to parallel the praise and worship of the afflicted after Yahweh ended their affliction (Ps 22:24–25).

The narrative in Gen 31 talks of the reconciliation of Jacob and Laban (Gen 21: 43–49). Each party partakes of a meal to seal their reconciliation. They invoke God as the witness of their reconciliation (v. 46). When his brothers come to Egypt the second time, Joseph invites them to his house for a meal and offers them the best Egyptian hospitality (43:24–25). This gesture is for him to know his brothers' real attitude towards each other, especially towards their youngest brother, who receives five portions from Joseph's meal. Joseph seems to notice the absence of hostility among his brothers. Instead, they enjoy themselves with Benjamin (vv. 26, 34).[14] When he eventually reveals himself, Joseph is now above "vindictiveness and retaliation."[15] He confesses to his brothers that God sent him ahead of them to save their lives (45:5).

Moses, who ran away from Egypt, arrived at Midian and was welcomed in Reuel's family (also known as Jethro) with a meal (Exod 2:20). Reuel's invitation to Moses to join the meals eventually made Moses part of Reuel's household (vv. 21–22).[16] When Moses became the leader of Israel, Jethro came and visited him at the wilderness in Sinai. There he offered sacrifices to Yahweh. He also ate with Aaron and the elders of Israel before God's presence (Exod 18:12). The shared meal meant "the ritual celebration of the reunion of the Israelites with the Midianites."[17]

Another occurrence in the OT concerning meals indicates acceptance and change of status. Ruth, a Moabitess, was invited to Boaz's meal. Daniel I. Block states that this occasion was "a glorious demonstration of compassion, generosity, and acceptance."[18] This also "offer[ed] protection even for despised Moabites."[19] The acceptance of Ruth into the family of Boaz paved the way for the coming of the Messiah. She became the ancestor of David, the king of Judah (Ruth 4:18–22). She is mentioned as one of the women in the genealogy of Jesus (Matt 1:5–6).

In the monarchic context, when a king offers a meal to a certain person, it means favor from the monarch and a better status. David commands Solomon, the successor to his throne, to let the sons of Barzilai eat on the king's table (1 Kgs 2:7). This is to reciprocate "the support and hospitality of Barzilai"[20] when David ran away from Absalom (2 Sam 19:31–39). To eat at the king's table means to receive "a regular royal allowance of food and clothing, with a house and land to support him and his family."[21] The sons of Barzilai receive a new status as members of the royal family.[22]

Jehoiachin, a captive and prisoner of the Babylonian kingdom, was released from prison and given "a seat above the seats of the kings who were with him in Babylon" (2 Kgs 25:29). He also regularly dined at the king's table. His situation elevated his status from a mere captive and prisoner to "a place of special honor by the Babylonian king."[23]

Isaiah prophesies that "on this mountain the LORD of hosts will make for all peoples a feast of rich food" (Isa 25:6a). The feasting is a loyalty oath of the people of Israel towards Yahweh. The feast carries an invitation extended not only to the people of Israel but to all peoples. The guests are of lowly and humble standing, but in the feast, they are elevated "to an unprecedented status."[24]

The occurrence of the feast/meal in the OT is an integral part of the restoration of honor. The feast/meal indicates the deliverance of the weak and the afflicted. During this occasion, Yahweh restores the honor of the afflicted, accepts of the outcast, and bestows enjoyment and satiation to the invitees. At the same time, he is honored in return through the people's praise and worship because of the deliverance he affords them. Yahweh and the people pass from shame to honor.

Summary

The theological implications indicate six things about Yahweh. First, Yahweh is a faithful patron who actively involves himself in the lives of his people. He is the source of provision, protection, help, deliverance, salvation, and rescue. He keeps the honor of his clients so long as they remain faithful to him.

Second, Yahweh is holy. He is morally perfect, pure, and awesome. Because he is holy, he is also reliable to save his people and he will repeatedly do so. Third, Yahweh forsakes and abandons those who sin. His chastisement of sin follows, which may lead to humiliation and shame. Confession of sin and genuine repentance are ways to avert his chastisement.

Fourth, Yahweh defends the honor of his people. He avenges the taunts of the enemies of his people by destroying them and restoring his people. He also prohibits the taunting of the vulnerable and the marginalized. Fifth, Yahweh covers nakedness. He does not leave his people vulnerable, destitute, and defenseless. He removes their reproach by restoring them into his relationship. Sixth, Yahweh is the ultimate host in the feast/meal. He elevates the status of everyone involved in this feast.

Psalm 22 shows that Yahweh may abandon his people, even in their innocence, to his shame. Yahweh may have reasons to abandon others because of their sins that cause their shame. In Ps 22, he has no reason at all. However, in his holiness, he remains reliable to deliver and restore the honor of his people, an idea prevalent in Scriptures. This psalm reveals that the enemies take advantage of the distress of God's people in the seeming absence of Yahweh in their lives. The same is true with other instances in the Scriptures. Yet when the psalmist in Ps 22 and God's people cry to him, Yahweh answers, delivers, rescues, and saves them from their humiliation.

This psalm also discloses that after deliverance, a rite of passage from shame to honor is done through the fellowship feast/meal. In this event, Yahweh and the attendees receive honor. Although the attendees receive honor, Yahweh is the center of honor because of his ability to deliver, as indicated in the Scriptures. Most of all, the psalmist's experience of deliverance from shame and the restoration of his honor though Yahweh's power as creator and warrior king may also be experienced by God's people. Those who call upon Yahweh's name will never be put to shame (Joel 2:26–27, Rom 10:13).

---

[1] Gen 14:19, 22; Exod 9:29, 19: 5; Deut 10:14; Job 41:11; Pss 24:1, 50:10–12, 74:16, 89:11, 95:4–5, 104:24; Jer 46:10; Dan 2:20.

[2] Eugene E. Carpenter, *Exodus 1–18*, ed. William B. Barrick, Evangelical Exegetical Commentary (Bellingham, WA: Lexham, 2016), 98. Eugene E. Carpenter describes that the Israelites were subjected to "drudgery, rigor, work conditions, toil, and psychological abuse." Ibid. Their oppressions delayed their immediate response to Moses call for them to go out of the land of Egypt. Ibid.

[3] Deut 28:20, 31:16; Judg 2:12f., 10:6, 13; 1 Sam 8:8; 2 Kgs 21:22, 22:17; Isa 65:11; Jer 2:13, 17, 19; 5:7, 19; 16:11; 19:4; Hos 4:10.

[4] H. Mark Abbott, *A Psalm-Shaped Life* (Eugene, OR: Wipf & Stock, 2011), 3.

[5] John Ramsey, *For Your Names' Sake* (Morrisville, NC: Lulu Press, 2008), 125.

[6] Douglas Connelly, *The Book of Psalms* (Nashville: Nelson, 2008), E-book edition, ch. 3, "Songs of God's Care (Psalms 22–30)," para. 14.

[7] Ibid.

[8] Cooper Sr., *Ezekiel*, 313.

[9] Lé, *The Naked Christ*, 124.

[10] Ibid., 128.

[11] Skinner, *Genesis*, 300. See also Mathews, *Genesis 1–11:26*, 217; Reyburn and Fry, *A Handbook on Genesis*, 386; Coats, *Genesis*, 137.

[12] Wenham, *Genesis 16–50*, 80.

[13] Ibid., 81.

[14] See also Henry and Scott, *Matthew Henry's Concise Commentary*; Gen 43:26.

[15] Elwell, *Evangelical Commentary*, 34.

[16] See also Douglas K. Stuart, *Exodus*, NAC 2 (Nashville: Broadman & Holman, 2006), 100.

[17] Noel D. Osborn and Howard A. Hatton, *A Handbook on Exodus*, UBS Handbook Series (New York: United Bible Societies, 1999), 435.

[18] Daniel I. Block, *Judges, Ruth*, NAC 6 (Nashville: Broadman & Holman, 1999), 667.

[19] Ibid.

[20] Mordekhai Cogan, *1 Kings: A New Translation with Introduction and Commentary*, AB 10 (New Haven: Yale University Press, 2008), 174.

[21] Donald J. Wiseman, *1 and 2 Kings: An Introduction and Commentary*, TOTC 9 (Downers Grove, IL: InterVarsity Press, 1993), 83.

[22] Those who receive the king's dole out "would be generally members of the administration and champions of military repute. Many of those would either be already part of the king's family or would marry into the family." Walton, Matthews, and Chavalas, *The IVP Bible*, 357.

[23] Roger L. Omanson and John Ellington, *A Handbook on 1 and 2 Kings*, ed. Paul Clarke et al., UBS Handbook Series (New York: United Bible Societies, 2008), 1365.

[24] Dan G. Johnson, *From Chaos to Restoration: An Integrative Reading of Isaiah 24–27*, JSOTSup 61 (Sheffield: JSOT Press, 1988), 62.

Summary

This chapter presents the summary and conclusion of the study. This research investigated the honor and shame values present in Ps 22. It looked into the scholarly works that specifically dealt with the interpretation of Ps 22 to examine the depth of their study in the honor and shame perspective. The survey revealed that scholars differ on the literalness of the psalmist's experience. It revealed that some scholars consider the psalmist's suffering as figurative. The belief that David's experiences are figurative denies the possibility that David literally went through all the misery described in the psalm. The figurative attribution of the experiences in the psalm dismisses the case of drawing its sociocultural background. However, some scholars attribute the experiences to the king of Israel, Babylonian exiles, an unnamed individual, David, and the Messiah. This paper holds that the experiences are specific to David and may apply to other personalities such as the Messiah.

Some scholars comment on the honor and shame material in the psalm but fall short of attributing it to the honor and shame perspective. The views refer to filial relationship, humiliation, meals, and deliverance. These views connect with the attribution of shame and the restoration of honor to either the psalmist or God. Also, most scholars hold that the psalm is messianic. Thus, they attribute the psalmist's humiliation to Jesus's suffering at his crucifixion.

Additionally, scholars indicate that the language of honor and shame occurs in the book of Psalms. One scholar mentions explicitly that the honor and shame terms appear also in Ps 22. A particular study on Ps 22 in the perspective of honor and shame needs some more amplification. This study was conducted from this viewpoint.

The second chapter discussed some values of honor and shame in some specific Mediterranean and Mesopotamian lands. It considered specifically the means of forsakenness/abandonment, taunt speeches, nakedness, and feast/meal. It also looked into the values of patronage, kinship/family, and trust. This research affirmed that the said values and means in the specific Mediterranean and Mesopotamian lands are closely related with the practices of Israel during the united monarchical period.

Patronage is a value in which a person of lesser status attaches himself/herself to a patron—a person of higher status. The system is reciprocal. Egypt; the Levantine societies, especially Palestine; and Israel practice patronage. Also, Egypt and the Levant have different gods as their patrons. Israel has Yahweh as its patron.

Forsakenness/abandonment is a means of group dis-attachment. The person, a king or anybody, forsaken or abandoned by the gods or God himself is put to shame. He/she must appease the gods for his/her honor's restoration. For Israel, God initiated the reconciliation to defend his honor and to restore Israel's honor. Akkadian texts and Assyrian epics record abandonment of kings, who faced shame when abandoned by their patron gods. But those who remained with the gods were honored. In the biblical culture, the main pillar of the culture is the value of kinship or family-centeredness. Honor is always bound with the family's honor, whether ascribed or acquired. Separation from family means loss of honor and acquisition of shame.

In the ANE, kinship can be among humans or between God as the patron and humans as clients. In sum, kinship provides honor, protection, and relationship. The fundamental human value of trust is associated with the human behavior of loyalty, commitment, and solidarity. The people trust the deities as a watcher, provider, or protector. For Israel, trusting in these gods ends in shame. God alone is trustworthy. He provides deliverance, protection, help, and eventually honor.

Taunt speeches are means to challenge others to defend one's honor or to publicly shame others verbally. Failure to defend oneself verbally means loss of honor and subjection to ridicule, taunt, and shame. In the Israelite and Mediterranean contexts, it is a means of social control. The Egyptian concept of Ma'at prohibits ridicule and insult of the weak and vulnerable. God promised to remove Israel's reproach and shame.

Nakedness expresses the dishonor or shame of a person. In ancient Israel, Egypt, and Assyria, nakedness equates to poverty, humiliation, powerlessness, lack of security, and disability. Egypt resolves nakedness by clothing the naked, a symbol of their pride.

Feast/meal is a means of communicativeness. It either ascribes honor to the invited or shame to the neglected. The invitee and the invited form a bond of belongingness. It marks the transition in the life of a person, from shame to honor. To sum up, the chapter presented that the values and means studied here existed in the specific Mediterranean and Mesopotamian lands. These values and means reflect similarities with and differences from the values and means found in Ps 22.

The third chapter presented the literary and linguistic analyses of Ps 22. The literary analysis highlighted three themes: God as savior and king, deliverance, and trust. It noted the psalm's genre as a lament (vv. 2–22) with praise (vv. 23–32). The psalmist in this psalm lamented God's seeming distance and failure to deliver him from the attacks of the enemies that affected his social, emotional, and physical well-being. The prayer ended with a statement that God, also known as Yahweh, answered his prayer of deliverance.

The praise accentuated the psalmist's call to praise and worship Yahweh and affirmed Yahweh's righteous deeds. The lament had three sections: complaint against God (vv. 2–12), complaint against his enemies (vv. 13–19), and call for deliverance highlighting Yahweh's deliverance of the psalmist (vv. 20–22). The praise formed a three-section chiasm: the psalmist's call to praise (vv. 23–24) paired with the people's praise (vv. 30–32), the reason to praise (vv. 25, 28–29), and the acts of praise and feasting (vv. 26–27).

This section of the paper also analyzed the honor and shame passages that reflected the means of forsakenness/abandonment, taunt speech, nakedness, and feast meal and the value of patronage, kinship/family, and trust. These values and means are also tied with deliverance. The analysis of the honor and shame passages explored the textual criticism, grammar, and syntax. The analysis of the textual criticism revealed that in most instances, the integrity of the Hebrew text is intact. The lexical analysis presented the different terms related to each value and means of honor and shame. The interpretation of the passages and the honor and shame implication followed.

For patronage, the vocatives אֵלִי (v. 2), אֱלֹהַי (v. 3), and יְהוָה (v. 9) refer to God/Yahweh as the personal patron of David, the psalmist. The terms suggest that God/Yahweh acts as a father, creator, and king who is a merciful and gracious divine patron of Israel. The related terms קָדוֹשׁ, יָשֵׁב, תְהִלָּה, and יִשְׂרָאֵל (v. 4) attribute honorific titles to God/Yahweh. This picture of God/Yahweh prompted David's petitions for salvation, rescue, and deliverance. The implication indicates that God/Yahweh honors his commitment as a patron to his client by serving as savior, protector, deliverer, and creator.

For forsakenness/abandonment, the term עֲזַבְתָּנִי (v. 2) indicated that God/Yahweh, the psalmist's patron, refused to accept or acknowledge his relationship with the psalmist, the client. The phrases רָחוֹק מִישׁוּעָתִי and דִּבְרֵי שַׁאֲגָתִי (v. 2) intensified the abandonment and heightened the distance of the psalmist's welfare and prosperity and the rejection of his pleas. The phrases לֹא תַעֲנֶה and לֹא־דוּמִיָּה (v. 3) sealed God's abandonment of the psalmist. The interrogative לָמָה (v. 2) expressed the psalmist's wondering as the reason for the falling out of his relationship with God/Yahweh. The abandonment implied loss of economic prosperity, emotional support, and reliable help that only God/Yahweh could provide to the psalmist. The honor and shame implication meant that the abandonment left the psalmist shamed, vulnerable, and ridiculed.

The family-centeredness or kinship provided solution to the abandonment. The term אֲבֹתֵינוּ (v. 5) referred to Abraham, Isaac, Jacob, and the long line of ancestors of Israel. It recalled God's/Yahweh's deliverance of the fathers of Israel from their bondage in Egypt. The deliverance became the paradigm of later generations every time they called for Yahweh's help, salvation, and deliverance when in trouble, distress, and oppression. It became the psalmist's as well. The vocative אַתָּה (vv. 4, 10, 20) and the phrases בֶּטֶן גֹחִי (v. 10) and הָשְׁלַכְתִּי מֵרֶחֶם (v. 11) emphasized the close affinity of the psalmist with God. It also implied that God/Yahweh, who served as adoptive father, cared for and attributed honor to the psalmist as to a natural-born son. The honor included salvation and deliverance. The honor and shame implication of the family-centeredness and kinship showed Yahweh's/God's salvific and redemptive power towards the fathers, which brought them out of their slavery. This salvific and redemptive power was also extended to the psalmist. Thus, he had claims to an ascribed honor.

The term בָּטַח (vv. 5–6) indicated the fathers' strong confidence and reliance upon God/Yahweh. In response to the fathers' trust, God/Yahweh did three things for them: תְּפַלְּטֵמוֹ, נִמְלָטוּ, and לֹא־בוֹשׁוּ (vv. 5–6). David's allusion to God's/Yahweh's deliverance of the fathers showed his total confidence that God/Yahweh would do to him what he had done to the fathers. God/Yahweh alone was trustworthy. The honor and shame implication indicates that when God's/Yahweh's people are in a state of oppression and defeat, God/Yahweh is trustworthy enough to rescue, deliver, and not to put his people to shame. David desired to experience the fathers' deliverance also.

The taunt speech indicated the shame the psalmist underwent in the hands of his enemies. The terms תּוֹלַעַת and וְלֹא־אִישׁ illustrated the psalmist's shameful condition: a worthless person and a defeated warrior (v. 7). The terms חֶרְפָּה, בָּזָה, רֹאַי, לָעַג יַפְטִירוּ בְשָׂפָה, and יָנִיעוּ רֹאשׁ exhibited that the enemies' gestures of contempt (v. 8) were all attempts to shame the psalmist.

The twist in the enemies' taunts were the insults upon Yahweh, indicating his untrustworthiness to save, rescue, and provide honor to the psalmist. Yet, Yahweh was the psalmist's progenitor and adoptive father who cared, protected, and ascribed him with honor. The honor and shame implication indicates that although the psalmist is shamed and separated from humanity and Yahweh's capability to deliver was undermined, his honor was intact because Yahweh was able to take care of him.

For nakedness, the phrases יְחַלְּקוּ בְגָדַי and עַל־לְבוּשִׁי יַפִּילוּ גוֹרָל (v. 19) specified the enemies' forceful removal of the psalmist's garments and clothing as the final act of putting him to shame. When the enemies stripped the psalmist naked, they reduced him to nothing and made him vulnerable and shamed. The honor and shame implication presents that the victorious enemies had the honor but the defeated psalmist had shame ascribed to him.

For feast/meal, the terms יֹאכְלוּ and אָכְלוּ, both having the same root, indicated a festive meal hosted by Yahweh (vv. 27, 30). Attendance to the festive meal meant the restoration of honor and relationship. The attendees formed a bond to praise, worship, and serve Yahweh. The feast was in honor of Yahweh, who brought help, rescue, salvation, and deliverance to the psalmist and the afflicted. The honor and shame implication indicated that festive meals were occasions for a change of status, an ascribed honor for both Yahweh and humanity.

Also, the analysis of the honor and shame passages confirms the shame and honor aspects of Ps 22. The first section of the analysis outlined David's shame, causing distress. The shame he went through were the following: (a) God abandoned him, causing him shame; (b) the broken relationship resulted in his loss of self-worth and sense of humanity; (c) the despicable situation of the psalmist prompted the enemies to taunt him; (d) the taunting led to the enemies' full-blown war, resulting to the psalmist's nakedness—a symbol of total defeat. The war left the psalmist without honor.

The second section showed the values and means that would confirm the psalmist's honor. The psalmist's honor came from (a) the patron-client relationship, (b) kinship/family, (c) trust relationship, and (d) festive meal. The patron-client relationship pointed out Yahweh as the patron and the psalmist as the client. Yahweh provided help, salvation, and deliverance from which came the preservation of the psalmist's honor. The adoption of the psalmist into the kinship of Yahweh secured his honor. The psalmist's trust relationship with Yahweh assured him of the deliverance and rescue which kept him away from shame. The festive meal provided an occasion for the change of his status, from defeat to victory and from shame to honor. Also, Yahweh received his honor during this festive meal. The participants of this festive meal praised, worshipped, and prostrated before him for the things he had done. Lastly, the NT use of Ps 22 reveals the presence of the means of abandonment, taunt speech, nakedness, and the value of kinship.

The fourth chapter presented the role of deliverance in the restoration of David's honor. It presented the cause of shame and the term used for the deliverance from shame. The psalmist used ten synonymous deliverance terms to indicate his urgent need of deliverance from shame. (a) The psalmist's abandonment and rejection by God brought him shame and caused him despair. The provisions attached to the patron-client relationship were essentially lost. Salvation, יְשׁוּעָה, from God was the way for the restoration of the patronage relationship. In relation to salvation, עָנָה, "answer" and דּוּמִיָּה, "repose" were needed for the restoration of relationship. The word עָנָה expresses the hope for God's beneficial act to respond helpfully for the resolution of the broken relationship. The word דּוּמִיָּה indicates a wish for relief from not having the right relationship with God. Both words imply a resolution to end the shame of abandonment and rejection and restore the psalmist's welfare and kinship with God.

(b) The allusion to the fathers' deliverance indicated that the psalmist experienced affliction just like the fathers. Three deliverance terms פָּלַט, "to be delivered"; מָלַט, "to be rescued from danger"; and לֹא־בוֹשׁוּ , "not put to shame" indicate a progression in the deliverance. The restoration of honor is the apex of this deliverance. (c) The enemies taunted the psalmist to let Yahweh rescue, deliver and protect him. They intended to shame the psalmist for trusting in Yahweh, who was insignificantly inutile to save the psalmist. The terms פָּלַט, "to be rescued"; נָצַל, "to be delivered"; and חָפֵץ, "to be protected" meant that Yahweh delivered the psalmist from personal and relational shame, provided care and protection to the psalmist and restored the psalmist's relationship with Yahweh and humanity, which also meant the restoration of honor.

(d) The psalmist's enemies had totally cast him to nakedness, which was the lowest point of the psalmist's shame. The terms the psalmist used to express his desire for deliverance—אֱיָלוּת, עָזַר, נָצַל, יָשַׁע, and עָנָה— convey protection, aid, and help in battle. The ultimate aim of this deliverance was to reverse the shameful status of the psalmist. It was the victory over the enemies which would ascribe honor to him and cast shame upon the enemies. Thus, deliverance restored the psalmist's honor.

The fifth chapter presented the theological implications of the study. The theological implications described Yahweh as a faithful patron who protects and provides. Also, Yahweh's holiness reflects his separateness from humanity's shameful status. Because of his separateness, he faithfully rescues and delivers his people from their enemies, keeping them from being shamed. Yahweh forsakes and abandons those who sin and become infidel. Only genuine confession and repentance can avert social forsakenness. Yahweh's response to the taunts of the enemies is to defend the cause of his people and his name. Yahweh promises his people that they are not going to hear the taunts of their enemies anymore. He also covers the nakedness of his people to restore their honor. In his mercy and grace, he does not leave his people destitute, a state of nakedness, forever. He appears in and hosts a festive meal. During these festive meals, he brings blessings and reconciliation. Every person who takes part in this festive meal belongs to his family and kingdom.

Conclusion

This paper answered the following questions: (a) "What are the honor and shame social values existing in the Mediterranean and Mesopotamian lands that relate to the honor and shame social values found in Psalm 22" This paper considers David, the king of the united kingdom of Israel, as its author. It holds that the probable honor and shame background of Ps 22 existed in the mentioned Mediterranean and Mesopotamian lands. It searched the backgrounds related to honor and shame present in the Mediterranean and Mesopotamian lands such as the means of forsakenness/abandonment, taunt speech, nakedness, and feast/meal and the values of patronage, kinship/family, and trust relationship. The study of the background found that honor values and means are employed to promote the welfare, prosperity, and deliverance and to strengthen the honor. The shame means are used to destroy honor and ascribe shame. This paper concludes that the values and means in the specific Mediterranean and Mesopotamian lands have differences from and similarities with the values and means present in Ps 22. The values and means in these Mediterranean and Mesopotamian lands may have influenced the writing of Ps 22.

(b) "What are the literary and linguistic clues that unveil the honor and shame context of Ps 22?" The literary and linguistic analyses revealed that honor and shame terms and phrases appear in Ps 22. These analyses established that the terms and phrases related to the values and means found in the places of concern also existed in the 10th-century BC monarchical period. The purpose of the values and means found in the Mediterranean and Mesopotamian background is comparable to the purpose of the values and means that occur in Ps 22. This paper concludes that the psalm displayed the different values and means noted. It also concludes that the intent of these values and means were either to raise the honor of Yahweh and the psalmist or to destroy their honor and attribute shame upon them.

(c) "What are the terms expressing the psalmist desire for deliverance in the context of honor and shame?" This paper found that the psalmist used ten synonymous terms to indicate his desire for deliverance. The reason for the desire for deliverance is abandonment, humiliation, defeat, and enslavement which demonstrated the psalmist's shame. The terms indicated deliverance, rescue, protection, aid, help in war, and victory over enemies. The psalmist's deliverance is an evidence to the reversal of his state, from shame to honor. His deliverance meant the restoration of his honor.

The psalmist's change of status from shame to honor was brought about by his deliverance that took place in the values of patronage, kinship/family, trust and the means of feast/meal. The primary agent in the psalmist's deliverance was Yahweh alone. This study concludes that since the psalmist was shamed, significantly his deliverance should also come through the values and means that would restore his honor. Also, Jesus was shamed yet his honor was restored.

(d) "What are the theological implications of the psalm?" This paper outlined six theological implications for this study: (1) Yahweh is a patron, (2) Yahweh is holy, (3) Yahweh abandons/forsakes, (4) Yahweh responds to taunts, (5) Yahweh covers nakedness, and (6) Yahweh restores honor at the feast/meal. The theological implication showed that Yahweh was actively involved as an agent in the social values of honor and shame, especially in the deliverance of the psalmist and his people Israel.

In conclusion, the psalmist experienced the shame of abandonment/rejection, taunting, and nakedness. He could not save himself from this humiliation. Yet, he continued to trust in Yahweh, his faithful patron and the active agent of his deliverance from shame and the restoration of his honor. His honor was preserved because Yahweh adopted him into his kinship/family. His change of status, from shame to honor, happened during the feast/meal hosted by Yahweh as he was restored into the fellowship of the universal humanity and to God/Yahweh himself. Also, Yahweh's honor was restored for the people praised, worshipped, and bowed down before him.

As a faithful patron to the psalmist, Yahweh remains a faithful patron to his people then and now. He may abandon them because of their sins, but he remains reliable to save his people from their shame and to restore their honor. His people may experience humiliation but they can cry to him because he is ready to defend them and cover their reproach. He will eventually restore his people into his fellowship, elevating their status into honor.

Recommendations

At the beginning of this study, this dissertation attempted to show the honor and shame social values and means existing in Ps 22 and their connection with deliverance as a restoration of honor. Because of the limitation of time and space, the study presents some specific social values and means. With this, further study possibilities are opened. This paper recommends research on Ps 22's sociocultural context to strengthen this psalm's honor and shame aspect. Further, a comparative study of Ps 22's honor and shame values with Jesus's passion experience may also be worthwhile research due to the messianic characteristic of this psalm. The social and missiological implications of the honor and shame in this psalm may also be essential research for applying this psalm in the sociological and missiological perspectives.

BIBLIOGRAPHY

Abbott, H. Mark. *A Psalm-Shaped Life*. Eugene, OR: Wipf & Stock, 2011.

Alden, Robert L. *Job*. NAC 11. Nashville: Broadman & Holman, 1993.

Alexander, T. Desmond, and Brian S. Rosner, eds. *New Dictionary of Biblical Theology*. Downers Grove, IL: InterVarsity Press, 2000.

Allen, Leslie C. *Ezekiel 1–19*. WBC 28. Dallas: Word, 1994.

Allen, Willoughby C. *Matthew*. 3rd ed. ICC. Edinburgh: T&T Clark, 1907.

Alter, Robert. *The Art of Biblical Poetry*. Chicago: HarperCollins, 1985.

Andersen, Arnold, Leigh Cohn, and Tom Holbrook. *Making Weight: Men's Conflicts with Food, Weight, Shape and Appearance*. Carlsbad, CA: Gurze Books, 2010.

Andersen, Francis I. *Job: An Introduction and Commentary*. TOTC 14. Downers Grove, IL: InterVarsity Press, 1976.

Arnold, Bill T. *Introduction to the Old Testament*. New York: Cambridge University Press, 2014.

—————., and Bryan E. Beyer, eds. *Readings from the Ancient Near East: Primary Sources for Old Testament Study*. Encountering Biblical Studies. Grand Rapids: Baker Academic, 2002.

Arnold, Bill T., and John H. Choi. *A Guide to Biblical Hebrew Syntax*. New York: Cambridge University Press, 2003.

Asher-Greve, Julia, and Deborah Sweeney. "On Nakedness, Nudity, and Gender in Egyptian and Mesopotamian Art." Pages 111–62 in *Images and Gender: Contributions to the Hermeneutics of Reading Ancient Art.* Edited by Silvia Schroer. London: Academic Press, 2006.

Augustine of Hippo. *Expositions on the Book of Psalms.* Edited by Philip Schaff. Translated by A. Cleveland Coxe. Vol. 8. A Select Library of the Nicene and Post-Nicene Fathers of the Christian Church. New York: Christian Literature, 1888.

Avrahami, Yael. "בוש in the Psalms: Shame or Disappointment?" *JSOT* 34.3 (2010): 295–313.

Bailey, John A. "Initiation and the Primal Woman in Gilgamesh and Genesis 2–3." *JBL* 89.2 (1970): 137–50.

Bailey, Kenneth E. *Poet and Peasant: A Literary-Cultural Approach to the Parables in Luke.* Grand Rapids: Eerdmans, 1976.

Baker, Warren, and Eugene E. Carpenter. *The Complete Word Study Dictionary: Old Testament.* Word Study Series. Chattanooga, TN: AMG, 2003.

Balch, Daniel L. "Rich and Poor, Proud and Humble in Luke-Acts." Pages 214–33 in *The Social World of the First Christians: Essays in Honor of Wayne A. Meeks.* Edited by L. Michael White and O. Larry Yarbrough. Minneapolis: Augsburg Fortress, 1995.

Balz, Horst Robert, and Gerhard Schneider. *Exegetical Dictionary of the New Testament.* Edinburgh: T&T Clark, 1990.

Balz, Horst Robert. "Ἅγιος." *EDNT* 17–20.

———. "Γυμνότης, Ητος, ἡ." *EDNT* 265–66.

Barker, Kenneth L., and Waylon Bailey. *Micah, Nahum, Habakkuk, Zephaniah*. Edited by E. Ray Clendenen. NAC 20. Nashville: Broadman & Holman, 1999.

Bashoor, M. Scott. "'Let Me Not Be Ashamed': Divine Protection from Shame in Psalm 25." PhD diss., The Master's Seminary, 2002.

Batten, Alicia J. "Clothing and Adornment." *BTB* 40.3 (2010): 148–59.

Bauer, Bruce L., ed. *Shame and Honor: Presenting Biblical Themes in Shame and Honor Contexts*. Berrien Springs, MI: Andrews University Press, 2014.

Bechtel, Lyn M. "The Perception of Shame within the Divine-Human Relationship." Pages 72–94 in *Uncovering Ancient Stones: Essays in Memory of H. Neil Richardson*. Edited by Lewis M. Hopfe. Winona Lake, IN: Eisenbrauns, 1994.

———. "Shame as a Sanction of Social Control in Biblical Israel: Judicial, Political, and Social Shaming." *JSOT* 16.49 (1991): 47–76.

———. "What If Dinah Is Not Raped? (Genesis 34)." *JSOT* 62 (1994): 19–36.

Bellini, Peter J. *Truth Therapy: Renewing Your Mind with the Word of God*. Eugene, OR: Wipf & Stock, 2014.

Bello, Moreno Dal. *For God so Loved...Who?* Morrisville, NC: Lulu Press, 2017.

Bentzen, Aage. *Forelæsninger over indledning til de gammeltestamentlige Salmer*. Copenhagen: Gad, 1932.

———. *Fortolkning til de gammeltestamentlige Salmer*. Copenhagen: Gad, 1939.

Bergen, Robert D. *1, 2 Samuel*. NAC 7. Nashville: Broadman & Holman, 1996.

Birkeland, Harris. *Die feinde des individuums in der Israelitischen Psalmenliteratur: ein beitrag zur kenntnis der Semitischen literatur-und religionsgeschichte*. Oslo: Grøndahl & Søns, 1933.

Bloch-Smith, Elizabeth. "Acculturating Gender Roles: Goddess Images as Conveyors of Culture in Ancient Israel." Pages 1–18 in *Image, Text, Exegesis: Iconographic Interpretation and the Hebrew Bible*. Edited by Izaak J. de Hulster, Joel M. LeMon, Andrew Mein, and Claudia V. Camp. London: T&T Clark, 2015.

Block, Daniel I. *The Gods of the Nations: A Study in Ancient Near Eastern National Theology*. Eugene, OR: Wipf & Stock, 2013.

———. *Judges, Ruth*. NAC 6. Nashville: Broadman & Holman, 1999.

Blomberg, Craig L. *Matthew*. Edited by David S. Dockery. NAC 22. Nashville: Broadman & Holman, 1992.

Bodenhamer, Kim Williams. "Poetry, Biblical." *Lexham Bible Dictionary*. E-book edition.

Böhl, F. M. Th. de Liagre, and B. Gemser. *Die Psalmen 1*. Nijkerk, Netherlands: Callenbach, 1946.

Boice, James Montgomery. *Genesis: Creation and Fall, Genesis 1–11; An Expositional Commentary*. Vol. 1. Grand Rapids: Baker Books, 1982.

———. *Psalms*. Grand Rapids: Baker Books, 2005.

Bok, Sissela. *Lying: Moral Choice in Public and Private Life*. New York: Vintage Books, 2011.

Bonhoeffer, Dietrich. *Ethics*. Edited by Clifford J. Green. Translated by Reinhard Krauss, Charles C. West, Douglas W. Stott, and Dietrich Bonhoeffer. Dietrich Bonhoeffer Works 6. Minneapolis: Augsburg Fortress, 2005.

Botha, P. J. "The 'Enthronement Psalms': A Claim to the World-Wide Honour of Yahweh." *OTE* 11.1 (1998): 24–39.

————. "Honour and Shame as Pivotal Values in Ephrem the Syrian's Vision of Paradise." *Acta Patristica et Byzantina* 10 (1999): 49–65.

Botha, P. J. "'The Honour of the Righteous Will Be Restored': Psalm 75 in Its Social Context." *OTE* 15.2 (2002): 320–34.

————. "Psalm 54: The Power of Positive Patterning." *Verbum et Ecclesia* 21.3 (2000): 507–16.

————. "Psalm 118 and Social Values in Ancient Israel." *OTE* 16.2 (2003): 195–215.

Botterweck, G. Johannes and Helmer Ringgren, eds. *Theological Dictionary of the Old Testament*. Translated by John T. Willis et al. 8 vols. Grand Rapids: Eerdmans, 1974–2006.

Bowditch, Phebe Lowell. *Horace and the Gift Economy of Patronage*. Berkeley: University of California Press, 2001.

Brannan, Rick. *The Lexham Analytical Lexicon to the Greek New Testament*. Bellingham, WA: Lexham, 2011.

Bratcher, Robert G., and Howard A. Hatton. *A Handbook on Deuteronomy*. UBS Handbook Series. New York: United Bible Societies, 2000.

Bratcher, Robert G., and William David Reyburn. *A Handbook on the Book of Psalms*. UBS Handbook Series. New York: United Bible Societies, 1991.

Bratcher, Robert G., and Eugene Albert Nida. *A Handbook on the Gospel of Mark*. UBS Handbook Series. New York: United Bible Societies, 1993.

Bridge, Sheila. *How to Feel Good Naked: Learning to Love the Body You've Got*. Oxford: Monarch Books, 2012.

Bridges, Jerry. *The Pursuit of Holiness: Run in Such a Way as to Get the Prize 1 Corinthians 9:24*. Carol Stream, IL: Tyndale House, 2014.

Briggs, Charles Augustus, and Emilie Grace Briggs. *The Book of Psalms*. ICC 1. London: T&T Clark, 1976.

Bromiley, Geoffrey W., ed. *International Standard Bible Encyclopedia*. 4 vols. Grand Rapids: Eerdmans, 1979–1988.

Brooks, James A. *Mark*. NAC 23. Nashville: Broadman & Holman, 1991.

Brown, Francis, S. R. Driver, and Charles A. Briggs. *The New Brown, Driver, Briggs, Gesenius Hebrew and English Lexicon with an Appendix Containing the Biblical Aramaic*. Peabody, MA: Hendrickson, 1979.

Broyles, Craig C. "Interpreting the Old Testament: Principles and Steps." Pages 13–62 in *Interpreting the Old Testament: A Guide for Exegesis*. Edited by Craig C. Broyles. Grand Rapids: Baker Academic, 2001.

Broyles, Craig C., ed. *Interpreting the Old Testament: A Guide for Exegesis*. Grand Rapids: Baker Academic, 2001.

Brueggemann, Walter. *Genesis*. IBC. Atlanta: John Knox, 1982.

Bullinger, E. W. *Figures of Speech Used in the Bible: Explained and Illustrated*. New York: E. & J. B. Young, 1898.

Butler, Bradley S. "Dog." *Holman Illustrated Bible Dictionary*, 438.

Buttenwieser, Moses. *The Psalms: Chronologically Treated with a New Translation*. Chicago: University of Chicago Press, 1938.

Calvin, John. *John Calvin's Commentaries on the Psalms 1–35*. Altenmünster, Germany: Jazzybee Verlag, 2012.

———. *Psalms*. Calvin's Commentaries. Albany, OR: Ages Software, 1998.

Carpenter, Eugene E. *Exodus 1–18*. Edited by William B. Barrick. Evangelical Exegetical Commentary. Bellingham, WA: Lexham, 2016.

Carson, D. A. *New Bible Commentary: Twenty-First Century Edition*. Leicester: Inter-Varsity Press, 1994.

———, Walter W. Wessel, and Walter L. Leifeld. *The Expositor's Bible Commentary: Matthew, Mark, Luke*. Edited by Frank E. Gaebelein. Vol. 8. Grand Rapids: Zondervan, 1984.

Charney, Davida H. *Persuading God: Rhetorical Studies of First-Person Psalms*. Hebrew Bible Monographs 73. Sheffield: Sheffield Phoenix, 2017.

Childs, Brevard S. *Introduction to the Old Testament as Scripture*. Philadelphia: Fortress, 1979.

Chrisholm, Robert B. "The Major Prophets." Pages 259–339 in *Holman Concise Bible Commentary: Simple, Straightforward Commentary on Every Book of the Bible*. Edited by David S.

Dockery. Holman Reference. Nashville: Broadman & Holman, 1998.

Clarke, Adam. *The Holy Bible Containing the Old and New Testaments: The Text Printed from the Most Correct Copies of the Present Authorized Translation, Including the Marginal Readings and Parallel Texts; Job to Malachi.* Vol. 2. Cincinnati: H. S. & J. Applegate, 1851.

Clines, David J. A., ed. *Dictionary of Classical Hebrew.* 9 vols. Sheffield: Sheffield Phoenix, 1993–2016.

Coats, George W. *Genesis, with an Introduction to Narrative Literature.* FOTL 1. Grand Rapids: Eerdmans, 1983.

Cogan, Mordekhai. *1 Kings: A New Translation with Introduction and Commentary.* AB 10. New Haven: Yale University Press, 2008.

Cole, R. Alan. *Mark: An Introduction and Commentary.* TNTC 2. Downers Grove, IL: InterVarsity Press, 1989.

Cole, Steven J. "Psalm 22: The Sufferings and Glory of Christ." *Internet Ministry: Where the World Comes to Study the Bible*, 18 April 2013. https://bible.org/seriespage / psalm-22-sufferings-and-glory-christ.

Connelly, Douglas. *The Book of Psalms.* Nashville: Nelson, 2008.

Cook, Stephen L. *The Social Roots of Biblical Yahwism.* Atlanta: SBL Press, 2004.

Cooke, G. A. *A Critical and Exegetical Commentary on the Book of Ezekiel.* ICC. Edinburgh: T&T Clark, 1936.

Cooper, Lamar Eugene, Sr. *Ezekiel.* NAC 17. Nashville: Broadman & Holman, 1994.

Cottrill, Amy C. *Language, Power, and Identity in the Lament Psalms of the Individual.* Edited by Andrew Mein and Claudia V. Camp. LHBOTS. New York: T&T Clark, 2008.

Craigie, Peter C. *The Book of Deuteronomy.* NICOT. Grand Rapids: Eerdmans, 2007.

—————. *The Old Testament: Its Background, Growth, and Content.* Nashville: Abingdon, 1986.

—————. *Psalms 1–50.* WBC 19. Dallas: Word, 2004.

Crane, Jonathan K. "Shameful Ambivalences: Dimensions of Rabbinic Shame." *AJSR* 35.1 (2011): 61–84.

Croft, Steven J. L. *The Identity of the Individual in the Psalms.* JSOTSup 44. Sheffield: JSOT Press, 1987.

Crook, Zeba A. "Reciprocity: Covenantal Exchange as a Test Case." Pages 78–91 in *Ancient Israel: The Old Testament in Its Social Context.* Edited by Philip F. Esler. Minneapolis: Augsburg Fortress, 2006.

Dahood, Mitchell J. *Psalms 1:1–50; Introduction, Translation, and Notes.* AB 16. New Haven: Yale University Press, 2008.

Daiches, Samuel. "The Meaning of כָּאֲרִי in Psalm 22, v. 17." *JRAS* 1.2 (1933): 401–3.

Danker, Frederick W., Walter Bauer, William F. Arndt, and F. Wilbur Gingrich. *Greek-English Lexicon of the New Testament and Other Early Christian Literature.* 3rd ed. Chicago: University of Chicago Press, 2000.

David, Rabbi Boruch. *Adam and Eve: The Rest of the Story Secrets from the Ancient Wisdom of the Jews.* Bloomington: Xlibris, 2016.

Davidson, Richard M. *Principles of Biblical Interpretation*. Berrien Springs, MI: Andrews University Press, 1995.

———. "Psalms 22, 23, and 24: A Messianic Trilogy?" Paper presented at the ETS Annual Meeting of the Old Testament Psalms Session. San Diego, CA, 20 November 2019.

———. "Shame and Honor in the Beginning: A Study of Genesis 4." Pages 43–76 in *Shame and Honor: Presenting Biblical Themes in Shame and Honor Contexts*. Edited by Bruce L. Bauer. Berrien Springs, MI: Andrews University Press, 2014.

Davies, Philip R. *Scribes and Schools: The Canonization of the Hebrew Scriptures*. Louisville: Westminster John Knox, 1998.

Davies, W. D., and Dale C. Allison Jr. *A Critical and Exegetical Commentary on the Gospel according to Saint Matthew*. ICC 1. New York: T&T Clark, 2004.

Dearman, J. Andrew. *Jeremiah, Lamentations*. Grand Rapids: Zondervan, 2011.

Declaissé-Walford, Nancy L. "An Intertextual Reading of Psalms 22, 23, and 24." Pages 139–52 in *The Book of Psalms: Composition and Reception*. Edited by Peter W. Flint and Patrick D. Miller. Leiden: Brill, 2005.

Deiros, Pablo Alberto. "Cultura." *Diccionario Hispano-Americano de La Misión*, 120–21.

Delitzsch, F. *Psalms*. Grand Rapids: Eerdmans, 1980.

DeMaris, Richard E., and Carolyn S. Leeb. "Judges–(Dis)Honor and Ritual Enactment." Pages 177–90 in *Ancient Israel: The Old Testament in Its Social Context*. Edited by Philip F. Esler. Minneapolis: Augsburg Fortress, 2006.

DeSilva, David A. *4 Maccabees*. Sheffield: Sheffield Academic, 1998.

————. "Exchanging Favor for Wrath: Apostasy in Hebrews and Patron-Client Relationships." *JBL* 115.1 (1996): 91–116.

————. "Grace." *EDB* 524–26.

————. "Honor and Shame." *Dictionary of the Old Testament: Pentateuch; A Compendium of Contemporary Biblical Scholarship*, 431–36.

DeSilva, David A. "Honor and Shame." *Dictionary of the Old Testament: Wisdom, Poetry and Writings* 3:287–300.

————. *Honor, Patronage, Kinship and Purity: Unlocking New Testament Culture*. Downers Grove, IL: InterVarsity Press, 2000.

————. *An Introduction to the New Testament: Contexts, Methods and Ministry Formation*. 2nd ed. Downers Grove, IL: InterVarsity Press, 2018.

————. "Patronage." *DNTB*, 766–71.

————. *Perseverance in Gratitude: A Socio-Rhetorical Commentary on the Epistle to the Hebrews*. Grand Rapids: Eerdmans, 2000.

"Dignity." In *Lexico Dictionaries: English*. Oxford University Press. Accessed May 15, 2020. https://www.lexico.com/en/definition/dignity.

Dille, Sarah J. "Honor Restored: Honor, Shame, and God as Redeeming Kinsman in Second Isaiah." Pages 232–50 in *Relating to the Text: Interdisciplinary and Form-Critical Insights on the Bible*. Edited by Timothy J. Sandoval, Carleen Mandolfo, and Martin J. Buss. New York: T&T Clark, 2003.

Dobbs-Allsopp, F. W. *Lamentations*. IBC. Louisville: Westminster John Knox, 2011.

Douglas, J. D., and Merrill C. Tenney. "Baal (Deity)." *Zondervan Illustrated Bible Dictionary*, 149–50.

Driver, Samuel Rolles, and George Buchanan Gray. *A Critical and Exegetical Commentary on the Book of Job*. 3rd ed. ICC. Edinburgh: T&T Clark, 1921.

Duell, Prentice. *The Mastaba of Mereruka: By the Sakkarah Expedition*. Chicago, IL: University of Chicago Press, 1938.

Duhm, B. *Die Psalmen: Eklärt*. Charleston, SC: Nabu, 1899.

Dumitrescu, Cristian. "The Gospel of Shame and Honor: Atonement through Asian Eyes." Pages 219–37 in *Shame and Honor: Presenting Biblical Themes in Shame and Honor Contexts*. Edited by Bruce L. Bauer. Berrien Springs, MI: Andrews University Press, 2014.

Dykstra, Pearl A. "Kin Relationship." *Encyclopedia of Human Relationships*, 951–54.

Eaton, John H. *Kingship and the Psalms*. 2nd ed. BibSem 3. Sheffield: JSOT Press, 1986.

Ebeling, Jennie R. "Gatekeeper." *EDB*, 484.

Edwards, James R. *The Gospel according to Mark*. Edited by D. A. Carson. PNTC. Grand Rapids: Eerdmans, 2002.

Eisenstadt, S. N., and Luis Roniger. *Patrons, Clients and Friends: Interpersonal Relations and the Structure of Trust in Society*. Themes in the Social Sciences. Cambridge: Cambridge University Press, 1984.

Ellingworth, Paul, and Eugene Albert Nida. *A Handbook on the Letter to the Hebrews*. UBS Handbook Series. New York: United Bible Societies, 1994.

Elwell, Walter A. *Evangelical Commentary on the Bible*. Baker Reference Library 3. Grand Rapids: Baker Books, 1989.

Elwell, Walter A., and Barry J. Beitzel, eds. *Baker Encyclopedia of the Bible*. Grand Rapids: Baker Books, 1988.

———. "Names, Significance Of." *BEB* 2:1522–24.

Erickson, Paul A., and Liam D. Murphy, eds. Readings for a History of Anthropological Theory. 5th ed. Vol. 5. Toronto: University of Toronto Press, 2017.

Erith, L. E. P. *Genesis*. Edited by Charles Gore, Henry Leighton Goudge, and Alfred Guillame. A New Commentary on Holy Scripture: Including the Apocrypha 1. New York: MacMillan, 1928.

Espero, Jose Manuel S. "The Authorship of Psalm 22." MA Thesis, Adventist International Institute of Advanced Studies, 2004.

Evans, Craig A., and Stanley E. Porter Jr. *Dictionary of New Testament Background*. Downers Grove, IL: InterVarsity Press, 2000.

Ewald, Heinrich. *Syntax of the Hebrew Language of the Old Testament*. Edinburgh: T&T Clark, 1891.

Fant, Clyde E., and Mitchell G. Reddish. *Lost Treasures of the Bible: Understanding the Bible through Archaeological Artifacts in World Museums*. Grand Rapids: Eerdmans, 2008.

Fee, Gordon D., and Douglas K. Stuart. *How to Read the Bible for All Its Worth: A Guide to Understanding the Bible*. Grand Rapids: Zondervan, 2009.

Finger, Reta Halteman. *Of Widows and Meals: Communal Meals in the Book of Acts*. Grand Rapids: Eerdmans, 2007.

Floyd, Michael H. *Minor Prophets: Part 2*. FOTL 22. Grand Rapids: Eerdmans, 2000.

Ford, J. M. "Defeat." Pages 42–45 in *Biblical Social Values and Their Meaning: A Handbook*. Edited by J. J. Pilch and Bruce J. Malina. Peabody, MA: Hendrickson, 1993.

Foster, Benjamin Read. *Before the Muses: Archaic, Classical, Mature*. 2nd ed. Vol. 1. Bethesda, MD: CDL, 1996.

Fowler, Donald. "Lion." *EDB*, 811.

France, R. T. *Matthew: An Introduction and Commentary*. TNTC 1. Downers Grove, IL: InterVarsity Press, 1985.

Frangipane, Francis. *Holiness, Truth, and the Presence of God: For Those Who Are Unsatisfied with Their Spiritual Life and Willing to Do Something About It*. Lake Mary, FL: Charisma Media, 2011.

Fredenburg, Brandon. *Ezekiel*. The College Press NIV Commentary. Joplin, MO: College Press, 2002.

Freedman, David Noel, ed. *Anchor Yale Bible Dictionary*. 6 vols. New York: Doubleday, 1992.

———, Allen C. Myers, and Astrid B. Beck, eds. *Eerdmans Dictionary of the Bible*. Grand Rapids: Eerdmans, 2000.

Frymer-Kensky, Tikva. "Gender and Law: An Introduction." Pages 17–24 in *Gender and Law in the Hebrew Bible and the Ancient Near East*. Edited by Victor H. Matthews, Bernard M. Levinson, and Tikva Frymer-Kensky. Sheffield: Sheffield Academic, 2004.

Futato, Mark D., and George M. Schwab. *The Book of Psalms, The Book of Proverbs*. Edited by Philip W. Comfort. Vol. 7. Cornerstone Biblical Commentary. Carol Stream, IL: Tyndale House, 2009.

Futato, Mark D. *Beginning Biblical Hebrew*. Winona Lake, IN: Eisenbrauns, 2003.

———, and George M. Schwab. *The Book of Psalms, the Book of Proverbs*. Edited by Philip W. Comfort. Vol. 7 of *Cornerstone Biblical Commentary*. Carol Stream, IL: Tyndale House, 2009.

Georges, Jayson. *Ministering in Patronage Cultures: Biblical Models and Missional Implications*. Downers Grove, IL: InterVarsity Press, 2019.

Georges, Jayson. "Psalms: An Honor-Shame Paraphrase (New Book)." *HonorShame*, 20 June 2018. http://honorshame.com/psalms-honor-shame-paraphrase-new-book/.

———. *Psalms: An Honor-Shame Paraphrase of Fifteen Psalms*. Charleston, SC: Time Press, 2018.

Gerstenberger, Erhard. *Psalms, Part 1: With an Introduction to Cultic Poetry*. FOTL 14. Grand Rapids: Eerdmans, 1988.

Giese, Curtis, and Paul Puffe. *Called To Be God's People, Abridged Edition: An Introduction to the Old Testament*. Eugene, OR: Wipf & Stock, 2015.

Gilmore, David, ed. *Honor and Shame and the Unity of the Mediterranean*. Washington, DC: American Anthropological Association, 1987.

Goelet, Ogden. "Nudity in Ancient Egypt." *Source* 12.2 (1993): 20–31.

Goldingay, John E. *Israel's Gospel*. Old Testament Theology 1. Downers Grove, IL: InterVarsity Press, 2003.

————. *Old Testament Theology: Israel's Faith*. Vol. 2. Downers Grove, IL: InterVarsity Press, 2006.

————. *Psalms: Volume 1; Psalms 1–41*. BCOTWP. Grand Rapids: Baker Academic, 2006.

Gottwald, Norman K. "The Participation of Free Agrarians in the Introduction of Monarchy to Ancient Israel: An Application of H. A. Landsberger's Framework for the Analysis of Peasant Movements." Pages 77–106 in *Social Scientific Criticism of the Hebrew Bible and Its Social World: The Israelite Monarchy*. Edited by Norman K. Gottwald. Missoula, MT: Scholars Press, 1986.

Gould, Ezra Palmer. *Mark*. ICC. Edinburgh: T&T Clark, 1922.

Gramm, Kent. *The Prayer of Jesus: A Reading of the Lord's Prayer*. Eugene, OR: Wipf & Stock, 2015.

Green, Barbara. *David's Capacity for Compassion: A Literary-Hermeneutical Study of 1–2 Samuel*. London: Bloomsbury, 2017.

Green, Kevin. "Baal." *Zondervan All-in-One Bible Reference Guide*, 93–94.

Greenberg, Mosheh. *Ezekiel 1–20: A New Translation with Introduction and Commentary*. AB 22. New Haven: Yale University Press, 1983.

Gren, Conrad R. "Forcing the Ambiguities of Psalm 22:16 and the Messiah's Mission." *JETS* 48.2 (2005): 283–99.

Grogan, Geoffrey W. *Psalms*. The Two Horizons Old Testament Commentary. Grand Rapids: Eerdmans, 2008.

Gugliotto, Lee J. *Handbook for Bible Study: A Guide to Understanding, Teaching, and Preaching the Word of God*. Hagerstown, MD: Review & Herald, 2000.

Gunkel, H. *Einletung in die Psalmen*. Edited by J. Begrich. 2 vols. Göttingen: Vandenhoeck & Ruprecht, 1933.

Gunkel, H. *The Psalms: A Form-Critical Introduction*. Philadelphia: Fortress, 1967.

Guthrie, Donald. *Hebrews: An Introduction and Commentary*. TNTC 15. Downers Grove, IL: InterVarsity Press, 1983.

Hagedorn, Anselm C. "Guarding the Parents' Honour: Deuteronomy 21:18–21." *JSOT* 88 (2000): 101–21.

―――, Zeba A. Crook, and Eric Clark Stewart. *In Other Words: Essays on Social Science Methods and the New Testament in Honor of Jerome H. Neyrey*. Sheffield: Sheffield Phoenix, 2007.

Hals, Ronald M. *Ezekiel*. FOTL 19. Grand Rapids: Eerdmans, 1989.

Hanson, Kenneth C., and Douglas E. Oakman. *Palestine in the Time of Jesus: Social Structures and Social Conflicts*. Minneapolis: Augsburg Fortress, 2008.

Harris, R. Laird, Gleason L. Archer Jr., and Bruce K. Waltke, eds. *Theological Wordbook of the Old Testament*. 2 vols. Chicago: Moody Press, 1980.

Harrison, R. K. *Introduction to the Old Testament with a Comprehensive Review of Old Testament Studies and a Special Supplement on the Apocrypha*. Grand Rapids: Eerdmans, 1973.

Hartin, P. J., and Daniel J. Harrington. *James*. SP 14. Collegeville, MN: Liturgical Press, 2003.

Hartley, John E. *The Book of Job*. NICOT. Grand Rapids: Eerdmans, 2007.

Hayes, John H. *Understanding the Psalms*. Eugene, OR: Wipf & Stock, 1976.

Heinemann, Mark H. "An Exposition of Psalm 22." *BSac* 147.587 (1990): 286–308.

Hendel, Ronald S. "Israel among the Nations: Biblical Culture in the Ancient Near East." Pages 43–76 in *Cultures of the Jews: A New History*. Edited by David Biale. New York: Schocken Books, 2002.

———. *Remembering Abraham: Culture, Memory, and History in the Hebrew Bible*. Oxford: Oxford University Press, 2005.

Henry, Matthew, and Thomas Scott. *Matthew Henry's Concise Commentary*. Oak Harbor, WA: Logos, 1997.

Herr, Larry G. "Archaeological Sources for the History of Palestine: The Iron Age 2 Period; Emerging Nations." *BA* 60.3 (1997): 114–83.

Hicks, John Mark. *1 and 2 Chronicles*. The College Press NIV Commentary. Joplin, MO: College Press, 2001.

Hirschfeld, A. Robert. *Without Shame or Fear: From Adam to Christ*. New York: Church Publishing, 2017.

Hobbs, T. Raymond. *2 Kings*. Edited by John D. W. Watts. WBC 13. Waco, TX: Word, 1985.

———. "Reflections on Honor, Shame, and Covenant Relations." *JBL* 116.3 (1997): 501–3.

Holland, Glenn Stanfield. *Gods in the Desert: Religions of the Ancient Near East*. Lanham, MD: Rowman & Littlefield, 2009.

Hoogendyk, Isaiah. *The Lexham Analytical Lexicon of the Hebrew Bible*. Bellingham, WA: Lexham Press, 2017.

Hopkin, Shon. "The Psalm 22:16 Controversy: New Evidence from the Dead Sea Scrolls." *Brigham Young University Studies* 44.3 (2005): 161–72.

Horn, Siegfried H. *Seventh-Day Adventist Bible Dictionary*. Rev. ed. Commentary Reference Series 8. Washington, DC: Review & Herald, 1979.

Hossfeld, Frank-Lothar, Erich Zenger, and Linda M. Maloney. *Psalms 2: A Commentary on Psalms 51–100*. Edited by Klaus Baltzer. Hermeneia: A Critical and Historical Commentary on the Bible. Philadelphia: Fortress, 2005.

House, Paul R. *1, 2 Kings*. NAC 8. Nashville: Broadman & Holman, 1995.

Inch, Morris A. *Psychology in the Psalms: A Portrait of Man in God's World*. 1st ed. Waco, TX: Word, 1969.

Izre'el, Shlomo. "The Amarna Letters from Canaan." *CANE* 4:2411–19.

"Introduction," [Psalm 22]. *SDABC*. Edited by Francis D. Nichol. Rev. ed. Vol. 3. Washington, DC: Review & Herald, 1976.

Jamieson, Robert, A. R. Fausset, and David Brown. *A Commentary, Critical and Explanatory, on the Whole Bible*. Vol. 1. Oak Harbor, WA: Logos Research Systems, 1997.

Jaynes, Julian. *The Origin of Consciousness in the Breakdown of the Bicameral Mind*. Boston: Houghton Mifflin, 1990.

Jenni, Ernst, and Claus Westermann. *Theological Lexicon of the Old Testament*. Peabody, MA: Hendrickson, 1997.

Jenson, Philip P. *New Bible Commentary: Twenty-First Century Edition.* Edited by D. A. Carson, R. T. France, J. A. Motyer, and G. J. Wenham. 4th ed. Leicester: Inter-Varsity Press, 1994.

Jeremias, Joachim. *The Proclamation of Jesus.* The New Testament Theology. New York: Scribner's Sons, 1971.

Johnson, Dan G. *From Chaos to Restoration: An Integrative Reading of Isaiah 24–27.* JSOTSup 61. Sheffield: JSOT Press, 1988.

Joshua, Nathan Nzyoka. *Benefaction and Patronage in Leadership: A Socio-Historical Exegesis of the Pastoral Epistles.* Carlisle, Cumbria: Langham, 2018.

Kaiser, Walter C. *Toward an Exegetical Theology: Biblical Exegesis for Preaching and Teaching.* Grand Rapids: Baker Books, 1981.

Kaltner, John. "Psalm 22:17b: Second Guessing 'The Old Guess.'" *JBL* 117.3 (1998): 503–6.

Kang, Bin. *Honor and Shame in 1 Samuel 1–7.* Carlisle, Cumbria: Langham, 2022.

Kang, Sa-Moon. *Divine War in the Old Testament and in the Ancient Near East.* Berlin: de Gruyter, 2011.

Karen, Robert. "Shame." *The Atlantic Monthly* 269.2 (1992): 40–70.

Karenga, Maulana. *Maat, the Moral Ideal in Ancient Egypt: A Study in Classical African Ethics.* African Studies: History, Politics, Economics, Culture. New York: Routledge, 2004.

Kaufman, Stephen A. *Targum Lexicon.* Cincinnati: Hebrew Union College, 2004.

Keel, Othmar. *Feinde und Gottesleugner: Studien zum Image der Widersacher in den Individualpsalmen.* Stuttgart: Katholisches Bibelwerk, 1969.

Keen, Craig. "A 'Quick' Definition of Holiness." Pages 237–38 in *The Holiness Manifesto.* Edited by Kevin W. Mannoia and Don Thorsen. Grand Rapids: Eerdmans, 2008.

Keener, Craig S. *Matthew.* 2nd ed. The IVP Bible Background Commentary: New Testament. Downers Grove, IL: InterVarsity Press, 2014.

Keil, Carl Friedrich, and Franz Delitzsch. *The Psalter.* Translated by James Martin. K&D 5. Peabody, MA: Hendrickson, 1996.

Kidner, Derek. *Psalms 1–72: An Introduction and Commentary.* TOTC 15. Downers Grove, IL: InterVarsity Press, 1973.

Kirsch, Jonathan. *King David: The Real Life of the Man Who Ruled Israel.* New York: Random House, 2009.

Kittel, Gerhard, Geoffrey W. Bromiley, and Gerhard Friedrich, eds. *Theological Dictionary of the New Testament: Abridged in One Volume.* Grand Rapids: Eerdmans, 1985.

Klaas, A. D. Smelik. "Ma'at." *DDD*, 534–35.

Klein, L. R. "Honor and Shame in Esther." Pages 149–75 in *A Feminist Companion to Esther, Judith and Susanna.* Edited by Athalya Brenner. FCB 7. Sheffield: Sheffield Academic, 1995.

Klein, Ralph W. *1 Samuel.* Edited by John D. W. Watts. WBC 10. Waco, TX: Word, 1983.

Klein, William W., Craig L. Blomberg, and Robert L. Hubbard Jr. *Introduction to Biblical Interpretation.* Rev. and exp. ed. Nashville: Nelson, 2004.

Kline, Meredith G. *Treaty of the Great King: The Covenant Structure of Deuteronomy: Studies and Commentary*. Eugene, OR: Wipf & Stock, 2012.

Klopfenstein, M. A. *Scham und Schande nach dem Alten Testament*. Zurich: TVZ, 1972.

Kloppenborg, John S. "Greco-Roman Thiasoi, the Ekklēsia at Corinth, and Conflict Management." Pages 187–218 in *Redescribing Paul and the Corinthians*. Edited by Ron Cameron and Merrill P. Miller. Atlanta: Society of Biblical Literature, 2011.

Knapp, Andrew. *Royal Apologetic in the Ancient Near East*. WAWSup 4. Atlanta: SBL Press, 2015.

Koehler, Ludwig, Walter Baumgartner, and Johann J. Stamm. *The Hebrew and Aramaic Lexicon of the Old Testament*. Translated and edited under the supervision of Mervyn E. J. Richardson. 4 vols. Leiden: Brill, 1994–1999.

Kohlenberger III, John R. and William D. Mounce, eds. *Kohlenberger/ Mounce Concise Hebrew-Aramaic Dictionary of the Old Testament*. Tulsa, OK: OakTree, 2012.

Köstenberger, A. J. "Nations." *NDBT*, 676–78.

Kraft, Charles H. *Power Encounter in Spiritual Warfare*. Eugene, OR: Wipf & Stock, 2017.

Kroeber, Alfred Louis. "What Anthropology Is About." Pages 130–39 in *Readings for a History of Anthropological Theory*. Edited by Paul A. Erickson and Liam Donat Murphy. 5th ed. Toronto: University of Toronto Press, 2017.

Laetsch, T. *The Minor Prophets*. St. Louis: Concordia, 1956.

Lambert, W. G., trans. "Ludlul Bēl Nēmeqi." Princeton, 1969.

Lange, John Peter, Philip Schaff, Carl Bernhard Moll, Charles A. Briggs, D. D. Forsyth, James B. Hammond, J. Frederick McCurdy, and Thomas J. Conant. *A Commentary on the Holy Scriptures: Psalms*. Bellingham, WA: Logos, 2008.

Laniak, Timothy S. *Shame and Honor in the Book of Esther*. SBLDS 165. Atlanta: SBL Press, 1998.

LaRondelle, Hans K. *Deliverance in the Psalms: Messages of Hope for Today*. Berrien Springs, MI: First Impression, 1983.

Lé, Dan. *The Naked Christ: An Atonement Model for a Body-Obsessed Culture*. Distinguished Dissertations in Christian Theology 7. Eugene, OR: Pickwick, 2012.

Leithart, Peter J. *A Great Mystery: Fourteen Wedding Sermons*. Moscow, ID: Canon, 2006.

Lemche, Niels Peter. *Ancient Israel: A New History of Israel*. 2nd ed. London: Bloomsbury, 2015.

————. "From Patronage Society to Patronage Society." Pages 106–20 in *The Origins of the Ancient Israelite States*. Edited by Volkmar Fritz and Philip R. Davies. Sheffield: Sheffield Academic, 1996.

————, and E. F. Maniscalco. *Prelude to Israel's Past: Background and Beginning of Israelite History and Identity*. Peabody, MA: Hendrickson, 1998.

Lemos, T. M. "Shame and Mutilation of Enemies in the Hebrew Bible." *JBL* 125.2 (2006): 225–41.

Lenzi, Alan. "The Curious Case of Failed Revelation in Ludlul Bēl Nēmeqi: A New Suggestion for the Poem's Scholarly Purpose." Pages 36–66 in *Mediating between Heaven and Earth: Communication with the Divine in the Ancient Near East*. Edited by C. L. Crouch, Jonathan Stökl, and Anna Elise Zernecke. New York: Bloomsbury, 2012.

Leyton, Cristian Alvarado. "Fictive Kinship." *Encyclopedia of Human Relationships*, 682–83.

Lichtenwalter, Larry L. "Toward the Moral Vision of Honor and Shame in Biblical Perspective: Worldview, Identity, Character." Pages 111–49 in *Shame and Honor: Presenting Biblical Themes in Shame and Honor Contexts*. Edited by Bruce L. Bauer. Berrien Springs, MI: Andrews University Press, 2014.

Liddell, Henry George, Robert Scott, Henry Stuart Jones, and Roderick McKenzie. *A Greek-English Lexicon*. Oxford: Clarendon, 1996.

Lind, Millard. *Yahweh Is a Warrior: The Theology of Warfare in Ancient Israel*. Scottdale, PA: Herald, 1980.

Linde, Charlotte. *Working the Past: Narrative and Institutional Memory*. Oxford: Oxford University Press, 2008.

Linville, James R. "Psalm 22:17b: A New Guess." *JBL* 124.4 (2005): 733–44.

Long, Burke O. *2 Kings*. FOTL 10. Grand Rapids: Eerdmans, 1991.

Long, Jesse C., Jr. *1 and 2 Kings*. Edited by Terry Briley and Paul Kissling. The College Press NIV Commentary. Joplin, MO: College Press, 2002.

Longman, Tremper, III. *How to Read the Psalms*. Leicester: Inter-Varsity Press, 1988.

———. *Psalms: An Introduction and Commentary*. Edited by David G. Firth. TOTC 15–16. London: Inter-Varsity Press, 2014.

Louw, Johannes P., and Eugene A. Nida, eds. *Greek-English Lexicon of the New Testament: Based on Semantic Domains.* 2nd ed. New York: United Bible Societies, 1989.

Luckenbill, Daniel David. *Ancient Records of Assyria and Babylonia.* Santa Barbara, CA: Greenwood, 1927.

Lyons, Michael A. "Psalm 22 and the 'Servants' of Isaiah 54; 56–66." *CBQ* 77 (2015): 640–56.

Machinist, Peter. "The Question of Distinctiveness in Ancient Israel." Pages 420–42 in *Essential Papers on Israel and the Ancient Near East.* Edited by Frederick E. Greenspahn. New York: New York University Press, 2000.

Malina, Bruce J. "Feast." Pages 76–79 in *Handbook of Biblical Social Values.* Edited by J. J. Pilch and Bruce J. Malina. 3rd ed. Eugene, OR: Wipf & Stock, 2016.

———. "Grace/Favor." Pages 83–86 in *Biblical Social Values and Their Meaning: A Handbook.* Edited by J. J. Pilch and Bruce J. Malina. Peabody, MA: Hendrickson, 1993.

———. "Hospitality." Pages 96–99 in *Handbook of Biblical Social Values.* Edited by J. J. Pilch and Bruce J. Malina. 3rd ed. Eugene, OR: Wipf & Stock, 2016.

———. *The New Testament World: Insights from Cultural Anthropology.* 2nd and rev. ed. Louisville: Westminster John Knox, 1993.

———. "Patronage." Pages 131–37 in *Handbook of Biblical Social Values.* Edited by J. J. Pilch and Bruce J. Malina. 3rd ed. Eugene, OR: Wipf & Stock, 2016.

Mangum, Douglas. *Lexham Theological Wordbook.* Bellingham, WA: Lexham, 2014.

Maré, Leonard P. "Honour and Shame in Psalm 44." *Scriptura* 113.1 (2014): 1–12.

Mark, Joshua J. "The Tales of Prince Setna." *Ancient History Encyclopedia*, 2 May 2017. https://www.ancient.eu/article/1054/the-tales-of-prince-setna/.

Mathew, Bincy. *The Johannine Footwashing as the Sign of Perfect Love: An Exegetical Study of John 13:1–20.* Tübingen: Mohr Siebeck, 2018.

Mathews, Kenneth A. *Genesis 1–11:26.* NAC 1A. Nashville: Broadman & Holman, 1996.

———. *Genesis 11:27–50:26.* NAC 1B. Nashville: Broadman & Holman, 2005.

Matthews, Victor H. "Honor and Shame in Gender-Related Legal Situations in the Hebrew Bible." Pages 97–112 in *Gender and Law in the Hebrew Bible and the Ancient Near East.* Edited by Victor H. Matthews, Bernard M. Levinson, and Tikva Frymer-Kensky. Sheffield: Sheffield Academic, 2009.

———. *The History of Bronze and Iron Age Israel.* Oxford: Oxford University Press, 2018.

Mays, James L. *Psalms.* Edited by James L. Mays. IBC. Atlanta: John Knox, 1994.

McClintock, John. "Benedictions." *Cyclopædia of Biblical, Theological, and Ecclesiastical Literature, Supplement—A–Z* 11:427–29.

McClintock, John, and James Strong. *Cyclopædia of Biblical, Theological, and Ecclesiastical Literature, Supplement—A–Z.* 11 vols. New York: Harper & Brothers, 1891.

———. "גָּבַר." *Cyclopædia of Biblical, Theological, and Ecclesiastical Literature, Supplement—A–Z* 3:760.

McComiskey, Thomas E. "Benediction." *BEB* 1:280.

McLaughlin, John L. *The Ancient Near East: An Essential Guide.* Nashville: Abingdon, 2012.

McVann, Mark. "Communicativeness (Mouth-Ears)." Pages 25–28 in *Handbook of Biblical Social Values.* Edited by J. J. Pilch and Bruce J. Malina. Updated ed. Peabody, MA: Hendrickson, 2000.

Mendenhall, George E. *Law and Covenant in Israel and the Ancient Near East.* Pittsburgh: The Biblical Colloquium, 1955.

Menn, Esther M. "No Ordinary Lament: Relecture and the Identity of the Distressed in Psalm 22." *HTR* 93.4 (2000): 301–41.

Merenlahti, Petri. *A Smaller God: On the Divinely Human Nature of Biblical Literature.* Eugene, OR: Cascade, 2015.

Merrill, Eugene H. *Deuteronomy.* NAC 4. Nashville: Broadman & Holman, 1994.

Merwe, Christo H. J. van der, Jackie A. Naudé, and Jan H. Kroeze. *A Biblical Hebrew Reference Grammar.* Biblical Languages Hebrew 3. Sheffield: Sheffield Academic, 2002.

Miller, Geoffrey P. "A Riposte Form in the Song of Deborah." Pages 113–27 in *Gender and Law in the Hebrew Bible and the Ancient Near East.* Edited by Victor H. Matthews, Bernard M. Levinson, and Tikva Frymer-Kensky. JSOTSup 262. Sheffield: Sheffield Academic, 1998.

———. "Verbal Feud in the Hebrew Bible: Judges 3:12-30 and 19-21." *JNES* 55, no. 2 (1996): 105–17.

Miller, Patrick D. *Interpreting the Psalms*. Philadelphia: Fortress, 1986.

———. "Trouble and Woe: Interpreting the Biblical Laments." *Int* 37.1 (1983): 32–45.

Miller, Stephen R. *Daniel*. Edited by E. Ray Clendenen. NAC 18. Nashville: Broadman & Holman, 1994.

Morris, Leon. *The Gospel according to Matthew*. Edited by D. A. Carson. PNTC. Grand Rapids: Eerdmans, 1992.

Moskala, Jiří. "Reflections on the Concept of Shame and Honor in the Biblical Creation and Fall Narratives." Pages 23–42 in *Shame and Honor: Presenting Biblical Themes in Shame and Honor Contexts*. Edited by Bruce L. Bauer. Berrien Springs, MI: Andrews University Press, 2014.

Motyer, J. A. "The Psalms." *New Bible Commentary: Twenty-First Century Edition*. Edited by D. A. Carson. Leicester: Inter-Varsity Press, 1994.

Mowinckel, Sigmund. *The Psalms in Israel's Worship*. The Biblical Resource Series. Grand Rapids: Eerdmans, 2004.

Moxnes, Halvor. "Honor and Shame." Pages 19–40 in *The Social Sciences and New Testament Interpretation*. Edited by Richard L. Rohrbaugh. Grand Rapids: Baker Academic, 1996.

Müller, Roland. *Honor and Shame: Unlocking the Door*. Philadelphia: Xlibris, 2000.

Murphy, Roland Edmund. *Introduction to the Wisdom Literature of the Old Testament*. Collegeville, MN: Liturgical Press, 1965.

Murphy, Todd J. *Pocket Dictionary for the Study of Biblical Hebrew*. The IVP Pocket Reference Series. Downers Grove, IL: InterVarsity Press, 2003.

Nakata, Ichiro. "Popular Concerns Reflected in Old Babylonian Mari Theophoric Personal Names." Pages 114–25 in *Official Cult and Popular Religion in the Ancient Near East: Papers of the First Colloquium on the Ancient Near East; The City and Its Life, Held at the Middle Eastern Culture Center in Japan (Mitaka, Tokyo, March 20–22, 1992)*. Edited by Eiko Matsushima. Heidelberg: Winter, 1993.

Navon, Ḥayim. *Genesis and Jewish Thought*. Translated by David Straus. New York: Ktav, 2008.

Neusner, Jacob. *A Theological Commentary to the Midrash: Pesiqta DeRab Kahana*. Lanham, MD: University Press of America, 2001.

Newcomb, Harvey. *The Young Lady's Guide to the Harmonious Development of Christian Character*. 3rd rev. and enlarged ed. Boston: James B. Dow, 1841.

Newman, Louis E. ללמד ולמד: *Studies in Jewish Education and Judaica in Honor of Louis Newman*. Edited by Alexander M. Shapiro and Burton I. Cohen. New York: Ktav, 1984.

Newsom, Carol A. *The Book of Job: A Contest of Moral Imaginations*. Oxford: Oxford University Press, 2009.

Neyrey, Jerome H. "Clothing." Pages 20–25 in *Handbook of Biblical Social Values*. Edited by J. J. Pilch and Bruce J. Malina. Update ed. Peabody, MA: Hendrickson, 2000.

———. "Dyadism." Pages 49–52 in *Biblical Social Values and Their Meaning: A Handbook*. Edited by J. J. Pilch and Bruce J. Malina. Peabody, MA: Hendrickson, 1993.

———. *Honor and Shame in the Gospel of Matthew*. Louisville: Westminster John Knox, 1998.

—————. "Nudity." Pages 119–25 in *Handbook of Biblical Social Values.* Edited by J. J. Pilch and Bruce J. Malina. Peabody, MA: Hendrickson, 1993.

—————. *Render to God: New Testament Understandings of the Divine.* Minneapolis: Augsburg Fortress, 2004.

Nichol, Francis D., ed. *The Seventh-day Adventist Bible Commentary.* Rev. ed. 7 vols. Washington, DC: Review & Herald, 1976-1980.

Nicholas, Mark. *The Rules: Ten to Live By.* Nashville: Transit, 2003.

"Nobility." In *Lexico Dictionaries: English.* Oxford University Press. Accessed May 15, 2020. https://www.lexico.com/en/definition/nobility.

O'Brien, Julia M. *Hosea.* Edited by Gail R. O'Day and David L. Petersen. Theological Bible Commentary. Louisville: Westminster John Knox, 2009.

Odell, Margaret S. "Hosea." *EDB* 609–10.

Olyan, Saul M. "Honor, Shame, and Covenant Relations in Ancient Israel and Its Environment." *Scriptura* 113.1 (2014): 1–12.

Omanson, Roger L., and John Ellington. *A Handbook on 1–2 Kings.* Edited by Paul Clarke, Schuyler Brown, Louis Dorn, and Donald Slager. UBS Handbook Series 2. New York: United Bible Societies, 2008.

—————. *A Handbook on the First Book of Samuel.* UBS Handbook Series. New York: United Bible Societies, 2001.

—————. *A Handbook on the Second Book of Samuel.* UBS Handbook Series. New York: United Bible Societies, 2001.

Oprisko, Robert L. *Honor: A Phenomenology*. New York: Routledge, 2012.

Osborn, Noel D., and Howard A. Hatton. *A Handbook on Exodus*. UBS Handbook Series. New York: United Bible Societies, 1999.

Osborne, Grant R. *The Hermeneutical Spiral: A Comprehensive Introduction to Biblical Interpretation*. Rev. and Expanded 2nd ed. Downers Grove, IL: InterVarsity Press, 2010.

Oswalt, John N. *The Book of Isaiah: Chapters 40–66*. NICOT. Grand Rapids: Eerdmans, 1998.

Packer, J. I., Merrill C. Tenney, and William White, eds. *Illustrated Manners and Customs of the Bible*. Nashville: Nelson, 1997.

Parkinson, R. B. *The Tale of Sinuhe*. Oxford: Oxford University Press, 2009.

———. *The Tale of Sinuhe and Other Ancient Egyptian Poems, 1940–1640 BC*. Oxford: Oxford University Press, 1998.

Partner, Peter. *God of Battles: Holy Wars of Christianity and Islam*. New York: HarperCollins, 1998.

Patzia, Arthur G., and Anthony J. Petrotta. "Holy War." *Pocket Dictionary of Biblical Studies*, 59–60.

Payne, J. B. "Psalms, Book Of." *Zondervan Pictorial Encyclopedia of the Bible*, 1056–82.

Pedersen, Johannes. *Israel: Its Life and Culture*. London: Oxford University Press, 1926.

Perdue, Leo G. *Proverbs*. IBC. Louisville: Westminster John Knox, 2000.

Perowne, J. J. Stewart. *The Book of Psalms: A New Translation with Introductions and Notes, Explanatory and Critical.* Grand Rapids: Zondervan, 1976.

Perschbacher, Wesley J. *New Testament Greek Syntax: An Illustrated Manual.* Chicago: Moody Press, 1995.

Petersen, David L., Joel M. LeMon, and Kent Harold Richards, eds. *Method Matters: Essays on the Interpretation of the Hebrew Bible in Honor of David L. Petersen.* Society of Biblical Literature Resources for Biblical Study 56. Atlanta: SBL Press, 2009.

Pfandl, Gerhard, and Angel Manuel Rodriguez. "Reading Psalms and the Wisdom Literature." Pages 163–82 in *Understanding Scripture: An Adventist Approach.* Edited by George W. Reid. Silver Spring, MD: Biblical Research Institute, 2005.

Pfoh, Emanuel. *The Emergence of Israel in Ancient Palestine: Historical and Anthropological Perspectives.* London: Routledge, 2016.

Pham, Xuan Huong Thi. *Mourning in the Ancient Near East and the Hebrew Bible.* JSOTSup 302. Sheffield: Sheffield Academic, 1999.

Pilch, J. J. *A Cultural Handbook to the Bible.* Grand Rapids: Eerdmans, 2012.

———. "Compassion." Pages 28–31 in *Biblical Social Values and Their Meaning: A Handbook.* Edited by J. J. Pilch and Bruce J. Malina. Peabody, MA: Hendrickson, 1993.

———. *Introducing the Cultural Context of the Old Testament.* Vol. 1. New York: Paulist, 1991.

————. "Trust." Pages 178–80 in *Handbook of Biblical Social Values*. Edited by J. J. Pilch and Bruce J. Malina. Update ed. Peabody, MA: Hendrickson, 2000.

————, and Bruce J. Malina, eds. *Biblical Social Values and Their Meaning: A Handbook*. Peabody, MA: Hendrickson, 1993.

Piper, Ronald A. "Glory, Honor and Patronage in the Fourth Gospel: Understanding the 'Doxa' Given to Disciples in John 17." Pages 281–309 in *Social Scientific Models for Interpreting the Bible: Essays by the Context Group in Honor of Bruce J. Malina*. Edited by J. J. Pilch. Leiden: Brill, 2001.

Pitt-Rivers, J. A. "Honor." *IESS* 6:503–04.

————. "Honour and Social Status." Pages 19–77 in *Honour and Shame*. Edited by John G. Peristiany. London: Weidenfeld & Nicholson, 1966.

Plantinga-Pauw, Amy. *Proverbs and Ecclesiastes: A Theological Commentary on the Bible*. Louisville: Westminster John Knox, 2015.

Pleins, J. David. "Poor, Poverty: Old Testament." *AYBD* 5:402–14.

Plevnik, Joseph. "Honor/Shame." Pages 95–104 in *Biblical Social Values and Their Meaning: A Handbook*. Edited by J. J. Pilch and Bruce J. Malina. Peabody, MA: Hendrickson, 1993.

Pohlig, James M. "Ezekiel 18 in the Context of Shame Cultures and Guilt Cultures." Pages 122–24 in *Global Perspectives on the Bible*. Edited by Mark Roncace and Joseph Weaver. Upper Saddle River, NJ: Pearson, 2014.

Pritchard, James B., ed. *Ancient Near Eastern Texts Relating to the Old Testament*. 3rd ed. Princeton: Princeton University Press, 1969.

Putnam, Frederic Clarke. *Hebrew Bible Insert: A Student's Guide to the Syntax of Biblical Hebrew*. Quakertown, PA: Stylus, 2002.

Raabe, Paul R. *Obadiah: A New Translation with Introduction and Commentary*. Edited by William Foxwell Albright and David Noel Freedman. AB 24D. New York: Doubleday, 1996.

Race, Marianne, and Laurie Brink. *In This Place: Reflections on the Land of the Gospels for the Liturgical Cycles*. Eugene, OR: Wipf & Stock, 2008.

Ramsey, John. *For Your Names' Sake*. Morrisville, NC: Lulu Press, 2008.

Reif, Stefan C. "The Fathership of God in Early Rabbinic Literature." Pages 505–25 in *Family and Kinship in the Deuterocanonical and Cognate Literature*. Edited by Angelo Passaro. Berlin: de Gruyter, 2013.

Reis, Harry T., ed. *Encyclopedia of Human Relationships*. Vol. 2. Thousand Oaks, CA: Sage, 2009.

Reyburn, William David. *A Handbook on the Book of Job*. UBS Handbook Series. New York: United Bible Societies, 1992.

———, and Euan McGregor Fry. *A Handbook on Genesis*. UBS Handbook Series. New York: United Bible Societies, 1998.

Reymond, Robert L. *A New Systematic Theology of the Christian Faith*. 2nd ed. Nashville: Nelson, 2010.

Richards, E. Randolph, and Brandon J. O'Brien. *Misreading Scripture with Western Eyes: Removing Cultural Blinders to Better Understand the Bible*. Downers Grove, IL: InterVarsity Press, 2012.

Roberts, Jimmy Jack McBee. *The Bible and the Ancient Near East: Collected Essays.* Winona Lake, IN: Eisenbrauns, 2002.

Roberts, Mark D. *Ezra/Nehemiah/Esther.* The Preacher's Commentary 11. Nashville: Nelson, 2004.

Rohrbaugh, Richard L. *The New Testament in Cross-Cultural Perspective.* Eugene, OR: Cascade, 2007.

Rosenbaum, Stanley Ned. "The Concept 'Antagonist' in Hebrew Psalmography: A Semantic Field Study." PhD diss., Brandeis University Press, 1974.

Ross, Allen P. *A Commentary on the Psalms: Volume 1 (1–41).* Wheaton, IL: Victor Books, 1985.

———. *Psalms.* Edited by John F. Walvoord and Roy B. Zuck. Vol. 1. The Bible Knowledge Commentary: An Exposition of the Scriptures. Wheaton, IL: Victor Books, 1985.

———. "The 'Thou' Sections of Laments: The Bold and Earnest Prayers of the Psalmists." Pages 135–50 in *The Psalms: Language for All Seasons of the Soul.* Edited by Andrew J. Schmutzer and David M. Howard Jr. Chicago: Moody Press, 2013.

Russell, A. Sue. *In the World but Not of the World: The Liminal Life of Pre-Constantine Christian Communities.* Eugene, OR: Wipf & Stock, 2019.

Ryken, Leland. *Sweeter than Honey, Richer than Gold: A Guided Study of Biblical Poetry.* Bellingham, WA: Lexham, 2015.

———. "Taunt." *Dictionary of Biblical Imagery,* 841–42.

———, Jim Wilhoit, and Tremper Longman III, eds. *Dictionary of Biblical Imagery.* Downers Grove, IL: InterVarsity Press, 1998.

Sadgrove, Michael. *I Will Trust in You: A Companion to the Evening Psalms*. London: Society of Promoting Christian Knowledge, 2012.

Sahlins, Marshall. *Stone Age Economics*. Chicago: Aldine, 1972.

Saller, Richard P. *Personal Patronage under the Early Empire*. Cambridge: Cambridge University Press, 2002.

Sanchez, Joel. "Honor and Shame in the Ancient Near East." *Crucified Life Ministries*, 12 December 2015. http://crucifiedlifemin.com/auto-draft-2/.

Santos, Narry F. *Turning Our Shame into Honor: Transformation of the Filipino Hiya in the Light of Mark's Gospel*. Manila, Philippines: Lifechange, 2003.

Sasson, Jack M., ed. *Civilizations of the Ancient Near East*. Vol. 4. Peabody, MA: Hendrickson, 2000.

Sawyer, W. Thomas. "Banquet." *Holman Illustrated Bible Dictionary*, 170.

Schäder, Jo-Mari. "Patronage and Clientage between God, Israel and the Nations: A Social-Scientific Investigation of Psalm 47." *JSem* 19.1 (2010): 235–62.

Schaefer, Konrad. *Berit Olam: Studies in Hebrew Narrative and Poetry; Psalms*. Edited by David W. Cotter, Jerome T. Walsh, and Chris Franke. Collegeville, MN: Liturgical Press, 2001.

Schloen, J. David. *The House of the Father as Fact and Symbol: Patrimonialism in Ugarit and the Ancient Near East*. Studies in the Archaeology and History of the Levant 2. Winona Lake, IN: Eisenbrauns, 2001.

Schmeekle, Maria. "Extended Families." *Encyclopedia of Human Relationships*, 572–74.

Schoors, A. *I Am God Your Saviour: A Form-Critical Study of the Main Genres in Is. 40–55*. Leiden: Brill, 1973.

Schroeder, Christoph O. *History, Justice, and the Agency of God: A Hermeneutical and Exegetical Investigation on Isaiah and Psalms*. Leiden: Brill, 2001.

Sheppard, Gerald T. "'Enemies' and the Politics of Prayer in the Book of Psalms." Pages 61–82 in *The Bible and the Politics of Exegesis: Essays in Honor of Norman K. Gottwald on His Sixty-Fifth Birthday*. Edited by Norman Karol Gottwald, David Jobling, Peggy Lynne Day, and Gerald T. Sheppard. Cleveland, OH: Pilgrim, 1991.

Shramek, Dustin. "Honor and Shame in the Psalter." *His Peace upon Us*, August 2009. https://hispeaceuponus.files.wordpress. com/2009/08/honor-and-shame-in-the -psalter1.pdf.

Sills, David L. and Robert K. Merton, eds. *International Encyclopedia of the Social Sciences*. New York: Macmillan, 1968–.

Simkins, Ronald A. "Patronage and the Political Economy of Monarchic Israel." *Semeia* 87 (1999): 123–44.

Simpson, William Kelly, ed. *The Literature of Ancient Egypt: An Anthology of Stories, Instructions, Stelae, Autobiographies, and Poetry*. 3rd ed. New Haven: Yale University Press, 2003.

Skinner, John. *A Critical and Exegetical Commentary on Genesis*. ICC. New York: Scribner Sons, 1910.

Smith, Dennis Edwin. *From Symposium to Eucharist: The Banquet in the Early Christian World*. Minneapolis: Augsburg Fortress, 2002.

Smith, Henry Preserved. *A Critical and Exegetical Commentary on the Books of Samuel*. ICC. New York: Scribner's Sons, 1899.

Smith, Mark S. "El." *EDB* 384–86.

Smith, W. R. *Lectures on the Religion of the Semites, First Series: The Fundamental Institutions*. Edinburgh: Black, 1889.

Sneed, Mark R. *The Social World of the Sages: An Introduction to Israelite and Jewish Wisdom Literature*. Minneapolis: Augsburg Fortress, 2015.

Spicq, Ceslas. *Theological Lexicon of the New Testament*. Translated and edited by James D. Ernest. 3 vols. Peabody, MA: Hendrickson, 1994.

Spurgeon, C. H. *The Treasury of David: An Expository and Devotional Commentary on the Psalms*. Grand Rapids: Baker Books, 1978.

———. *The Treasury of David: Spurgeon's Classic Work on the Psalms*. Grand Rapids: Kregel, 1976.

———, and David O. Fuller. *Psalms*. Grand Rapids: Kregel, 1976.

Stager, Lawrence E. "Forging an Identity: The Emergence of Ancient Israel." Pages 123–75 in *The Oxford History of the Biblical World*. Edited by Michael D. Coogan. New York: Oxford University Press, 2001.

Stefanovic, Zdravko. *Daniel: Wisdom to the Wise; Commentary on the Book of Daniel*. Nampa, ID: Pacific Press, 2007.

Stiebert, Johanna. *The Construction of Shame in the Hebrew Bible: The Prophetic Contribution*. JSOTSup 346. Sheffield: Sheffield Academic, 2002.

Stockitt, Robin. *Restoring the Shamed: Towards a Theology of Shame.* Eugene, OR: Cascade, 2012.

Strawn, Brent A. "Psalm 22:17b: More Guessing." *JBL* 119.3 (2000): 439–51.

Strong, James. *A Concise Dictionary of the Words in the Greek Testament and The Hebrew Bible.* Bellingham, WA: Logos Bible Software, 2009.

———. *The New Strong's Dictionary of Hebrew and Greek Words.* Nashville: Nelson, 1997.

Stuart, Douglas K. *Exodus.* NAC 2. Nashville: Broadman & Holman, 2006.

Stuart, Douglas K. *Old Testament Exegesis: A Handbook for Students and Pastors.* 4th ed. Louisville: Westminster John Knox, 2009.

Swanson, James. *Dictionary of Biblical Languages with Semantic Domains: Hebrew (Old Testament).* Oak Harbor, WA: Logos Research Systems, 1997.

Swartley, Keith E. *Encountering the World of Islam.* Downers Grove, IL: InterVarsity Press, 2014.

Sweeney, Marvin A. *Isaiah 1–39: With an Introduction to Prophetic Literature.* FOTL 16. Grand Rapids: Eerdmans, 1996.

Swenson, Kristin M. "Psalm 22:17: Circling around the Problem Again." *JBL* 123.4 (2004): 637–48.

Sztompka, Piotr. *Trust: A Sociological Theory.* Cambridge: Cambridge University Press, 1999.

Tate, Jeanne Choy. *Something Greater: Culture, Family, and Community as Living Story.* Eugene, OR: Wipf & Stock, 2013.

Taylor, Michelle Ellis. "Dog." *EDB*, 352.

Tennent, Timothy C. *Theology in the Context of World Christianity: How the Global Church Is Influencing the Way We Think About and Discuss Theology.* Grand Rapids: Zondervan, 2007.

Terrien, Samuel L. *The Psalms: Strophic Structure and Theological Commentary.* Grand Rapids: Eerdmans, 2003.

Tesh, S. Edward, and Walter D. Zorn. *Psalms.* The College Press NIV Commentary. Joplin, MO: College Press, 1999.

Thomas, R. L. *New American Standard Hebrew-Aramaic and Greek Dictionaries.* Updated ed. Anaheim, CA: Foundation Publications, 1998.

Thompson, Henry O. "Yahweh (Deity)." *AYBD* 1011–12.

Toon, Peter. "Remember, Remembrance." *Baker's Evangelical Dictionary of Biblical Theology*, 668–69.

Toorn, K. van der, Bob Becking, and Pieter W. van der Horst, eds. *Dictionary of Deities and Demons in the Bible.* 2nd ed. Grand Rapids: Eerdmans, 1999.

Toorn, K. van der. "Yahweh." *DDD* 910–19.

Toth, Lina. *Transforming the Struggles of Tamars: Single Women and Baptistic Communities.* Eugene, OR: Wipf & Stock, 2014.

Tucker, W. D., Jr. "Is Shame a Matter of Patronage in the Communal Laments?" *JSOT* 31.4 (2007): 465–80.

———. "Psalms 1, Book Of." *Dictionary of the Old Testament: Wisdom, Poetry and Writings*, 579–93.

————, and Jamie A. Grant. *Psalms*. NIVAC. Grand Rapids: Zondervan, 2018.

Tuell, Steven Shawn. *First and Second Chronicles*. IBC. Louisville: Westminster John Knox, 2001.

Vall, Gregory. "Psalm 22:17B: 'The Old Guess.'" *JBL* 116.1 (1997): 45–56.

VanGemeren, Willem, ed. *New International Dictionary of Old Testament Theology and Exegesis*. 5 vols. Grand Rapids: Zondervan, 1996.

Vesely, Patricia. *Friendship and Virtue Ethics in the Book of Job*. Cambridge: Cambridge University Press, 2019.

Wallace, Daniel B. *The Basics of New Testament Syntax: An Intermediate Greek Grammar*. Grand Rapids: Zondervan, 2000.

Waltke, Bruce K. "Psalms, Theology Of." *NIDOTTE* 4:1100–1115.

————, James M. Houston, and Erika Moore. *The Psalms as Christian Lament: A Historical Commentary*. Grand Rapids: Eerdmans, 2014.

Waltke, Bruce K., and M. O'Connor. *An Introduction to Biblical Hebrew Syntax*. Winona Lake, IN: Eisenbrauns, 1990.

Waltke, Bruce K., and Charles Yu. *An Old Testament Theology: An Exegetical, Canonical, and Thematic Approach*. Grand Rapids: Zondervan, 2007.

Walton, John H., Victor H. Matthews, and Mark W. Chavalas. *The IVP Bible Background Commentary: Old Testament*. Downers Grove, IL: InterVarsity Press, 2000.

Walvoord, John F., and Roy B. Zuck, eds. *The Bible Knowledge Commentary: An Exposition of the Scriptures*. Vol. 1. Wheaton, IL: Victor Books, 1985.

Watson, David F. *Honor Among Christians: The Cultural Key to the Messianic Secret*. Philadelphia: Fortress, 2010.

Watson, Wilfred G. E. *Classical Hebrew Poetry: A Guide to Its Techniques*. JSOTSup 26. Sheffield: JSOT Press, 1984.

Watts, John D. W. *Isaiah 34–66*. Edited by John D. W. Watts. Rev. ed. WBC 25. Nashville: Nelson, 1999.

Weanzana, Nupanga, Samuel Ngewa, Tewoldemedhin Habtu, and Zamani Kafang. "Psalms." Pages 605–772 in *Africa Bible Commentary: A One-Volume Commentary Written by Seventy African Scholars*. Edited by Tokunboh Adeyemo. 2nd ed. Grand Rapids: Zondervan, 2010.

Weber, Stuart K. *Matthew*. HNTC 1. Nashville: Broadman & Holman, 2000.

Weiner, James Blake. "Interview: Nudity in the Ancient World." *Ancient History Encyclopedia*, 18 December 2018. https://www.ancient. eu/article/1295/interview -nudity-in-the-ancient-world/.

Weiser, Artur. *The Psalms: A Commentary*. Translated by Herbert Hartwell. 5th and rev. ed. OTL. Philadelphia: Westminster, 1962.

Wendland, Ernst R. *Contextual Frames of Reference in Translation: A Coursebook for Bible Translators and Teachers*. London: Routledge, 2014.

———. *Studies in the Psalms: Literary-Structural Analysis with Application to Translation*. Dallas: SIL International, 2017.

Wenham, Gordon J. *Genesis 16–50*. Edited by John D. W. Watts. WBC 2. Waco, TX: Word, 1994.

Wesley, John. *Explanatory Notes upon the Old Testament*. Vol. 2. London: William Pine, 1765.

Wessel, Walter W. *The Expositor's Bible Commentary: Matthew, Mark, Luke.* Vol. 8. Edited by Frank E. Gaebelein. Grand Rapids: Zondervan, 1984.

West, Christopher. *Theology of the Body Explained: A Commentary on John Paul II's "Gospel of the Body."* Herefordshire, UK: Gracewing, 2003.

Westbrook, Raymond. "Patronage in the Ancient Near East." *JESHO* 48.2 (2005): 210–33.

Westbury, Joshua R., et al., eds. *Lexham Figurative Language of the Bible Glossary.* Bellingham, WA: Lexham, 2016.

Westermann, Claus. *Genesis 1–11.* Neukirchen-Vluyn: Neukirchener Verlag, 1974.

———. *The Living Psalms.* Edited by J. R. Porter. Grand Rapids: Eerdmans, 1989.

Wheatley, Alan B. *Patronage in Early Christianity: Its Use and Transformation from Jesus to Paul of Samosata.* Eugene, OR: Wipf & Stock, 2011.

White, R. E. O. "Psalms." In *Evangelical Commentary on the Bible*, 3:367–98. Baker Reference Library. Grand Rapids: Baker Books, 1995.

Williamson, P. R. "Covenant." *NDBT* 419–30.

Wills, Lawrence M. *Not God's People: Insiders and Outsiders in the Biblical World.* Lanham, MD: Rowman & Littlefield, 2008.

Wilson, Gerald Henry. *The Editing of the Hebrew Psalter.* SBLDS 76. Chico, CA: Scholars Press, 1985.

Wiseman, Donald J. *1 and 2 Kings: An Introduction and Commentary.* TOTC 9. Downers Grove, IL: InterVarsity Press, 1993.

Wright, N. T. *The Case for the Psalms: Why They Are Essential.* New York: HarperCollins, 2013.

Wu, Jackson. *Reading Romans with Eastern Eyes: Honor and Shame in Paul's Message and Mission.* Downers Grove, IL: InterVarsity Press, 2019.

Yee, Gale A. *Poor Banished Children of Eve: Woman as Evil in the Hebrew Bible.* Minneapolis: Augsburg Fortress, 2003.

"*Yĕšûʾâ.*" *Blue Letter Bible*, 2020. https://www.blueletterbible.org/kjv/gen/1/1/s_1001.

Young, Edward J. *An Introduction to the Old Testament.* Grand Rapids: Eerdmans, 1964.

Zaracho, Rafael. "Communicating the Gospel in a Shame Society." *DMBF* 39.2 (2010): 271–81.